# TO HELL IN A DAY COACH

*By Peter Lyon*

To Hell in a Day Coach:
An Exasperated Look at American Railroads

Success Story:
The Life and Times of S. S. McClure

# TO HELL IN
# A DAY COACH

## AN EXASPERATED LOOK AT AMERICAN RAILROADS

## by Peter Lyon

J. B. LIPPINCOTT COMPANY

Philadelphia and New York

1968

# CONTENTS

v

# TO HELL IN A DAY COACH

# A PRELIMINARY ENCOURAGEMENT

What! a book about railroads, when we are already on our way to putting a man on the moon? In the jet age, a book about railroads, those shabby and decrepit antiques, so noisome, so thickly encrusted with an antediluvian soot?

And yet the railroads continue to be provocative, to be vexatious; as much so today, in their Götterdämmerung, as in the time of their ascendency. "The business of America," said Calvin Coolidge, "is business"; and to those who are interested in business the history of American enterprise affords no more absorbing chronicle than that of the railroads. Indeed, without the American railroads there could have been no American business. With a web of rails we bound our continental spaces together and spurred them into production; on a skeleton of rails we fleshed out our commerce and hardened our industrial muscles. It is not too much to say that the railroads hauled an underdeveloped nation out of debt and carried it much of the way toward industrial supremacy in the world.

Here was a valuable load of freight, and the railroads soaked the United States an exorbitant rate for the job. Up soared their revenues, and up soared their power and their influence, up to incalculable heights. The men who administered the affairs of the railroads were lordly fellows who acknowledged or flouted the law as it fitted their convenience, who trafficked in congressmen like so many chattels, who dangled state legislatures like seals from their watch fobs, who took it for granted that the U. S. Army would squash any strike by their workmen, and who deigned in their spare time to instruct Presidents in the conduct of national affairs.

By 1905, when the American railroads were only seventy-five years old, no other industry approached them in capital investment, in revenues, or in power. A competent observer estimated that their officers controlled one sixth of the wealth of the United States and that their capital was "ten times that of the combined banks and trust companies of the country." No industry seemed more secure, and certainly the captains of no industry were more complacent. Of this euphoric time, John Moody, the most authoritative financial journalist of his day, could later write: "Railroad bankruptcy was now impossible in the United States." Contemporary economists, peering confidently into the same crystal ball, agreed with him.

But in the sixty years since then, while the national economy has steadily expanded, the fortunes of the railroads, except in wartime, have as steadily shrunk. During the 1930s several railroad companies bellied up, importunately contesting which might first be run through the wringer of bankruptcy; these companies operated one third of the nation's total mileage of railroad tracks. Many other companies contrived to avert receivership only by virtue of fat federal loans.

The railroads can no longer be usefully measured against other industries. Today there are single corporations (General Motors, Standard Oil of New Jersey, and American Telephone and Telegraph) each of which boasts greater revenues than the entire railroad industry and each of which clears a net profit that puts the net profit of the entire railroad industry to shame. Today the railroads haul less than half the nation's freight and less than a ludicrous two per cent of its passengers— fewer people than travel by automobile, fewer than travel by airplane, fewer than by bus, fewer than by any other mode of

2

transportation, unless you count pogo sticks.

What has happened to the railroads? In 1905 they were ogres, feared and detested, collectively portrayed as an octopus or as a school of man-eating sharks. Today they seem to be more like a kitten, not a playful kitten with claws that can scratch but a poor, bedraggled kitten that has fallen down a well and mews and whimpers piteously to be pulled out.

What has become of the railroad executives who once swaggered about, entertaining Presidents and senators in their private cars? Today they have forsaken their own railroads, preferring to travel on airplanes, for after all they still deem themselves men of consequence, for whom every millisecond is a matter of transcendent importance. Today they snivel in the public market place, begging the governors of states for a free handout.

It is an extraordinary transformation and, as might be expected, the spokesmen for the railroads, who have had a long period of leisure in which to scratch their heads and puzzle over the matter, know just whom to blame for what they insist is a national crisis in transportation. They have leveled a whole fistful of accusing fingers: at the federal government; at the Interstate Commerce Commission; at their employees, the members of the Railroad Brotherhoods; at their competitors, the automobile, the airplane, the bus, the truck, the barge, and the pipeline; but first, last, and always most passionately, at the federal government.

Agents for the railroads have been howling their complaints and mounting their indictments for so many years, so stubbornly and with such a sense of outrage, that today it is next to impossible to calm their cholers and charm them into a coherent discussion of their woes. As soon as the suggestion is put that perhaps the technological changes of the last fifty years have presented the traveler or the shipper of freight with a variety of seductive choices, one or two of which may conceivably be superior to the railroads, their agents commence to twitch. Veins pound in their foreheads. The dialogue hots up infernally. "If only" is their recurrent snarl.

3

"If only the government had let us alone . . ."

"If only we were treated equally . . ."

"If only it weren't for the featherbedding . . ."

"If only our competitors had to pay taxes . . ."

"If only the government had let us alone . . ."

"If only the government *would* let us alone, even *now*, we could . . ."

That there is a modicum of truth in these jeremiads must be admitted; not much, to be sure, but enough to measure on a torsion balance.

For example, the Interstate Commerce Commission, which regulates the railroads, affords a fair example of how successive Congresses, in their infinite wisdom, can contrive a truly impressive bureaucratic snarl. In 1887 the Commission comprised five commissioners and a staff not much bigger. In response to "the public necessity and convenience," the Commission has bloated up to eleven commissioners and a secretariat of nearly twenty-five hundred persons; the law under which it operates has swollen from a lean statute of ten pages to one of more than four hundred pages; its responsibilities have multiplied like bunnies, and so have its regulations; today its procedures are labyrinthine in method and glacial in dispatch. But if the railroads are to some extent hobbled by regulations dating from the days when a spittoon was still a useful and elegant accessory in the depot, the officers of the railroads, as we shall see, have themselves cannily opposed revision or repeal of some of those regulations. And if, on matters of substance, the Commission has been known to waver and wobble for as long as nine years before making up its collective mind as to what it should do, this bureaucratic indecision had its origin, once again, in the conference rooms of the great railroad companies.

But the railroad men reserve most of their indignation for the government policy that has allocated vast sums of public funds (i.e., taxpayers' money) for the construction of airports, highways, and inland waterways, and for research to improve the technology of aviation and motor transport. In the last

4

twenty years federal, state, and local governments (i.e., the taxpayers) have spent some two hundred billions of dollars on highways, cloverleafs, overpasses, underpasses, tunnels, and bridges for the use of automobiles, trucks, and buses. More billions have gone for airports, air navigation systems, and direct subsidies to companies operating helicopters.

The anguish of the railroad executive may be imagined. To see all this money going to soothe and support his rivals is to ulcerate the duodenum of every sensitive vice-president. In 1965 the federal government spent one billion three hundred million dollars to assist the airlines. There was also talk of another billion dollars to develop a supersonic airplane. No wonder, say the railroad men, that their freight revenues have dwindled and their passenger revenues all but disappeared. Moreover, railroad companies are obliged to pay taxes on their tracks, depots, and other real estate, while highways, airports, and waterways get off scot free.

Isn't it scandalous, and a shame?

Well, no; or, at most, not much.

There is nothing new about federal assistance to those who would travel to and fro. The sovereign power of the United States of America, pursuant to Article I, Section 8, paragraph 3 of the Constitution thereof, has been aiding and abetting private enterprise to stimulate transportation between and among the several states ever since 1802, when Congress appropriated money for the building of the Cumberland Road. This particular turnpike was still the nursling of the federal government as late as 1844, when it had been pushed as far west as Missouri. By that time the voracious railroads had for fourteen years been gobbling private and public funds alike, and there was little to spare for turnpikes or wagon roads.

If there is one mode of transportation whose way was smoothed by public funds and by grants of public lands, it is the railroad. The iron horse was fed and watered at the public trough for more than fifty years. No man knows precisely how much of the public's funds was handed over to the railroad promoters by one or another set of politicians; a conservative

5

student of the matter estimated that by 1870 the states alone had given $228,500,000 in cash, while another $300,000,000 had been paid over by counties and municipalities. The federal government and the various states gave, in addition, about 184,000,000 acres of the public lands to the railroads; this represents nearly one tenth of the land area of the continental United States. The state of Texas was most generous of all: at one point (in 1882) her legislators were embarrassed to find that they had actually given away about eight million more acres than they had in their power to bestow; as it finally turned out, they forked over to twelve railroad companies more than thirty-two million acres, which is more real estate than can be fitted inside the boundaries of the state of New York.

The railroad press agents insist that all these public lands were worthless stuff, merely desert and prairie, until the railroads came to make it valuable. They are fond of quoting an obscure politician, William Rufus Devane King, senator from Alabama, who was later Vice-President in the memorable administration of Franklin Pierce. In 1850, King joined a debate in the Senate as to whether land should be granted to the Illinois Central Railroad Company. "We are met by the objection," King said, "that this is an immense grant—that it is a great quantity of land. Well, sir, it is a great quantity; but it will be there for five hundred years; and unless some mode of the kind proposed be adopted, it will never command ten cents."

Never command ten cents? The argument was specious then; it is specious now. To this day several railroad companies are profitable concerns, thanks only to those land grants. Some companies are making more money by exploiting the mineral rights in the lands given them years ago than they can make by operating their railroads.

The national economy was undeniably strengthened when the continent was crisscrossed by a half-dozen railroads. Those railroads coaxed farmers from halfway around the world to come with their plows and break the plains; altogether, the railroads made possible the commercial brigandage in which

6

today we all rejoice. The government assisted them in their depredations, yet now, when the same helping hand is extended to their rivals, they howl. It is not a pleasant sound. When the conversation turns to matters of subsidy and grants from the public purse, only those railroad officials who are utterly lost to shame will not cough with embarrassment and discreetly seek to change the subject.

In the sweet spirit of conciliation, however, let us suppose that the railroad men are right: they are fettered by archaic regulations; they are harshly and inequitably treated by an arbitrary and exigent government. "In fact," says a representative of the Association of American Railroads, "lopsided transport policies sometimes seem diabolically designed to sidetrack trains forever." Good: we shall postulate a sinister plot hatched by a government probably socialist, certainly creeping toward socialism, the leaders of which have sworn to bring the railroads to their knees. But can even such a paranoid fantasy begin to explain the long, steady decline of the railroad industry from its pre-eminence fifty or sixty years ago to its inelegant posture today?

Here is a puzzle. For it is a fact that the railroad is a remarkably efficient form of transportation, and why its operators have not easily, even derisively, squelched their competition is hard to see.

A railroad is a device for rolling people or commodities from one place to another. When it comes to rolling many people in a short time, as in hauling commuters to a city, the railroad is incomparably superior to all other such devices: cheaper, quicker, safer, needing less real estate and fewer operators to do the job, able to keep rolling in fair weather or foul, cleaner, and quieter. On *one* track, a railroad can haul fifty thousand persons an hour. To haul the same number in the same time over a highway requires ten thousand cars traveling in *four* lanes and requires further that the weather be fair, that there be no accidents or mechanical breakdowns, and that each driver carry four passengers in his car. (To set

7

such conditions is to provoke a hollow, mirthless laugh.) Moreover, the trains, once emptied of their passengers, can be sent about their other business, while the automobiles, having poisoned the city's air, now encumber the city's streets until the evening, when they will poison the city's air all over again.

The mad and wonderful problem of commutation will be examined in detail later on, as will the perplexing problem of longer, more casual journeys on the railroad. For the moment, it is enough to note that the railroads, despite their several inherent advantages, have managed to work themselves into a sweet pickle.

When it comes to rolling commodities, the railroads' competitive edge is even more startling. Consider just the basic physics of the thing. As it rolls along, the steel wheel of engine, car, or caboose touches, at any given moment, very little of its curve to the flat of the steel rail. (The surface contact is about the size of a dime.) The less contact, the less resistance; the less resistance, the less friction; the less friction, the greater efficiency. If $x$ equals the force required to move a loaded steel-wheeled freight car over steel rails, then $4x$ will be required to move a comparable load in a hull through water and $7\frac{1}{2}x$ to move it on rubber tires over a concrete highway. For this reason and others, such as the greater efficiency of its more powerful diesel engine, a train averages 192 ton-miles to the gallon of fuel, while a truck gets only 58 ton-miles to the gallon.

But perhaps the most telling advantage of the railroad over its rivals lies in manpower. A train hauling one hundred freight cars has a crew of five. To haul a comparable load by truck takes hundreds of drivers. If you want to move one hundred thousand tons of freight from New York to San Francisco, you must pay for:

43,416 man-days by highway
11,158 man-days by water
3,220 man-days by rail*

*For this example, as for the other technical information in this discussion, I am indebted to the editors of Railway Age, a weekly trade magazine.

8

Nevertheless, the railroads' share of freight revenues has steadily declined. There are some categories of freight (the products of mines, the products of forests) that have traditionally been considered a captive property of the railroads. Yet even here the tonnage is down, the revenues are down.

From first to last, it is a remarkable phenomenon. The men who run the railroads seem to have positively booted the commuters, and the passengers generally, away from their ticket windows and off their trains. They seem to have totally ignored the shippers of freight or to have taken them too much for granted.

Their plant dwindles. "There is much surplus railroad mileage in this country today," Stuart T. Saunders said, in 1962. (Mr. Saunders is chairman of the board of the Pennsylvania Railroad, the biggest in the country.) When a railroad company rips up a mile of track, it stands to gain as much as five thousand dollars in cash for salvaged material and will annually save three thousand dollars in maintenance costs and as much as two thousand in taxes. Moreover, the land can then be profitably sold, perhaps to the government (i.e., to the taxpayers) for use as a highway, after which the press agents for the railroad can complain bitterly about tax-free competition from trucks, buses, and automobiles. (The Boston & Albany Railroad sold eleven miles of its tracks and right of way to the Massachusetts Turnpike Authority for eight million dollars.) The total mileage of track diminishes steadily, from 430,000 miles in 1930 to less than 373,000 miles today.

Their industry's share of the gross national product dwindles, too. In 1930 railroad revenues accounted for 5.8 per cent of the gross national product; in 1966 they accounted for only 1.4 per cent.

Enough of these somber statistics. The picture seems plain enough: a giant industry, vital to the national economy, has for a half century been on the skids to—what? receivership? bankruptcy? nationalization? The signal blocks ahead are hard to make out.

Any examination of the strange and foolish plight of the

9

railroads will uncover vaulting ambition, dumb luck, sly cunning, gross stupidity, incomprehensible arrogance, and naked greed—in short, all the characteristics that have caused the American to be so universally loved and admired. The present inquiry, however, must be prefaced by one further statistic, one that intrudes like a fanfare in a dirge, to wit: despite the fact that the railroads seemed to have been staggering along on very unsteady pins, in 1966 their shareholders were paid five hundred and two million dollars in cash dividends, more than in any other year in the industry's history. How was it possible?

# 1

---

*How the railroads began. Futile efforts toward state ownership. Railroad financiers go into politics: the genesis of the New York Central. The pirates swoop down: Vanderbilt and Drew. The North Western Ring. The Erie War.*

---

THE OFFICERS of a corporation, hoofed and hustled by their shareholders, quite naturally strive for the highest possible net profit. So also the officers of a railroad corporation, but with a difference. Railroad corporations are special: they were chartered by the various states to build and operate railed *public highways* and to levy taxes (in the form of passenger fares and freight rates) on those persons who elected to use the highways. From the outset it was quite clear, at least in charter and law, that the railroads were public thoroughfares, like turnpikes or canals (which also impose a tax, or toll, on their users); that the railroad corporations were quasi-public in nature, having been formed to serve the public convenience and necessity; and that rates were to be charged fairly and equitably, to one and all alike.

So was established a delicious tension, a tug of war between the natural greed for private profit and the irksome obligation to serve the public interest, and its consequences are the salient aspects of the economic history of the nation during the last half of the nineteenth century and for a good part of the twentieth, as well. Elsewhere in the world, in nations wearied by constant struggle, one government after another resolved the conflict by nationalizing the railroads. Under the benign influence of a merciful Providence, however, nationalization was successfully resisted in these two-fisted United States, as a result of which connoisseurs have been diverted, ever since about 1840, by an unending procession of rate wars, back stabbings, raids on the public purse, bankruptcies, corruptions of legislatures, double crosses and triple crosses, virtuosities of stock manipulation, legal swindles, panics and severe depressions, larcenies, extortions, and tyrannies, together with the stupidities, otiosities, effronteries, impertinences, and discourtesies customarily associated with railroad management.

No time was lost in establishing the ground rules for the tug of war. Long before the first ten thousand miles of track had been laid down in the United States—which is to say, before 1850—the policy of railroad management in respect of the public interest had been set and had hardened: it was to ignore the public interest, dismiss it, sweep it under the rug, and carry on. What public interest, indeed? The railroads were the private property of the railroad corporations or, to be more precise, of the associations of capitalists who owned the stock of those corporations; and the railroads would be operated for their benefit.

Such an attitude is hard to reconcile with the fact of the flood of public funds that had been let loose to build the railroads. To select a typical example: the Baltimore & Ohio Railroad Company was given, between 1827 and 1850, thirteen million dollars of taxpayers' money by the state of Maryland and the cities of Baltimore and Wheeling, West Virginia; it was also given, tax free, some choice real estate. Again: a committee of the New York state legislature would later reckon that the state and various cities and towns had given New York railroad corporations, among other goodies, $40,039,496.82 either in cash or by investment, and that only about one quarter of this sum had ever been repaid. The New York & Erie Railroad Company alone got nearly thirteen millions of public money. (One should bear in mind that these were hard-earned ante-bellum dollars, each one equivalent to about three dollars today.)

12

Why did these public subventions not carry with them the assurance that the public interest would be scrupulously respected? The difficulty, of course, was that a corporation bent on the beautiful pursuit of profit is a single-minded entity, whereas the public interest was, as always, vague, amorphous, and proclaimed by many contradictory voices.

Throughout the 1840s there were anguished outcries against the railroad companies from scores of citizens, protesting high and discriminatory freight rates, poor passenger service, filthy accommodations, watered stock and other financial monkeyshines, a regrettable trend toward monopoly, and the policy of giving free passes to politicians, favored shippers, and newspaper editors. As early as 1843 the squawk went up: State ownership of the railroads! To no avail.

All public clamor was ignored, for the railroad executive and the state politico, having early and separately sniffed out the source of potential profit, had inevitably become the same man. Let us trot out for inspection a couple of these hybrids, so swiftly homogenized—Erastus Corning and Dean Richmond.

Corning, an austere and imperious man, was a wealthy hardware merchant and iron manufacturer of Albany, New York, who in 1833 was elected president of a small railroad that was to run between two upstate New York cities—the Utica & Schenectady. Although he served without salary, he had an agreeable arrangement with the infant enterprise: while the road was being built, and thereafter, President Corning bought all its iron and hardware from E. Corning & Company at a toothsome price and also pocketed the commissions for the iron rails imported from England.

Moreover, President Corning soon grasped the peculiar importance of politics to railroading. By the terms of its charter, the U&S was forbidden to haul any freight whatsoever, for its tracks paralleled the state-owned Erie Canal and the state legislators were determined to protect the canal's income against all competition. Presently Corning got himself elected mayor of Albany. Before long he was a power in the Albany Regency, a clique of Democratic politicians that ran the affairs

13

of the state. By 1842 he was a state senator and, sure enough, in 1844 the charter of the U&S was amended so that it might haul freight in the winter months when the canal was frozen. Three years later the railroad was carrying freight the year round but paying tolls for the privilege. By 1851 the U&S was free of all restrictions on its freight business, and naturally Corning was scheming as to how he might further enhance his net profits.

Richmond, a big, ugly, affable man from Buffalo, at the western end of the state, was president of the Buffalo & State Line Railroad. Too shrewd to bother about political preferment, he chose instead to ride herd on the Democratic party as its state chairman. Since the Whigs were all but extinct and the Republicans were yet to be heard from, the state chairman of the Democratic party was admirably fixed to influence legislators; Richmond's headquarters, Room 57 at the Delavan House, across the street from the Albany railroad station, came to be a home away from home for a quorum of the state legislature, and for years Richmond's hand could be glimpsed, moving as adroitly as that of a three-card-monte man, behind every legislative act affecting the young railroads.

Before long, one of Richmond's trained seals on the Railroad Committee of the New York Senate came up with a remarkable suggestion: why not link the eight or ten small railroads that reached from Albany to Buffalo into one big railroad? Not a bad idea, said Corning. Not bad at all, said Richmond. And so was born what was then the biggest corporation in the country, the New York Central Railroad. Who was elected president of the new corporation? Erastus Corning. And who was vice-president? Dean Richmond.

While the New York Central was being capitalized, a little water was allowed to seep in—not much: maybe twelve million dollars, maybe twenty-four million; the estimates of the historians vary—enough, at any rate, to sweeten the disposition of Messrs. Corning and Richmond and their directors.

Corning was particularly pleased. Not because of his salary as president of the New York Central, for he had none; rather

14

because of the net profit realized by E. Corning & Company from the sale of iron and hardware to the big new railroad: it was estimated to be two hundred and fifty thousand dollars a year.

And now we have to introduce two personages of impeccable social standing, the brothers Robert and George Schuyler, who were to cause Dean Richmond all kinds of carks and cares over the next few years. The Schuylers, inheritors of a proud and illustrious name, nephews of Alexander Hamilton, were partners in a New York brokerage business and men of consequence in the commercial community. Each served as president of the New York & Harlem Railroad Company, and Robert was, as well, an officer of the New York & New Haven, the Illinois Central, and the Vermont Valley. In the summer of 1854 it appeared that the two brothers were also both crooked and stupid: Robert had fraudulently issued millions of dollars' worth of spurious securities and had stolen a fortune in relatively sound securities; George, a meaner fellow, had contented himself with such petty thefts as the rents from office space illegally leased.

When the newspapers got hold of the story, they set up a brouhaha that reverberated for weeks. Stockjobbing! Wicked practices! Men in high places! It went to show what everybody had known all along. More important, the rumpus underlined the fact that the directors of the railroad companies were unable to act as trustees of properties confided to their care by the public. And that was what their charters and the common law demanded of them. A special law would have to be passed. Dean Richmond's discomfiture may be imagined.

In 1855 the New York state legislature enacted a statute establishing a Board of Railroad Commissioners, the first in the history of the nation. The commissioners were to supervise freight tariffs, keep an eye peeled on the financial shenanigans of railroad officials, and generally protect the public interest.

In their first year the commissioners bustled about. They asked questions; they called for reports on revenues; they scrutinized dividend rates. The public air was filled with excitement. In their second year the commissioners hesitated. They were not so sure. What were they doing in Albany, anyway? Now that they thought about it, why should they not vote to dissolve their commission?

And so they did; and the legislature, acting with unprecedented alacrity, ratified their decision; and the governor nimbly put his seal upon it.

How came such a remarkable reversal of public policy? More than twenty years passed before the answer was let slip. It was then revealed that matters had been smoothed by a judicious application of the old grease. Was it $125,000 or $25,000? The witness before an investigating committee could not remember precisely. But he vividly recalled whose had been the master hand administering the grease: it was that of Dean Richmond.

Here was a nice instance of how the public could be obliged to pay (in passenger or freight charges) the cost of thwarting the popular will. Nor was it an isolated instance. Edwin D. Worcester, the treasurer of the New York Central, later acknowledged that the company had spent, from 1853 to 1867, more than a half-million dollars to buy laws at Albany. To be sure, Worcester did not characterize the purchase as a betrayal of the public interest. He called it "protecting [the company's] stockholders against injurious legislation."

So, back and forth, the tug of war.

As railroad executives, Corning and Richmond were lucky. Thanks to geological happenstance, theirs was the only trunk line from Vermont to Georgia that could reach back from the coast into the hinterland without having to climb over a range of mountains. And, in their case, the hinterland meant the Great Lakes; it meant Cleveland, Detroit, and Chicago; it meant hefty freight revenues and a busy traffic in passengers. Aside from this special good fortune, Corning and Richmond were representative of the first generation of railroad masters, merchants by training and temperament, no more dishonest and no more inconsiderate of the public interest than a hundred others.

The second generation was something else again. The second generation included the speculators, the gamblers, the buccaneers who took a positive delight in throttling the public interest, dragging it down a dark alley, raping it, and leaving it for dead. The second generation included Daniel Drew and Cornelius Vanderbilt.

For more than forty years Drew and Vanderbilt were alternately partners and rivals, but they were always cronies, always as thick as thieves. They played whist and euchre with each other, they raced their trotters on the Bloomingdale Road. When Vanderbilt concluded that his son Billy was a blockhead, Drew agreed to hire the youngster as a clerk in his brokerage business (at one hundred and fifty dollars a year) and to try to instruct him in wile. (Billy could have found no better tutor.)

Their greatest delight, however, they took in trying to outfox each other in the stock market—which is to say, in the railroad business.* Only multimillionaires could comfortably test their skill in this game, but both Drew and Vanderbilt were multimillionaires before 1850. By that time each considered the skinning of the average plump merchant to be dull sport, akin to shooting a sitting bird. Each looked forward with relish to inventing a stratagem that would confound the other.

In 1850 these two were the reigning magnates of the steamship business. At fifty-six Vanderbilt was a tall, robust, big-beaked man, fluent with profanity, who seemed to swagger even when he was sitting down. Drew was three years younger, a spare, wiry man, wrinkled and weathered from his years as a cattle drover. He walked with a stealthy tread, like a cat; he chose to dress himself as dowdily as possible; he affected the bland, who-me? air of a hedgerow parson. His speech had a country twang and a barnyard flavor, but he never swore and neither did he drink spirits, for at least on Sunday he was a pious Methodist.

*Until late in the century, railroad securities were almost the only ones listed on the New York Stock Exchange. The man of speculative disposition was, perforce, limited in the play of his fancy.

At first both men had viewed the newfangled railroads with suspicion. "I'm a steamboat man," Vanderbilt told a promoter who wanted him to invest in an early railroad; "I'm a competitor of these steam contrivances that you tell us will run on dry land. Go ahead. I wish you well, but I never shall have anything to do with them." Drew controlled the People's Line, which enjoyed a monopoly on the Hudson River; his steamboats were vast, elegant, luxurious vessels that had cost upward of six hundred thousand dollars apiece. When the president of the hungry, new Hudson River Railroad suggested that he and Drew should regulate their passenger fares, Drew showed his teeth in a grin. "You can regulate your railroad fares as you choose," he retorted, "but the only way you can regulate my steamboat fares is to buy the People's Line, and that I don't believe you have money enough to do."

Yet they had kept a wary eye on this new competition. In 1845 they had bought control of the Providence & Stonington Railroad, since it connected with their steamboats on the New York-to-Boston run. In 1849 Drew had linked his People's Line to two small railroads and some Lake Champlain side-wheelers and so had established a North & South Through Line between New York and Montreal. In 1851, when the New York & Erie Railroad at last reached Lake Erie, its directors found there a steamboat company newly established by Drew and all prepared to feast off the east-west traffic. And, despite his show of reluctance, Vanderbilt had by 1850 invested in a half-dozen railroads in Pennsylvania, New Jersey, New York, and Connecticut.

In short, neither Drew nor Vanderbilt stood pat on his monopoly. What others had built, they were now ready to take over.

They moved first into the Erie. That unfortunate road could prosper only at Drew's sufferance: when he chose, he could link his steamboats at Albany with the New York Central so that passengers might travel from New York to Buffalo more cheaply and far more comfortably than was possible on the Erie. The directors of the Erie sensed their plight, but

18

only dimly. In 1854, finding themselves short of funds, they turned trustfully to Drew, like so many woolly lambs. They expected to find a nice comfy ewe. What they got was a wolf.

At Drew's suggestion, Vanderbilt gave the road a short-term loan of four hundred thousand dollars. Drew himself loaned the road nearly one million dollars and went on the board of directors. The Erie became his personal plaything. Its stock began to go up and down like a yo-yo, responsive only to his whim. Public interest? He had never heard of it.

Drew's method was simplicity itself. As a director (and before long as treasurer) he knew the Erie's every weakness and could probe each one to his profit whenever he chose. There was, for example, the question of competition, not only with the Central but also with the B&O and the Pennsylvania. Among these four trunk lines, rate wars raged incessantly, interrupted only by brief, ineffectual truces. A war drove the price of Erie's shares down, to Drew's profit. A truce brought them up again, and Drew purred. Who had started the war? Who had stopped it? Drew was not talking. "It's the still hog," he said, "that eats the most."

In the fall of 1854, representatives of the four trunk lines met in a New York hotel and agreed to fix their rates for passengers and freight. At once a howl went up. The editor of The New York Times perceived "a combination of railroad companies against the public."

> Their charters were obtained [said the editor of The Times], their stock was subscribed and their routes were fixed on the plea that by their *competition* the rates of travel would be reduced, their speed would be increased, the prices of transportation would be diminished and the public at large would reap immense benefits in various ways.

The railroad compact called for a fare of nine dollars from New York to Buffalo, but of course it was promptly dishonored. The Erie announced a rate of six dollars and fifty cents, and up went the Erie's stock, Drew having bet that it would. The Central thereupon scheduled a train to meet Drew's steamboats at

Albany, cutting the fare to four dollars, and down went the Erie's stock, Drew having bet that it would.

Rate wars, mismanagement, and Drew's sedulous policy of stock manipulation drove the New York & Erie into receivership in 1859. It emerged two years later as the Erie Railway Company; Drew and Vanderbilt sat next to each other on the board of directors.

For his part, Vanderbilt coveted the two roads leading north from New York City. The New York & Harlem was a poor thing that wound around through farmland, reaching perhaps two thirds of the way to Albany; shares of its stock were cheap, selling for twelve or fifteen dollars. The Hudson River Railroad, on the other hand, had been put through to Albany in 1851 and was operated at a handsome profit, interchanging freight and passengers with the New York Central. For a man of the Commodore's grand monopolistic bent, what point was there in controlling only one of them?

The old pirate began by bribing the New York city council and the New York state legislature in order to secure the rights to valuable franchises for the Harlem. These foolish politicians having presumed to double-cross him by revoking the franchises they had granted and then gambling that the railroad's stock would drop, Vanderbilt proceeded to take them to the cleaners. He rigged three corners on the stock exchange, two of them simultaneously, a feat that called for all the available millions even of the Commodore. In one corner he squeezed the members of the city council, in another he squeezed the state legislators, and then he hung them out to dry. By the end of the summer of 1864, Vanderbilt had both railroads under his thumb and neither one had cost him a cent; indeed, he had cleared a substantial profit on the transactions. It was a pretty demonstration of what could be accomplished by a man who had nothing but guile, determination, and a few million dollars.*

*The shorts caught in the Hudson corner of June–July, 1863, gambled that the price of the stock would go below 125; they were obliged to settle at 175. The shorts caught in the first Harlem corner had succeeded

20

The Commodore now fixed a calculating eye on the New York Central. While Corning and Richmond were still in control, they had quarreled with the officers of the Hudson River Railroad over the division of revenue from freight consigned between New York and Buffalo; Vanderbilt had forthrightly demanded of the Central a tribute of one hundred thousand dollars a year, failing which he proposed to urge all merchants and manufacturers to ship their goods over the competitive Erie. At length the Central's officers appreciated the force of this argument and agreed to make the payment.

But now Corning had retired and Richmond was dead, and the gang of freebooters who seized control of the Central in December, 1866, at once declared war on Vanderbilt by canceling the annual blackmail.

The Commodore struck back at once. In January, 1867, during the coldest freeze of midwinter, he served notice that the Hudson River Railroad would carry passengers and freight only to its terminus, East Albany, a half mile short of the Hudson River, a mile short of any connection with the Central on the far bank.

What price the public interest? No ferries could cross the frozen river; the snow fell. Trains were stalled in great drifts east and west of Albany and travelers bound either way had to trudge on ice, lugging their baggage, supporting their sick, piggybacking their children.

The New York state legislature, eighty-five of the members of which were more often than not on Vanderbilt's payroll, presumed to summon their boss to a legislative inquiry. He chose to be now genial, now arrogant. Why had he ordered his trains stopped a half mile from the river?

---

in hammering *its* stock from 116 in May, 1863, down to 73, on June 25; they settled in August at about 180. In the second Harlem corner (April–June, 1864) the shorts bet that the stock would go down at least to 75, but Vanderbilt and his allies succeeded in driving it up to 285.

According to a shaky tradition, Drew was caught in both Harlem corners and shorn of more than one million dollars; after the second Harlem corner he is supposed to have invented a rueful rhyme:

"He that sells what isn't his'n
Must buy it back or go to prison."

"I was not there, gentlemen," Vanderbilt said.

"But what did you do when you heard of it?"

"I did not do anything."

"Why not? Where were you?"

"I was at home, gentlemen, playing a rubber of whist, and I never allow anything to interfere with me when I am playing that game. It requires, as you know, undivided attention."

But what of the rights of the people to travel over these railed highways? Why had Vanderbilt permitted a squabble between his corporation and another to put the public to such a gross inconvenience?

"I have always served the public to the best of my ability," Vanderbilt retorted. "Why? Because, like every other man, it is my interest to do so, and to put them to as little inconvenience as possible. I don't think there is a man in the world who would go further to serve the public than I."

Counsel for the legislature's railroad committee paused, perhaps eying the heavens and waiting for a thunderbolt to strike. "Did you not know," he asked, "that the law provides a remedy for all wrongs, and that railroad corporations have no right to take the redress of their own wrongs into their own hands, to the detriment of the public?"

"The law, as I view it," said Vanderbilt, "goes too slow for me when I have the remedy in my own hands."

"Could not the Hudson River Railroad enforce their claim for the one hundred thousand dollars through the courts of the law?"

"They might; I will not give an opinion on that point. I stated a while ago that I, for one, will never go to a court of law when I've got the power in my own hands to see myself right. Let the other parties go to law if they want, but by God I think I know what the law is; I have had enough of it."

All bowed before the majesty of the Commodore's millions, for this was the Gilded Age. The management of the Central quaked and collapsed. The stock of the railroad declined sharply (Vanderbilt grabbed thousands of shares at bargain-basement prices), and the most influential shareholders, painfully disturbed, could see only one solution. A group of them representing nearly half of the Central's stock invited Vanderbilt to be their chief and sovereign lord; only this, they wrote him, "would result in larger dividends to the stockholders and greatly promote the interest of the public."

Here was a striking formulation, yoking the two desiderata quite as if they were not mutually exclusive. The stockholders could be sure the Commodore would addess himself diligently to beefing up the dividends (so long as he owned a substantial block of the stock), but what possessed them to prattle about the public interest?

They had good reason. The fact was that popular pressure against the management of the railroads had been building steadily and apace, especially since the end of the Civil War. Even before Vanderbilt had moved to gobble up the New York Central and so materially advance the goals of monopoly, another group of capitalists from New York had pointed the way by organizing what was called the North Western Ring. These men—William B. Ogden, Charles Butler, and Samuel J. Tilden were the ring's leaders, and Russell Sage also had a hand in it—had in 1865 combined seven or eight small railroads in Michigan, Illinois, and Wisconsin into one big railroad, which they called the Chicago & North Western. In the process they had manipulated securities so as to rob farmers, merchants, and other such small investors of an estimated twenty million dollars; their railroad dominated the farmland for eleven hundred miles around Chicago, and their control of the rate for shipping grain threatened to impoverish the farmers even further. When in 1866 a young journalist named James Parton presumed to publish a small pamphlet exposing their frauds, Tilden got a crooked Tammany judge to enjoin the publication and managed to impound and destroy all but a few copies of it.*

*Parton went on to become a biographer and historian of some repute. His pamphlet, which was called *Manual for the Instruction of "Rings," Railroad and Political,* was reprinted in 1876, when Tilden was campaigning for election as President, and it may be presumed to have cost him some votes.

The North Western Ring and others like it inflamed the popular temper against the railroad promoters yet more feverishly. Conventions of businessmen were called in Chicago and Detroit *ad hoc*, associations of farmers began to agitate, petitions were addressed to Congress; and all this ferment culminated in a National Board of Trade and in another, shorter-lived sodality that staggered along under the burden of what is surely the most grandiloquent handle in our history, to wit: The National Anti-Monopoly Cheap Freight Railway League, for Promoting Reform in Railroad Management, by Securing Equal Rights & Cheap Transportation, with Consequent Increased Development of Our Industrial Energies & National Resources.

In 1867 this outfit was hot stuff. The scheme its members advocated was wonderfully simple: the federal government, in co-operation with the various state governments, to build railroads as necessary; thereafter, any shipper to use them, transporting his freight in his own rolling stock; rates to be a fraction of what the railroad monopolists charged; and, as a consequence, everybody to join hands and dance to the music of the spheres. Since politicians always scurry to endorse sufficiently popular panaceas, a swarm of governors, senators, and congressmen leaped aboard this particular band wagon, which had got up considerable steam and was rolling along splendidly when all of a sudden it ground to a halt and everybody fell off. What had happened? Lobbyists for the railroads had been at work, of course, convincing the politicians with their long-green convincers; more important, however, was the fact that commodity prices went up faster than freight rates.

It should be noted that the Cheap Freight League was never concerned with the railroad passenger, nor indeed with the larger aspects of the public interest. Its members were only businessmen who were vexed because they were not getting a bigger slice of the profits from the gross national product. When the prices they put on their commodities were not too severely shaved by the freight rates they had to pay, they forgot all about the evils of monopoly.

24

And so Cornelius Vanderbilt advanced, unimpeded, and engorged the New York Central with no audible carminative effect whatsoever.

With the Central under his belt, Vanderbilt concluded that he had best control the Erie, too. Here, as he knew he would, he ran smack dab into the private preserve of his old friend Daniel Drew, who had posted his property with signs warning all trespassers to keep off. Nevertheless the Commodore kept on and so precipitated the great Erie War.

As a public spectacle of greed, the Erie War stands alone in our history. Other scandals have involved bigger sums of money or more eminent personages; only the Erie War was shamelessly fought in the open, where it could be seen—and smelled—by everybody. The newspapers reported the whole sordid affair: the deceptions and betrayals of the two chief combatants, Vanderbilt's attempt to seize the Erie with the brute strength of his millions, Drew's sly use of fishy securities, the corruption of the Supreme Court of the State of New York, Drew's flight to New Jersey with the six million dollars in cash he had wrung from Vanderbilt on the stock market, the Commodore's plot to kidnap Drew and fetch him back to New York, the quite open bribery of legislators in Albany on behalf of a law to legalize recent felonies, and the cynical concordat that finally ended hostilities.

If the early skirmishes are included, the Erie War lasted about seven months, from early October, 1867, to late April, 1868. On March 3, 1868, the Erie's general superintendent filed a report on the condition of the road:

> The iron rails have broken, laminated and worn out beyond all precedent, until there is scarce a mile . . . between Jersey City and . . . Buffalo, where it is safe to run a train at the ordinary . . . speed, and many portions of the road can only be traversed safely by reducing the speed . . . to twelve or fifteen miles an hour, solely on account of the rotten and worn-out condition of the rails. Broken wheels, rails, engines, and trains off the track, have been of daily, almost hourly, occurrence for the last two months. . . . The condition of the iron at the present

time is such as to give me much anxiety and apprehension for the safety of trains. . . .

Two days later there was a serious wreck, but it came on the Central. On March 15, Vanderbilt, who had just spent something like eight million dollars in a single week of desperate gambling on the stock market, ordered all wages on the Central to be cut by ten per cent. His workmen promptly went on strike and stayed out for two weeks, when their wages were restored. On April 15 the Erie's Buffalo Express was crawling around a curve at thirty miles an hour, in hilly country northwest of New York City, when four of its nine cars snapped their couplings and plunged into a gorge below. Forty persons were killed, seventy-five were injured. George Templeton Strong, a New York lawyer, made an entry in his diary:

> Another railroad accident (so-called) on the Erie Road. Scores of people smashed, burned to death, or maimed for life. We shall never travel safely till some pious, wealthy, and much beloved railroad director has been hanged for murder, with a "gentlemanly conductor" on each side of him. Drew or Vanderbilt would do to begin with. . . .

In these circumstances, the principals of the Erie War met to sign their peace treaty.

Vanderbilt got one million dollars in cash, three and one half million dollars for fifty thousand shares of the suspicious Erie stock he had bought from Drew, some worthless bonds, and two seats on the Erie's board of directors.

Vanderbilt's brokers got $429,250 in cash.

A Tammany politician named Peter Sweeny got $150,000 for being a Tammany politician in the right place.

Drew got his enormous profits, less $550,000, the fee he had to pay to the Erie Railway Company for discharge of all claims against him.

Jay Gould and Jim Fisk, two young men who had been Drew's lieutenants in the Erie War, got control of the Erie Railway Company, and God help it. (One of the first men elected to the Erie's board of directors under the Gould-Fisk regime was William Marcy Tweed, the most notorious boss of

Tammany Hall in the long and malodorous history of that political organization.)

The next of kin in the wreck of the Buffalo Express got nothing.

The stockholders of the Erie got ten million dollars of debt, at least as much in ill-will, and a shocking bad road.

No doubt about it, Vanderbilt had been flummoxed. He had hoped to grasp in his fist all the railroads connecting New York City with the continent and to control them utterly, but Drew had overreached him. Moreover, the New York merchants had made unmistakably clear their antagonism to his ambitions. Much as they despised Drew, they feared Vanderbilt's monopoly even more.

Rubbing his bruises, the Commodore withdrew and considered. To satisfy his greed, there was only one course open to him: to inflate the capitalization of the New York Central. On the Saturday night before Christmas, 1868, he convened the Central's directors in secret session. (He chose a Saturday so that his schemes might not be foiled by injunctions granted on behalf of indignant shareholders; that the meeting was called in the Christmas season was a charming coincidence.) He proposed that there be a new issue of stock, puffing up the Central's capitalization by an exhilarating eighty per cent. It was done.*

A pesky state law—the General Railroad Act of 1850—restricted dividends to ten per cent of a railroad's actual cost. In 1869 the state legislature agreed with Vanderbilt that such a curb was intolerable. The law was changed. No bribe was necessary; most of the legislators had long since invested in the New York Central.

In the same year, with the kind consent of the legislature,

*Later, when a stockholder's suit was filed against this remarkable fraud, Vanderbilt testified with his customary equanimity. The Central's earnings, he declared, would justify the inflation. He was asked about the New York & Harlem, his smallest road. Did he plan to water its stock, too? Not for the moment, he said; but maybe later on. "I use the Harlem," he said, "just as though it all belonged to me, and that is the way I shall control every other road as long as I control any—as though it all belonged to me."

27

Vanderbilt consolidated the Central and the Hudson River Railroad, and, since one is twice as big as two, he concluded that the new corporation's capital structure should be doubled. After this last influx of water, the NYC&HRR's book value was about ninety million dollars, of which, mirabile dictu, twenty million was actually cash investment. The balance, to quote the report of a tardy investigating committee, represented "nothing except imagination and audacity."

The Commodore was naturally determined to pay an eight per cent dividend on the full ninety million. To do so he gouged all those who shipped freight over his road. (A law restricting fares to two cents a mile protected the passengers; in this restraint can be detected the germ of the implacable hatred that most railroad executives have for their passengers.) New York City merchants and upstate farmers alike were ruthlessly squeezed.

The farmers were particularly bitter, for they paid more than did midwest farmers to send their produce to the New York market. In the midwest, Vanderbilt had to compete with the other trunk lines; east of Buffalo he could charge the farmers whatever he chose. Before long upstate New York, which had been the most productive agricultural region in the country, was impoverished. Was this progress? The editor of an upstate New York agricultural journal made a wry joke: "They load our farms on their freight cars and carry them [west] without the consent of the owners (we give them credit for doing this free of charge)."

The merchants, on the other hand, still had a margin for profit. They could pass the exorbitant freight charges on to the consumer, in the form of higher prices for commodities. Every citizen of New York paid his tribute to Vanderbilt, a penny, a nickel, a dime, a dollar; and so Vanderbilt's hand stole into every citizen's purse, and so he got richer, and so everyone gradually forgot that the railroads had been chartered, in the first instance, by publicly elected officials and for the good of all.

So, back and forth, the tug of war.

# 2

*The Union Pacific and the Central Pacific. The Crédit Mobilier: graft and politics. Envious attempts to loot as much or more elsewhere. The Northern Pacific and the Panic of 1873. Sage and Gould grab the Union Pacific.*

AT PROMONTORY POINT, Utah, in the clear cold afternoon of May 10, 1869, before a gathering that included prostitutes from the nearby railroad camps, train crews, Irish and Chinese workmen, the 21st Infantry regimental band, a couple of Mormon bishops, and a pride of assorted dignitaries, Leland Stanford, the president of the Central Pacific Railroad, took in hand a sledge hammer of silver. He proposed to drive a spike of gold through a tie of laurel and so ceremonially connect the Central Pacific to the Union Pacific. A telegraph wire had been attached to the spike; it would carry the impact of Stanford's whack east to Washington, where, in response, a magnetic ball would drop from a pole above the dome of the Capitol; west to San Francisco, where cannon were primed to boom and firemen stood by to toll scores of bells; to every city of the land, at every point of the compass, where factory whistles would blow and citizens would cheer and cheer again the pride of the nation, the achievement that Horace Greeley had called "the grandest and noblest enterprise of our age," the railroad that had bridged a continent.

It was an epochal moment, quintessentially American. There had been speeches, lengthy prayers, and requests for divine blessing on this latest triumph of God's country. Stanford, a

29

man of impressive heft and dignity, who expanded on such occasions, stepped forward, acknowledging the patter of applause.

He lofted his hammer and swung it down. He missed the spike.

An anonymous telegrapher, alert for just such a boo-boo, banged his key to simulate the stroke of the hammer and the celebration proceeded on schedule across the nation.

After the cheers had died down, gradually it became clear that there was another aspect of the enterprise: the building of the railroad had been attended at every step by fraud and corruption.

The source of profit was the Pacific Railroad Act, signed into law by President Lincoln on July 1, 1862. The law authorized two companies to build and operate a railroad between Sacramento and the Missouri River. To help the companies build the road, the government granted them a strip of land two hundred feet wide for right of way; gave them ten alternate sections of the public domain in each mile, on both sides of the prospective road, over its entire length; and engaged to pay them from sixteen thousand dollars for each mile built on the flat up to forty-eight thousand dollars for each mile of mountainous terrain. These subsidies were to be repaid; they were secured by thirty-year bonds at six per cent interest, which gave the government a first mortgage on the road.

Here, it seemed, would be a truly national railroad. The intentions of the Congress were clear; they were "to promote the public interest and welfare by the construction of said railroad . . . and to secure to the Government at all times, but particularly in time of war, the use and benefit of the same for postal, military, and other purposes." To make sure that this brave project would never fall into the hands of a few greedy men, to be used by them for their own profit, the Congress stipulated that no one individual might own more than two hundred shares of the company.*

*This restriction applied only to the Union Pacific Railroad Company,

The man chiefly responsible for this legislation, which indeed he had helped to draft, was one Theodore D. Judah, a young engineer whose passion on behalf of a transcontinental railroad amounted to mild monomania. (In California they called him Crazy Judah.) He had infected many Californians with his enthusiasm; he had even got some Sacramento merchants to disgorge a little cash—not much, but enough to enable him to incorporate the Central Pacific Railroad Company, which was to build the western end of the road. Of these merchants, the most important were Mark Hopkins and Collis P. Huntington, who owned a hardware store; Leland Stanford, a wholesale grocer; and Charles Crocker, a dealer in dry goods.

These men knew nothing of railroads. They knew little of anything save how to bargain, make money, and hang on to what they had made in their strong, tight fists. Hopkins was the oldest of the four, a skinny man, cautious and stubborn and saving; a clerk. Stanford was big and stolid, ponderous and vain; of the four, he alone had got beyond grade school, but this was a matter of opportunity, not of intelligence. Crocker was also vain and stupid and stubborn, a whale of a man whose weight rarely dropped below two hundred and fifty pounds. Huntington was the ablest of the lot. He was a big, spare man, ruthless, grim, cold, crafty, and, in the phrase of some unknown eulogist, "scrupulously dishonest."

When Judah had first talked with these four men, they had listened suspiciously. A transcontinental railroad? It was too much for their pawky greed to comprehend. Their vision reached only to the Nevada silver mines, newly opened in 1860 and gushing out a great careless wealth. Freight was being hauled from Sacramento to the Nevada mining towns by horse and wagon at exorbitant rates; so much these merchants could understand. If they could only control that

---

which, by the terms of the original legislation, was to lay its tracks as far as the California border. The Central Pacific Railroad Company, which was to build the road between Sacramento and the state line, was a corporation chartered by the state of California.

market beyond the Sierra, that traffic rich beyond credulity, they would consider their tiny investment in a railroad a worth-while gamble. But when in 1862 Judah came back from Washington with the Pacific Railroad Act signed, sealed, and in his valise, the four merchants reconsidered. Here was land, here was real estate, millions of acres of it. Here was cash and, if they made no mistake, here was the chance for much more cash, far more than could be made from a few silver bonanzas. Here, if they played their cards right, was an empire.

They moved swiftly. They began to lay track in January, 1863; a few months later they had raised more than three million dollars from the state, some counties, and the cities of San Francisco and Sacramento, and much of this money was given to the railroad company outright, from public funds, for wasn't the railroad in the public interest? (The fact that Stanford had managed to get himself elected governor in 1862 helped in many ways, as in the subsequent agreement by the state to pay interest on two million dollars' worth of the company's seven-per-cent bonds.)

By August they had picked a quarrel with Judah: he wanted to build carefully and well, they wanted to build hastily and so collect the government subsidy. And then there was the matter of the stretch of land a few miles east of Sacramento. It was as flat as a floor, but wasn't the soil geologically the same as the soil at the base of the Sierra Nevadas, twenty-five miles away? And didn't that prove that the government should pay them forty-eight thousand dollars a mile, rather than sixteen thousand? Judah said no, and that was the end of Judah. His four partners forced him out of the company he had created and were off on their fraudulent own.

According to the law, President Lincoln was to fix the point at which the Sierra Nevadas began to rise. A state geologist, retained by Governor Stanford, fancied he could perceive "a regular and continuous ascent" beginning seven miles east of Sacramento. In Washington, a California congressman, Aaron Sargent, pestered Lincoln for a quick decision. The President accepted the opinion of the state geologist.

32

Sargent grinned and told a journalist: "My pertinacity and Abraham's faith moved mountains." The mountains moved westward some twenty-five miles, a miracle that cost the tax-payers eight hundred thousand dollars.

The settlement the four Sacramento merchants made with Judah has never been precisely elucidated. One story goes that they paid him one hundred thousand dollars and gave him options to buy their interests in the company for the same amount each. There is evidence that he got ninety-one thousand dollars worth of stock and ten thousand dollars in gold. At all events, Judah sailed for New York in October, 1863, confident that he would be able to oust his former partners from the management of the Central Pacific. A meeting had been arranged with some financiers of New York and Boston who, Judah was sure, would put up the money he needed to regain control. But on his way across the Isthmus of Panama he fell sick of yellow fever and died a week after he was carried off the steamer in New York.

Even if Judah had lived, it may be doubted that he would have prevailed over the merchants. Who did he imagine would supply the capital he needed? Not Vanderbilt, as has been commonly supposed, for Vanderbilt was never a railroad builder; even after the transcontinental railroad was an accom-plished fact, the Commodore's son-in-law, Horace F. Clark, speaking for the Vanderbilt interests, declined to invest in the road, arguing that its traffic was too trivial to be profitable. It seems more likely that Judah hoped to persuade some of the men who had helped him lobby for the Pacific Railroad Act, those shadowy figures who controlled the Union Pacific's end of the road. If this is so, it is a measure of Judah's naïveté. The Sacramento merchants were, to be sure, mean-spirited and grasping, but their counterparts on the east coast were far more practiced in guile and treachery and would have gutted Judah's dream far more swiftly.

Besides which, Huntington had reached New York several months before Judah, had opened an office as purchasing agent for the Central Pacific, and had at once got on the friendliest (if often competitive) footing with the Union Pacific's promoters. Before long he and some of them were working amicably together in Washington, seeking to change some of the clauses in the Pacific Railroad Act. They paid out nearly four hundred and thirty-six thousand dollars for fees, bribes, entertainment, and other evidences of their warm appreciation of how hard was the life of a congressman; and so, in July, 1864, up for vote came an amended bill—described as a wartime necessity—that doubled the size of the land grants to twelve thousand eight hundred acres per mile, permitted the companies to take timber, coal, and stone from public lands other than those already granted them, increased the federal subsidy in mountainous country, canceled the restriction on individual stock ownership, and, most significant of all, empowered the companies to issue first-mortgage bonds, thereby downgrading the government bonds to a second mortgage on the railroad.

The Honorable Elihu B. Washburne of Illinois was aghast. "The greatest legislative crime in history," he cried, to a House full of congressmen debilitated by the infernal heat of a Washington summer and anxious to adjourn. "The most monstrous and flagrant attempt to overreach the Government and the people that can be found in all the legislative annals of the country!" Richer by nearly one half million dollars, his colleagues laughed, passed the bill, and sent it on to the White House, where Lincoln at once signed it.

For his part, Huntington was impressed by the statecraft of which the Congress was occasionally capable. "An extraordinarily generous act," he murmured. He thereupon addressed himself to the delicate task of convincing the owners of mills and foundries glutted with cost-plus-fifty-per-cent army contracts that the Pacific Railroad was a quasi-public enterprise, that the War Department agreed with him, and that rails and locomotives should be forthwith dispatched to California. He was often to get quite cross, in future months, when equipment promised him was diverted to serve the southern battle fronts.

Meanwhile, in laggardly fashion, the eastern financiers were beginning to interest themselves in the Union Pacific. They were not prodded, as was Huntington, by a constant popular pressure to unite the two sea coasts; on the other hand, they knew the war would not go on forever; soon they would have to find other investments for their money. The permission to issue first-mortgage bonds, coaxed from the Congress by their agents, made the Union Pacific more attractive. All that was needed was a company for the transaction of certain interesting financial sleights of hand. A few of them undertook to establish such a company; it would be called the Crédit Mobilier of America.

Who were these men? To name them precisely is no easy task. They were mysterious to their contemporaries, and after a century of investigation the economic historians are still by no means certain of their identity. Charles Francis Adams, who as a journalist specialized in the disgraces of the railroads of the Gilded Age, estimated their number at nearly six dozen:

> Under one name or another [Adams wrote] a ring of some seventy persons is struck, at whatever point the Union Pacific is approached. As stockholders they own the road, as mortgagees they have a lien upon it, as directors they contract for its construction, and as members of the Crédit Mobilier they build it.

It would have been more accurate to say "and as members of the Crédit Mobilier they loot it," for the Crédit Mobilier was the corporate device by which the Pacific ring was able to rob railroad, government, and public alike. But to comprehend that simple and elegant device one must first inspect the ring itself.

The insiders of the Pacific ring included the shrewdest and most enterprising railroad men in the nation. In Boston there was the group of financiers, centering around John Murray Forbes, that had built the Michigan Central and later the roads that were to become the Chicago, Burlington & Quincy. In Chicago there was William B. Ogden, who had built the

35

first railroads into Chicago and who was elected the city's first mayor; and there was his brother-in-law Charles Butler, associated with him in building the roads into Chicago from Pennsylvania and out of Chicago west across Wisconsin and Minnesota (what are now the Chicago & North Western and the Chicago, Milwaukee, St. Paul & Pacific). In Philadelphia there were John Edgar Thomson, the president of the Pennsylvania Railroad, and his vice-president, Thomas A. Scott. In New York there were Erastus Corning and John V. L. Pruyn of the New York Central; there was John I. Blair, a director of the Delaware, Lackawanna & Western, who was scheming to plunder the public lands of Iowa by undertaking to build a railroad showily called the Sioux City & Pacific; and there was Russell Sage, an ally of Erastus Corning in the consolidation of the New York Central and a partner to Ogden and Butler in the wholesale bribery and looting of public lands that had attended the building of the railroads across Wisconsin and Minnesota. In New York there were also the investment bankers August Belmont and J. F. D. Lanier and the lawyer Samuel J. Tilden, who represented not only Sage and others of the North West Ring but also the Pennsylvania Railroad.

So long as the Pacific Railroad was considered a patriotic duty and a public responsibility, these men were prominent in the affairs of the Union Pacific. Ogden was the company's first president; Forbes conferred with President Lincoln as to how it could be more swiftly built; Tilden was one of its federal commissioners; Thomson, Pruyn, Blair, Belmont, and Lanier sat on its board of directors; Sage served as a trustee for the public funds raised to build it.

Then came the Crédit Mobilier, and everybody ducked out of sight. Dummies and stock nominees stepped forward as if by magic. Ogden, forewarned, had already resigned the presidency; Forbes, after a genteel deprecation of those who "hunt with the hounds and run with the hares," severed all visible connections with the plunderbund; Tilden busied himself with reform politics and before long got himself elected governor of New York; Thomson, Pruyn, Blair, Belmont, and Lanier all

36

resigned from the board of directors; and Sage, ever devious and reclusive, kept his mouth shut tight. If they were involved, their complicity was cloaked; if they had established and invested in the Crédit Mobilier, it could never be proved but only inferred; they could survive any consequent scandals unruffled.

To recite the few visible facts about its nativity, the Crédit Mobilier of America was born on March 26, 1864, by act of the Pennsylvania legislature and at the behest of Thomas C. Durant, a promoter who had won a certain reputation by manipulating the affairs of the Mississippi & Missouri Railroad (later absorbed by the Chicago, Rock Island & Pacific). Durant, after having been named the vice-president of the Union Pacific by the ring's insiders, had searched about for a corporation with a conveniently flexible charter, and George Francis Train, a flamboyant eccentric of the time, had found him just what he wanted. It was called the Pennsylvania Fiscal Agency; its charter permitted its officers to do almost anything, even violate the Eighth Commandment. Durant purchased this admirable contrivance, Train gave it its new and exotic name, and Durant was at once elected its president.

Ostensibly the Crédit Mobilier was a construction company, organized for the purpose of building the Union Pacific, and as such it was quite commonplace. A construction company, tightly held and having for its directors the same men who had formed and were promoting a railroad company, was essential to the building of a railroad, for only so could the promoters get rich quick, by buying cheap and selling to themselves at a yummy profit the ties, spikes, rails, rolling stock, and other hardware needed to build a road. If by some mischance the profit could not be taken in cash, it could always be taken in the securities of the railroad under construction. In this way the promoters could get a lock on the road and all its assets, including the virgin timber and the rich mineral rights that came with grants of land from the public domain.

Most of the insiders of the Pacific ring had routinely organized such companies during the previous decade—Thomson

37

in Pennsylvania, Ogden and Butler in Illinois and Ohio, Sage in Wisconsin and Minnesota, Blair in New Jersey and later in Iowa, and so on. In California, the four Sacramento merchants had as a matter of course organized such a company: it was first called The Associates and later the Contract & Finance Company. There was no other way to guarantee a return on investment; railroad financiers could not otherwise be coaxed to venture their funds.

In truth, the financiers rarely risked much of their own money on their railroads. They preferred to sell bonds to the public, i.e., to the chumps in this country and abroad. The bondholders provided the capital, they assumed almost all the risk, but, aside from their limited contractual returns, they never saw any of the profits. For a trifling investment of cash, a very few men controlled the common stock of both railroad company and construction company. This gave them the voting power.

The Crédit Mobilier was, except in one decisive respect, a typical construction company. Contracts to build the Union Pacific were let, at fancy fees, to contractors who were dummies controlled by the Crédit Mobilier. For example, when a competent engineer estimated the cost of a mile of road at $22,500, he was replaced by a more perceptive and more agreeable engineer; the contract was let at $50,000 per mile and the dummy contractor was paid in cash and Union Pacific securities. By this device, and others more arcane, the first two hundred and forty-seven miles of Union Pacific track were laid at a

| | |
|---|---|
| cost to the Union Pacific of | $12,974,416.24 and a |
| cost to the contractor of | $ 7,806,183.33, which left a |
| profit to the Crédit Mobilier of | $ 5,168,232.91. |

It was scarcely worth the trouble. Already the insiders of the Pacific ring had staked more than two million dollars of their own cash to promote this railroad, and all they had to show for it were their dividends: first-mortgage bonds worth one and one quarter million dollars and stock worth six and one half million dollars at par.* The insiders commenced to squabble amongst themselves. The Boston financiers having edged their way into a dominant position, a new contract was drawn in the summer of 1867 and finally ratified on October 1: Oakes Ames, the nominee of the Boston financiers, engaged to lay the next six hundred and sixty-seven miles of track at a

cost to the Union Pacific of    $57,140,102.94 and a
cost to himself of    $27,285,141.99, representing a
profit to the Crédit Mobilier of   $29,854,960.95

A respectable rate of profit. Oakes Ames, a manufacturer of shovels, a trustworthy Republican congressman from Massachusetts, and a member of the House Committee on Pacific Railroads, was the perfect dummy contractor for the shareholders of the Crédit Mobilier. Despite his impressive credentials, Ames was not, however, perfectly trusted: he was obliged to assign his contract to seven trustees, who could be relied upon for an equitable division of the loot.

Already in November, 1867, it was clear that the Crédit Mobilier was about to harvest an impressively plump and juicy melon. Cash was pouring in. The Treasury was steadily ladling out generous federal subsidies; the public was snapping up first-mortgage bonds with gratifying alacrity. It was, nevertheless, a ticklish moment for the insiders of the Pacific ring. Even as they rejoiced, they sensed the need for caution. When they stripped the Union Pacific of its securities, they were plundering a corporation with a federal charter. Five of its directors were appointed by the Secretary of the Interior to represent the government and protect the public interest; at any time, one of them might blow the whistle on the whole caper.†

Soon the remarkably profitable exploits of the Crédit Mobilier would be common gossip. What if some preternaturally conscientious congressman were to demand an investigation?

*Par for Union Pacific stock was 100. It was not publicly traded at this time; later the insiders insisted that it was privately traded at about 30.

†In 1862 John P. Usher was the Assistant Secretary of the Interior. In August of that year, soon after Lincoln had signed the first Pacific Rail-

To avert such a disaster, Oakes Ames undertook to execute an ingenious plan. When the Fortieth Congress assembled, in November, 1867, Ames had in hand some shares of the Crédit Mobilier and he either gave or sold, at a fraction of their real value, scores of them to the most influential politicians; he spread them around, as he said later, in an unhappier time, "where it would do us the most good." This procedure was not extraordinary, or at any rate not extraordinarily dishonest. John Blair was simultaneously equipping selected congressmen with blocks of stock in the Dubuque & Sioux City Railroad, Collis Huntington was passing out shares of the Central Pacific, and no doubt three or four other railroad financiers were doing the same. It was a normal business precaution. As Ames put it: "There is no difficulty in getting men to look after their own property." On Ames's list there were, among others, the Vice-President, the Speaker of the House of Representatives, a few senators, and the chairmen of the most important standing committees of the House. Since the Congress was controlled by the Republicans, it followed that Ames bagged some tolerably eminent specimens of the breed. James G. Blaine was one, James A. Garfield was another.

And now all seemed to have been corked up tight. It was time to slice the melon.

In the next thirteen months, six dividends were declared: dividends of ninety per cent in cash, one hundred and fifty-five per cent in first-mortgage bonds, and three hundred per cent in stock: a total of more than twenty million dollars. On November 1, 1868, the contract to build the last one hundred and twenty-five miles of the railroad was let at a

---

road Act, Usher arranged for the appointment of Samuel J. Tilden, the New York railroad lawyer, as a federal commissioner of the Pacific Railroad; the next day Usher wrote to Tilden, instructing him to put money in Usher's account at Winslow, Lanier & Company, a firm that specialized in floating railroad securities. Usher was named Secretary of the Interior in January, 1863, and he subsequently appointed the government directors of the Union Pacific. In May, 1865, Usher resigned and was at once engaged as counsel for (surprise!) the Union Pacific; he held that post for the rest of his life.

cost to the Union Pacific of $23,431,768.10 and an ultimate cost to the contractor of $15,629,633.62, leaving a profit to the Crédit Mobilier of $ 7,802,134.48.

All quite satisfactory. The last three dividends would be in securities worth about thirteen million dollars; when they had been distributed, an appreciable sum would remain in the treasury of the Crédit Mobilier to meet any contingent expenses. (A government commissioner would have to be paid $25,000 before he would approve the construction of part of the road; in 1871, $126,000 would have to be spent to get the Congress to pass an act permitting the Union Pacific to charge the government abnormally high rates for carrying the mails, federal troops, and various supplies; there would be a few other incidental expenses.)

Most important, however, was the fact that the insiders held 367,623 shares of Union Pacific stock, more than enough to maintain control of the road, *and the shares had not cost the insiders one cent.*

The job was done.

Yet there was a flaw. It was not that an honest government director of the Union Pacific, Jesse Lynch Williams, filed a report in December, 1868, charging frauds in the building of the road, for his report could have been suppressed; not that a dutiful congressman, wonderfully named Philadelph Van Trump, spilled the beans on the floor of the House in January, 1869, for he could have been ignored. The flaw was a more human thing: it was contained within those 367,623 shares of Union Pacific stock: it was the contest for ultimate control of the road.

The Crédit Mobilier was not tightly held by one group of financiers, as were the other railroad construction companies; three or four antagonistic groups were constantly jockeying for an advantage, each over the others. Back in January, 1868, just as the melon was about to be sliced, the representative of one group insisted he had been cheated out of a substantial block of Crédit Mobilier stock—which was, of course, about to

41

balloon into oodles of Union Pacific stock. Late in 1868, when still his demands were ignored, he recklessly brought suit for a judgment against Oakes Ames and other leading spirits of the Crédit Mobilier. That was the match to the fuse: so long for lawyers to confer and bicker, so long for an effort to settle out of court, so long for tempers to rise and erupt into inevitable litigation, and *boom!* there would follow the public disclosure of many private matters.*

The spectacular success of the Crédit Mobilier had by no means gone unnoticed in financial circles. Other railroad promoters, pricked by jealousy, had launched all kinds of greedy schemes. It has been estimated that, in the decade 1862–1872, not less than one billion dollars was invested in the construction of American railroads, most of it shoveled in by trusting souls abroad. During this time the Atchison, Topeka & Santa Fe was inching westward, the Missouri-Kansas-Texas was crawling south from Kansas towards New Orleans, the St. Louis-San Francisco was reaching into the southwest, and the Denver & Rio Grande was headed south. The Rock Island and the Kansas Pacific, liberally assisted by grants of public land, were expanding rapidly. The Texas & Pacific, chartered by the Congress in 1871 and heir to a potential of thirty-eight million acres of public land, had inspired lust in a dozen or more capitalists, who circled around Capitol Hill like so many vultures.

Of all these railroad schemes, however, the most impudent was that of the Northern Pacific, chartered by the Congress in 1864 and promoted by no less a personage than Jay Cooke,

*The suit was brought by one H. S. McComb, a man whose experience as a manufacturer of leather goods naturally qualified him to serve as a director of the Union Pacific and as a member of the executive committee of the Crédit Mobilier. From the evidence available it would appear that McComb was a dummy representing the interests of the Philadelphia group headed by Thomson and Scott of the Pennsylvania Railroad. Later, after the Crédit Mobilier affair had exploded, McComb was most circumspect in his sworn testimony before a congressional committee. Never would he say he owned any Crédit Mobilier stock; rather he would say, for example: "I am the holder in my own name of about eight hundred and fifty shares. . . ."

the Philadelphia banker who by hook and by crook had become the nation's most powerful financier. This Cooke approached banking with the strenuous exuberance of a man leading a big brass band. He hired swarms of press agents; during the Civil War he had harnessed eighteen hundred newspapers to help him peddle government bonds; he canvassed every hamlet across the land and sold one and one half billion dollars' worth of war bonds, and so acquired the reputation of having saved the Union. For his railroad schemes he mounted an even mightier propaganda. The Northern Pacific had been given the enormous grant of forty-seven million acres of the public lands, a banana-shaped tract reaching from the Great Lakes to the Pacific Northwest. Construction was actually begun in 1870, after a bill had been jammed through Congress that made Jay Cooke & Company the sole fiscal agents for the road and gave them two hundred dollars' worth of stock and a commission of twelve per cent on every thousand-dollar bond they sold. For such rewards Cooke was prepared to fabricate the most outrageous humbug. The Northern Pacific, he insisted, "has never been excelled in the merits of its appeal to the public"; the climate of the region through which it would pass was "a cross between Paris and Venice," and rumors were permitted to spread that orange groves and monkeys had been found by his surveyors; its gold bonds were "SAFE! PROFITABLE! PERMANENT!" Cooke even urged the holders of government bonds to convert them into Northern Pacific first-mortgage bonds, securities that, he claimed in advertisements in the financial columns of the most influential newspapers, were "safe beyond all question." In poured the money, a million dollars a month, to be invested in what had been nicknamed "Jay Cooke's Banana Belt."

In the meantime, while flame still crept along the fuse that led to the powder keg of the Crédit Mobilier, the first transcontinental railroad was joined in Utah, and all the dummies and stock nominees who had represented the insiders of the Pacific ring could be thanked, paid off, and retired, and their principals could once again surface and squabble in public for control of the railroad that had cost them nothing. In January, 1871, that road was burdened with a floating debt of five million dollars due in three months, and with ten million dollars' worth of income bonds, of questionable legality, that would mature within one to three years.

Who needed it? One passenger train a day sufficed to accommodate the traffic east or west; more often than not a solitary citizen could travel across the plains and over the mountains, having to himself one bleak day coach and one hideously uncomfortable sleeper. Union Pacific stock was traded at 9, its income bonds at 32, its land-grant bonds at 52.

Nevertheless, the officers of the Pennsylvania Railroad, aggressively imperialist, decided that they needed the Union Pacific. The Pennsylvania's dominion reached through Ohio and Illinois to Chicago and St. Louis; with a little luck and a little cash it might be extended at least as far as Denver. In 1871 Thomas Scott, the ambitious vice-president of the Pennsylvania, recruited as allies Andrew Carnegie, the steel master, and George Pullman, the manufacturer of sleeping cars, and got himself elected president of the Union Pacific. To the editor of The Railroad Gazette this smooth seizure of power was a crucial event in railroad history. The Pennsylvania, he declared, was "likely to control all the transcontinental traffic for many years to come."

Many railroad men, but three men chiefly, were uncomfortably aware of this grab for empire. In the west, Collis P. Huntington of the Central Pacific recognized that he was faced with an adversary of spirit and determination. In the east, Horace F. Clark, the son-in-law of Commodore Vanderbilt and the president of the railroad (the Lake Shore & Michigan Southern) that connected the New York Central with Chicago, found it intolerable that the Pennsylvania, his most puissant competitor, should capture such a rich prize. And in the financial district of New York City, in his drab suite of rooms at 25 William Street (which was also the executive suite for at least seven midwestern railroads), Russell Sage, somber and crafty, mentally audited his liquid assets and pondered a sure-pop campaign of acquisition. By training and temperament he was superbly equipped to devise such a scheme.

Clark was the first to move. He arranged a series of conferences with Levi P. Morton, the senior partner of the investment banking firm of Morton, Bliss & Company, which had held, presumably as nominee, eighteen thousand five hundred shares of the Crédit Mobilier.* Morton had close ties with the Boston insiders of the Pacific ring. The Boston group may have been particularly angry with Scott and the other officers of the Pennsylvania because the Philadelphia group was presumed to have instigated the litigation against Oakes Ames; at all events, the Boston group made common cause with Clark, and so, in March 1872, Clark deposed Scott as president of the Union Pacific.

Next—was it propter hoc, or only post hoc?—the Philadelphia group let leak some incriminating and remarkably outspoken letters that Oakes Ames had written to McComb, letters in which, among other indiscretions, Ames had listed by name many of the influential Republican politicians whom he had bribed with Crédit Mobilier stock. The letters were published in The New York Sun at a most embarrassing moment—the first weeks of the Presidential campaign of 1872— and other newspapers promptly spread them abroad. The fuse had at last reached the powder keg.†

*This is the same Morton who was elected Vice-President in the administration (1889–1893) of Benjamin Harrison and who later served (1895–1897) as governor of New York.

†McComb had earlier threatened that he would publish the letters. He testified that Ames retorted: "You can publish any letters that you have from me; everybody knows that members of Congress are bribed, and everybody does it." Ames of course later denied that he had ever said any such thing.

It is certain that political considerations played a part in the release of the damaging letters. McComb's lawyer was Jeremiah Black, a Democrat who had served President Buchanan both as Attorney General and as Secretary of State. In 1872 Black was counsel to the Pennsylvania Railroad; he was also an old friend and close associate of Samuel J. Tilden, who was the chairman of the New York State Democratic Committee and, in turn, an associate of Charles Dana, the editor of the Sun.

45

Now the nation could reflect on the fact that railroad corruption had reached all the way to the Vice-President, Schuyler Colfax; to the man nominated to succeed him, Senator Henry Wilson of Massachusetts; and to other dignitaries of almost equal pomp.

A congressional investigation was mandatory. In fact, such was the public dismay that *three* congressional committees were obliged to inquire into the scandals. Two of the committees addressed themselves to whitewashing the distinguished Republican statesmen whose names had so unfortunately been broadcast. The third, in a rare access of indignation, spread over the record a good part of the story of the Crédit Mobilier without, however, getting behind the dummies to name the men chiefly responsible for the plunder. The report of this third committee, filed in the spring of 1873, censured the Union Pacific's visible corporators so sharply that the Attorney General was forced to bring an action (civil, of course; not criminal) against the railroad, the Crédit Mobilier, and their officers, charging misappropriation of funds, unlawful sale of land-grant bonds and income bonds, and many other torts and malfeasances.*

The threat of this legal action sent the Union Pacific's stock tumbling down five points, to 25, a level at which a number of railroad financiers found it attractive. One of these was Jay Gould, who, after impoverishing the Erie, had at last been booted out and was looking for another railroad to exploit; but Gould had attempted, in December, 1872, to rig a corner in Chicago & North Western and had got so badly stung in the process that he had few funds for speculation. Another was Russell Sage, a director of two dozen railroad companies, who three months before had ordered a halt to further construction of the Milwaukee & St. Paul (now the Chicago, Milwaukee, St. Paul & Pacific) just because he had a hunch. Thanks to his hunches, Sage always had plenty of cash on hand.

*Five years later, the United States Supreme Court dismissed the suit, ruling that the government had no grounds for an action until after the railroad's bonds had matured, i.e., in 1895.

46

Gould's purse swung light and Sage's hung heavy, but both men were eying the Union Pacific covetously when something happened, abrupt and unexpected, that made the two men partners. In that same summer of 1873 Jay Cooke, the promoter of the Northern Pacific, had tried to float another fifteen million dollars' worth of bonds. It was too much. The issue was not subscribed. Too many demands had been made by greedy railroad promoters on the market for money. At 2:30 P.M. on September 18 the New York offices of Jay Cooke & Company were obliged to close their doors, and the panic of 1873 was on.

During its earliest days the panic was an authentic scourge, loud with wails and brimful of woe. On every hand banks and brokerage houses collapsed in a swoon, awaking only to find themselves in the icy grip of receivers. The New York Stock Exchange was shut down for ten days, the longest suspension in the history of that notably jittery organization. Everyone knew where to fix the blame for the misery. On the second day of the panic, even before the Stock Exchange halted its operations, the editor of The New York Times pointed an accusing finger:

> There has been a railroad mania and the banks have lent large sums of money on railroad bonds. . . . Last year over six thousand miles of new railroads were built, not five hundred miles of which were really needed or can be turned to any profitable use. The foreign markets have been glutted with these schemes. Many gross swindles . . . have been foisted upon these markets in the past two years. . . .

Twenty-five railroad companies had already defaulted on the payment of interest on their bonds, and more would soon follow suit. The men who had tried to grasp control of the Union Pacific were hit particularly hard. Thomas Scott of the Pennsylvania was deeply involved in the Northern Pacific; when the crash came he was in Europe seeking to float a bond issue on behalf of the Texas & Pacific, of which he had been elected the president; the collapse of his hopes for the bond issue brought him to the edge of a physical and nervous breakdown; he faced financial ruin. Vanderbilt was also in trouble. His son-in-law, Horace Clark, the president of both the Lake Shore and the Union Pacific, had died two months before, and when the Commodore took charge of the Lake Shore (at the age of eighty) he found that the company's treasury was empty and that the money for a recent dividend, amounting to more than two million dollars, had been borrowed on call from the Union Trust Company, a Vanderbilt bank. Nor could he save the Union Trust from receivership, for on the first day of the panic his brokers had to fight off a fierce raid by the bears on both the Lake Shore and the New York Central, a raid that left him grumbling about his own cash position. The bears had been led by his old enemy, Jay Gould, and they had very nearly succeeded. But how had Gould, notoriously a heavy loser in his recent attempt to corner the Chicago & North Western, been able to finance his raid? The Commodore shook his shaggy head in puzzlement. Only Russell Sage, ever reticent and evasive, could have supplied a clue. Vanderbilt was quite cross when he considered his affairs:

> There are a great many worthless railroads started in this country, without any means to carry them through [he growled to a reporter]. The roads get into difficulties, and bad language is heard all around. These worthless roads prejudice the commercial credit of our country abroad. Building railroads from nowhere to nowhere at public expense is not a legitimate undertaking. . . . When railroads are to be built, don't victimize the public to build them.

In short, so far as Vanderbilt was concerned the Union Pacific might rust and decay, at least until he was satisfied it would pay him dividends. This grumpy attitude precisely suited Russell Sage's convenience. Sage promptly swept the Union Pacific, the national railed highway, "the grandest and noblest enterprise of our age," into his capacious pocket.

# 3

*The six railway kings of 1875: William Henry Vanderbilt, Thomas Scott, Collis P. Huntington, John Murray Forbes, Jay Gould, and Russell Sage. How these men ran the country and how they corrupted it, politically and financially.*

As THE NINETEENTH CENTURY reached its three-quarter mark, a half-dozen men dominated the railroads of the republic and, in consequence, the republic itself, while in the background another half dozen patiently held their spears, awaiting the moment when, by violence or duplicity, by manipulation of the stock market or the ultimate logic of mortality, they might unseat their peerless leaders. Lest there be any doubt as to the prestige and prerogative of these men, let us summon to the witness stand a contemporary who was both objective and observant, the British historian, James Bryce:

> These railway kings [Bryce wrote later, in The American Commonwealth] are among the greatest men, perhaps I may say the greatest men, in America. . . . They have power, more power—that is, more opportunity of making their will prevail— than perhaps anyone in political life except the President and the Speaker who, after all, hold theirs only for four years and two years, while the railroad monarch may keep his for life.

Kings? They were lords of creation, at least of American industrial creation. Consider, for example, the riotous events in the Oil Regions of Pennsylvania during the winter of 1871-1872, when the independent oil producers and refiners were dismayed to learn that John D. Rockefeller and his associates had signed a secret and illegal contract with three railroad systems—the Pennsylvania, the New York Central, and the Erie—by the terms of which the railroads agreed to give to Standard Oil a fifty-per-cent rebate and a fifty-per-cent drawback on their shipments of crude oil.* That the contract was never enforced made no difference, for, while it was still secretly impending, Rockefeller was able to convince twenty-one of his twenty-six Cleveland competitors that they must sell to him—on his terms—or be wiped out. The lesson to be learned was that the railway kings could make an industry or break it. Writhe and wriggle as he might, the independent producer or manufacturer was at their mercy. The men who ran the railroads ran the national economy.

Of these men, the half dozen most important in 1875 were: in the east, Tom Scott of the Pennsylvania and William H. Vanderbilt of the New York Central; in the far west, Collis P. Huntington of the Central Pacific and the Southern Pacific; in the midwest, John Murray Forbes of the Burlington, and Russell Sage and Jay Gould who, in partnership, controlled the Union Pacific and several smaller roads.

In 1875 other men fretted impatiently and itched to conquer. John Garrett of the B&O was laying his rails toward Chicago; Jim Hill, a man of thirty-seven who, with his barbed-wire beard, his mane of long black hair, and his one blind eye, looked like what would today be termed a beatnik, sat in front of his coal-and-wood store on the levee at St. Paul, whittling away at a chunk of wood and talking, to anybody who would listen, about the possibilities of a godforsaken railroad called

*Standard Oil was to have been charged forty cents a barrel, while its twenty-six Cleveland competitors would have had to pay eighty cents; of that eighty cents, moreover, forty would have been paid back to Standard Oil by the railroad companies. This splendid scheme was devised by the officers of the South Improvement Company, a corporation chartered by the legislature of the commonwealth of Pennsylvania, a body that seems to have specialized in the legitimization of larceny. The moving spirit back of the South Improvement Company was Thomas Scott, vice-president of the Pennsylvania.

the St. Paul & Pacific; Henry Villard, a mettlesome journalist who had won the confidence of German investment bankers and had by them been appointed a receiver of the Kansas Pacific, was speculatively eying the shambles of the Northern Pacific left by the failure of Jay Cooke & Company; young Ned Harriman, who at twenty-two had borrowed the three thousand dollars needed to buy a seat on the New York Stock Exchange, was now, at twenty-seven, possessed of a substantial fortune and devoting all his spare time to the study of railroad maps; and J. Pierpont Morgan sat hunched behind his roll-top desk, a big black cigar cocked up in the corner of his mouth, thinking black thoughts about the untidy finances of the American railroads.

But in 1875 the czars of those railroads—the men with "opportunity to make their will prevail"—were still William Henry Vanderbilt, Scott, Huntington, Forbes, Gould, and Sage. They deserve a closer look.

At fifty-four, William Henry Vanderbilt, a stout, sedentary man with an amiable, rather piggish face set off by a champion cascade of Dundreary whiskers, had lived almost his entire life in the shadow of the bulldozer, his father, the brutal and autocratic Commodore. Contemptuously dismissed as a chucklehead, hired in sweet charity by Drew to clerk at one hundred and fifty dollars a year, Billy Vanderbilt at last contrived to impress his sire by cheating him in a commercial transaction. Had he been coached in this swindle by Drew? However that may be, "There's something in the boy, after all," the Commodore crowed to his friends, and he got Billy appointed as the receiver of a tottery railway on Staten Island. Two years later the road was being run at a profit and Billy had overnight become William. He was then forty-two years old.

His stretch in the doghouse had, however, left its mark. The son gradually assumed the father's responsibilities, but he showed a natural inclination to shun conflict and to seek compromise. It was the son who made the decision, in 1870, to give the Standard Oil Company an illegal rebate. In his prime, the

Commodore would have demanded and got a partnership with Rockefeller as the price for any rate concession; the son settled for a few shares of Standard Oil stock, acquired through the South Improvement Company. The father was instinctively predatory, lustful, and greedy; the son was patient, cautious, and stupid, with a marked talent, as we shall see, for putting his foot in his mouth.

In 1874 the son was elected president of the New York Central. In 1877 the father died, but still the son was in his shadow, for William H. was the well-publicized heir to more than eighty million dollars and, as well, to the exquisite headaches that afflict only a very rich man. Shall we pity him? The railroads of the continent were at his feet. His annual *income* was eight million dollars. Anything he willed he could have achieved. Just as the Commodore had seized hegemony of the northern region east of the Mississippi, so his son could have reached a long arm to the Pacific coast and put the entire United States of America in his thrall. The son put a tentative finger on the Union Pacific, then drew it back. He had the Rock Island in his grasp but let it slip. He bought control of the Chicago & North Western but never exploited it, since to do so would have involved an aggressive territorial war for which he had no stomach. He was better fitted for the defensive rate wars that raged incessantly amongst the eastern trunk lines.

Yet William was more than just a homely Dutch Fafnir, guarding the cave where the Vanderbilt gold was hoarded. He invested that gold, always prudently, always when securities were cheap ("I never sold a share short in my life," he once said), and watched with satisfaction as his hoard expanded in a steady arithmetical progression.

To defend is easier than to attack, and besides it gives a man more time at home with his children.

In 1875 Tom Scott had been president of the Pennsylvania Railroad for only one year, but for a dozen years he had been the driving force behind the road's spectacular growth from

Pittsburgh west to Chicago and St. Louis and from Philadelphia north to the port of New York and south to Washington. His swift ascent to power was the more remarkable because he started from scratch. Orphaned at twelve, young Scott had been obliged to go to work before he was out of grade school. Up he shot, like a rocketing pheasant: errand boy, clerk, station agent, superintendent of the Pennsylvania's western division, first vice-president of the company at thirty-seven—what was his secret? Fundamentally, it was his talent for exploiting the weaknesses of others, his ability to corrupt. In a time of feverish venality, Tom Scott stood alone, the acknowledged master of corruption.

Thanks to this talent, Scott was able to clobber the Pennsylvania's competition. For years the B&O had sought to build a line into Pittsburgh and for years the city's manufacturers had stood ready to welcome another railroad with glad cries, but Scott, with the assistance of a servile legislature in Harrisburg, always managed to bar the door. This legislature was the personal property not so much of the Pennsylvania Railroad as of Tom Scott. In 1864, after a vote had been taken on two of Scott's bills to block the B&O from entry into Pittsburgh, a member arose to ask: "Mr. Speaker, may we now go Scott free?" In 1869, when Jay Gould, then the president of the Erie, threatened to swoop down and snatch the Pennsylvania's freight traffic from the west, Scott's bill to prevent such lèse majesty was whipped through both houses of the legislature and signed by the governor in thirty-four minutes. It broke the record. Early in 1871, while John Garrett of the B&O dreamed of building a terminal station in Washington, Scott crooked a finger to summon General Grenville M. Dodge, a Republican politico who had been President Lincoln's crony and was then President Grant's trusted adviser. Dodge was also the engineer appointed by the Crédit Mobilier to build the Union Pacific (his wife having been given one hundred shares of the Crédit Mobilier to sweeten his pot) and was universally considered the slickest railroad lobbyist in the land. Obedient to Scott's summons, Dodge arrived in Washington and spoke urgently to a clutch of midwestern congressmen. Before long the Congress had authorized Scott to locate the Union Station at the end of the Pennsylvania's road into Washington.

As a consequence of Scott's energy and industry, the Pennsylvania Railroad was the most powerful corporation in the land. Its rails crisscrossed the guts of the richest industrial region—iron, coal, steel, petroleum—in the world and reached into the nation's most important centers of commercial activity. Its annual net profit, even in years of panic and severe depression, was six per cent on an investment of some four hundred million dollars.

Scott was not satisfied. He wanted nothing less than a coast-to-coast monopoly. He had organized two prototypal holding companies—the Pennsylvania Company and the Southern Railway & Security Company—that guaranteed a steady flow of traffic for the Pennsylvania from the midwest and the southeast, but without the traffic from the far west he felt cheated.

At fifty-two, Scott was at the height of his powers. He was a fellow of agreeable appearance: in repose he looked rather stern, like a Methodist bishop listening to an off-color story; but when he had a job to do, which is to say when he was one of the boys, bonhomie glowed from him like heat from a stove, and it was easy to see why Wendell Phillips said of him: "The members of twenty legislatures rustled like leaves in a winter's wind, as he trailed his garments across the country."

In 1875 the job Scott had to do was to chisel enough cash out of the federal treasury to build the Texas & Pacific west to San Diego and so make the Pennsylvania the keystone of a transcontinental system. One man blocked his way: Collis P. Huntington.

At fifty-four, Huntington was a massive monolith of a man, defying any trespass into his domain. He had and held what every other railroad king yearned for: a monopoly. If anything could set his mean, mercantile heart to pounding, it was the thought of his iron grip on the traffic to and from the Pacific coast. He was determined that never should anyone pry any part of it from him.

He had robbed a fortune from the state of California, the federal government, and the trustful public, but his millions had not changed him a whit. Frugality, tenacity, and industry: these were still the noblest virtues. To make money and to hang on to it: these were still the loftiest purposes his mind could envision. Philanthropy, art, religion, responsibility for the lot of his fellows, any slightest inkling of the ceaseless energy that strives toward a higher and fuller life—these notions he wholly ignored, and when they were thrust in his face, so that even he was obliged to take notice of them, he snorted with sincerest contempt.

Even a sense of his own comfort and pleasure was lacking. The center of his life was his office: a small, bleak room on the seventh floor of a drab building on Broad Street in the cramped, ugly financial district of Manhattan: no carpet on the floor, no curtains at the windows, a few straight-backed wooden chairs, a long table of oak covered with red felt and piled high with a litter of papers. One picture hung on his walls, a photograph of the shipyards at Newport News. (He had acquired the shipyards and the Chesapeake & Ohio Railroad, in 1869, at a bargain.) Everything was stripped down, everything geared for the transaction of business. His weekly schedule permitted him two days a week in this office; a third he spent in Boston; the other four he devoted to his work as a lobbyist, in Washington. Four of every seven nights he spent on trains. "I would feel better," he once said, "if I didn't have to spend most of my life on trains," but he was getting old then; it was one of the few complaints he ever addressed to his bitch goddess.

This curious creature had been born the son of a tightfisted Connecticut tinker, was schooled four months a year until he was thirteen, and hired out to work on a farm at fourteen. He had invested his earnings in a country store at fifteen and become a peddler and trader at sixteen. By then young Huntington knew everything he would ever need to know. He was already a hard-used, hard-bitten swindler, differing in no salient respect from the big bearded man who in 1875 sat at

55

his desk in New York, his skullcap pulled down over his bald head, bargaining, scheming, making policy for a nation's commerce, the apotheosis of a merchant.

The battle to keep Scott from California would be a long one, and fierce, but Huntington was ready to join it. Even before the Central Pacific was linked to the Union Pacific, he and his associates—Stanford, Hopkins, and Crocker—had organized a subsidiary, the Southern Pacific, of which Huntington was elected president, and they had let it be known that they planned to build a road south from San Francisco.

Their purpose, which was to confront and challenge any railroad promoter who might seek to reach California by the two southern approaches—at Fort Yuma, Arizona, or a couple of hundred miles north, at The Needles—was entirely greedy, but throughout southern California the news was greeted with ecstatic hurrahs. The six thousand citizens of Los Angeles were pathetically fearful that they might be passed over, quite as though Huntington would ever have dreamed of slighting a potential seaport and commercial junction. After their passions had been sufficiently roused, he deigned to bargain with them: if they would give to the Southern Pacific five per cent of the assessed valuation of all Los Angeles county, he would condescend to run his rails through their hamlet. Oh, joy! They showered him with gifts: two hundred thousand dollars in stock of the Los Angeles & San Pedro Railroad, nearly four hundred thousand dollars in cash (raised by the sale of municipal bonds), and sixty acres of land for a depot.

These goodies were ammunition for the war against Tom Scott or any other eastern interloper. In the meantime, Huntington and his associates prudently burned all the records of their construction company, the Contract & Finance Company, lest by some mischance they fall into the hands of a zealous congressional investigator, as had the records of the Crédit Mobilier. In its stead, Huntington and his partners organized a Western Development Company, by which they could enrich themselves still further while they built a road through the southwest.

In 1872, when the Congress, by amending an earlier act, chartered the Texas & Pacific and authorized Tom Scott to build westward to San Diego, Huntington was on hand to show why he customarily spent four days a week in Washington. Into the act went a paragraph, inserted at Huntington's behest, that empowered the Southern Pacific to build south from Los Angeles and meet the Texas & Pacific "at or near" Fort Yuma, on the Colorado River. By this exploit, the Southern Pacific acquired another five million acres of the public lands.

But Huntington was not satisfied. He at once ordered that tracks be laid south from San Bernardino to the Colorado River at Fort Yuma and began to lobby in Washington for authority to build eastward into Arizona until he should meet Scott and the Texas & Pacific working west. To Huntington, "at or near" Fort Yuma meant as far east of Fort Yuma as he could lay tracks before somebody stopped him. And who could stop him? Not the United States Army. Not its commander in chief, the President of the United States. They both tried, but neither of them was able to stop Collis P. Huntington.

John Murray Forbes was at this time the oldest of the railroad kings (in 1875 he was sixty-two) and he was unique among them in that he was a man of breeding and culture, a man concerned for the virtue of the republic, a man who could move with modesty and distinction in any society; in short, a gentleman. At this time Emerson was acidly contemplating American manners, or the lack of them, and mourning the disappearance of "our gentlemen of the old school," men like Washington and Adams and Hamilton and Jefferson; but when he thought of Forbes he took heart.

> Never [Emerson wrote of Forbes] was such force, good meaning, good sense, good action, combined with such domestic lovely behavior, such modesty and persistent preference for others. . . . Wherever he moved he was the benefactor. . . . Yet I said to myself, How little this man suspects, with his sympathy for men and his respect for lettered and scientific people,

57

that he is not likely, in any company, to meet a man superior to himself. And I think this is a good country that can bear such a creature as he is.

In fact, Forbes was born in Bordeaux, his parents having taken up residence in France whilst their elder children were being schooled there. Young Forbes was educated at an academy near Boston and later went to work in the counting-house of his uncles, James and Thomas Perkins, who were in the China trade. At seventeen Forbes was their representative in Canton and seven years later he was home again, with a fortune to invest as he chose. He was thirty-three when he formed a syndicate of Boston financiers to buy the Michigan Central Railroad from the state of Michigan for two million dollars, and a few years later he had put together several small roads to make the Chicago, Burlington & Quincy.

As a financier and manager of railroads during this time, Forbes stood alone. He frowned on the device of the construction company, of which the Crédit Mobilier was only the most flagrant example. He was actually concerned about the public interest in his roads, taking the position that, if they were to pay good dividends, the roads must be soundly built, must be conservatively financed, and must serve the public fairly and well. To the absolute monarchs of his day, such constitutional monarchy smacked of communism.

But it worked. The Burlington marched steadily across the prairie, spreading out through Kansas and Iowa and Nebraska, profitable, secure against the Panic of 1873 and the lean years of depression that followed.

In large part the Burlington prospered because of what was called the Iowa Pool, a "domestic lovely" combination in restraint of competition by which three well-managed rail-roads—the Chicago & North Western, the Rock Island, and the Burlington—amicably agreed to divide (and charge the same stiff prices for) all the traffic they got from the Union Pacific. The Iowa Pool was the envy of every railroad executive in the republic. Elsewhere the president of a railroad gave his word that he would abide by rates agreed upon with his

58

competitors, and in due time that president invariably broke faith, ignored his pledged word, and cheated every competitor in sight.

Not, however, in Iowa. The Iowa Pool had been formed on the pledged word of John Murray Forbes and, for that reason alone, it survived every vicissitude. Forbes's faith was strong enough to sustain even the rascals and the greedheads— but only locally, and only for a decade. Gresham's law operates for ethics in business as well as for currency.

In contrast to Forbes, Jay Gould was the youngest of the railroad royalty under present inspection. (In 1875 he was only thirty-nine.) Gould was a small man, saturnine and sickly, black-bearded and black-visaged, at once furtive and self-possessed, whose eyes glowed, who spoke softly, so softly during the several inquiries into his affairs that the congressional investigators were obliged to ask that he raise his voice, who gave the impression of being at arms against the world; a solitary, demoniac power of evil.

In the circumstances, it was natural for his contemporaries to think of Gould as His Satanic Majesty, Mephistopheles. One of Forbes's associates in the Burlington (which was considered a Boston road) fancied that Boston was Gould's pet aversion; a Boston railroad, this man wrote, "seems to have the same disagreeable influence upon him that holy water is said to have on his great prototype."

The historians have been more dispassionate. They have recognized that the comparison is unjust. The Devil was never so destructive as was Gould. Moreover, Gould was much less of a hypocrite. For example, in his testimony before a select committee of the New York state assembly early in 1873, just before he was booted out of the presidency of the Erie Railroad, Gould declared quite frankly his considered opinion of American politics:

We had to look after four states [Gould said], New York, New Jersey, Pennsylvania, and Ohio; and we have helped men in all of them. It was the custom, when men received nominations, [for them] to come to me for contributions, and I made them and considered them good paying investments for the company. In a Republican district I was a strong Republican, in a Democratic district I was Democratic, and in doubtful districts I was doubtful; in politics I was an Erie Railroad man every time.

Could anything have been fairer than that?

In the spring of 1875 Gould's reputation as a financial pest and disturber of the industrial peace was already secure. In 1869 when he had sought by speculation to corner the market in gold, even attempting, with unexampled impudence, to involve President Grant himself in the scheme, he had dealt the nation's economy a staggering blow and put Wall Street through the blackest of all its Black Fridays. When he was ousted from the Erie Railroad in March, 1873, it was in receivership, a physical and financial wreck. Yet in 1874, with the help of Russell Sage, Gould had somehow contrived to take control—real or nominal, it is not clear which—of the Union Pacific, the eastern section of the transcontinental railroad.

Gould had all of Tom Scott's ambition to achieve a national monopoly and, thanks to Sage's well-filled purse, plenty of cash to pursue that ambition. To preside over the Union Pacific, Sage and Gould had installed Sidney Dillon, a complaisant rascal who had served as president of the Crédit Mobilier without, however, having been too severely scorched in the process. Moreover, Sage and Gould had got control of the Pacific Mail Steamship Company, a line that operated between San Francisco and Panama while fattening off a generous federal subsidy.

Huntington, enviously studying this show of strength, wrote to his partner Mark Hopkins in April, 1875, that Gould had the power to set rates for freight across the whole country, "a power equal to the control of the whole link." But Gould was not concerned with building a rate structure. He preferred to disrupt, to smash agreements like the Iowa Pool, to create chaos, and so, after speculating amidst confusion and manipulating securities in a bewildered market, to emerge with an even bigger railroad system.

In short, Gould stood ready to antagonize and do battle simultaneously with Huntington, Scott, Forbes, and Vanderbilt. Sage was his only ally.

Russell Sage was born in August, 1816, a year that the farmers of upstate New York recalled as Eighteen Hundred and Starve-to-Death because, according to local tradition, it was a year without a summer. It is said that three feet of snow fell on the countryside west of Albany that June, and that ice froze a half-inch thick on the brooks and ponds. There is no evidence that Sage's heart ever thawed, from that chilly summer till the day he died, at the age of ninety, in 1906.

Sage was born in the farming country west of Albany. It is a curious fact, and one that could be profitably examined by some candidate for a Ph.D. in economic history, that a quorum of the commercial scoundrels who devoted their lives to robbing their countrymen blind were born within one hundred miles of Albany during the span of two decades. The center of the country's population lay well to the south, but here was the land that cradled the robber barons. Was it the soil? The climate? Some lapse in their religious training, characteristic of the region? At all events, at this time and within this charmed circle, Philip Armour was born, and Marshall Field and Cyrus Field and Charles Crocker and Collis P. Huntington and Sidney Dillon and Jay Gould and George Pullman and Leland Stanford and William C. Whitney and probably twice as many more. John D. Rockefeller was born just to the west of the charmed circle, and Mark Hopkins just to the north of it. Isaac Singer was born just too soon to fit within the span of two decades, and George Westinghouse just too late; otherwise they qualified.

Of them all, Sage was the most pernicious. Sage was an habitual liar, a perjurer, and a betrayer of his associates. He was a convicted usurer, saved from a term in jail only because his lawyer, Samuel J. Tilden (who was also born within the charmed circle), was able to bring political influence to bear on a crooked judge. Railroad companies controlled by Sage corrupted the governors and legislators of Wisconsin and Minnesota, at a cost of more than two million dollars and a profit of well over twenty millions. Sage fattened off the misfortunes of others; he was miserly and devious; he was scandalously unfaithful to his second wife, who was the daughter of a man he had defrauded.

In short, he was perfectly fitted to be Gould's partner.

The nature of their partnership has never been elucidated and probably never will be. One student of Sage's career has theorized that Sage, in his capacity of moneylender (a business that he practiced even whilst he was a member of the Thirty-Third Congress), held notes signed by Gould and so was able to force Gould to do his bidding.[*]

Certainly Gould was the front man. Sage, a spidery figure, preferred the shadows. The best guess about these partners would seem to be that Sage, twenty years older than Gould and vastly more experienced in chicane, began after the Panic of 1873 to use the younger man, letting him issue the statements and grant the interviews of an empire builder but at the

[*]This theory is advanced by Paul Sarnoff, who wrote *Russell Sage: The Money King*, New York, 1965, the only full-length biographical study ever made of Sage.

There are several glimpses of Sage at work, supplied by his contemporaries, that tend to support Mr. Sarnoff's thesis. For example, when Tom Scott in 1880 finally agreed to sell his interest in the Texas & Pacific, it was publicly reported that Gould had added the T&P to his empire. But a more circumstantial account later turned up in the papers of General Grenville Dodge, the T&P engineer who had arranged the deal. It seems that Gould *and Sage* traveled to Philadelphia to negotiate the transaction with Scott and ultimately to hand Scott three and one half million dollars. (To Gould the sum would have been an enormous one, but Sage was famous for having available large sums of cash at all times.) The deal having been made, Gould left the room, airily bidding General Dodge to express the T&P securities to his offices in New York. Sage thereupon took charge. He produced two suitcases into which he packed the securities; he would, he declared, personally place them in his own private boxes in his bank. Dodge was satisfied with a receipt from Sage's bank. The public report was, as so often is the case, wrong. The T&P was Sage's, not Gould's.

62

same time obliging him to suffer the obloquy as the investors in one Sage-Gould railroad enterprise after another were systematically rooked.

One of Sage's favorite techniques for self-enrichment in Wisconsin and Minnesota had been to take over small feeder roads and then unload them at huge profit on a big railroad, like the Milwaukee & St. Paul, in which his was the commanding voice. In 1874, when the shareholders of this road met to celebrate its expansion and to change its corporate name to the Chicago, Milwaukee & St. Paul Railway Company, they also voted to remove Sage from his vice-presidency. Sage could afford to shrug. There were some railroads that paralleled the Union Pacific—the Kansas Pacific and the Denver Pacific—and maybe, if Gould could be made to play his cards right, Sage could help him to make a dishonest dollar by buying them in and unloading them on the Union Pacific.

So stood things with Sage in 1875.

To sum up, five of these six men were as well fitted for positions of trust and authority as so many baboons. Their apologists have argued that they should not be singled out for censure, that they were merely typical of their venal times, that they were indeed superior men, being shrewder than most. This is nonsense. More than any others, these men made their times venal. These men made disdain for the law fashionable; these men corrupted legislature and judiciary; these men created the commercial climate; their ethics (to select a word at random) became the ethics of the emerging industrial society. The matter was put with baboonish elegance by one Milton H. Smith, who was president of the Louisville & Nashville Railroad for thirty-eight years (and who was another of those born within the charmed circle around Albany). "Society, as created," said this Smith, "was for the purpose of one man's getting what the other fellow has, if he can, and keep out of the penitentiary."

But, their apologists insist triumphantly, say what you will about these men, they got the railroads built! This is also nonsense. The railroads were built by the labor of exploited immigrants (or by convict labor, which was still cheaper) and paid for with money that came, more often than not, from public funds. These men built no railroads: they stole them; and in the process they loaded them down with a staggering debt structure that will never be removed, but only refunded.

The wounds these men and their like inflicted on the republic are still not healed. These men blighted their era, and, because the railroad industry more than any other apes the old ways of doing things and clings to the past, their contempt for the public interest is with us today, a malign legacy, apparently indestructible.

*The great rebellion. Farmers rebel: the Grangers. Railroad workers rebel: the strike of 1877. Shippers rebel: the war against the rate.*

OF THE MANY EXCELLENT REASONS for hating the men who controlled the railroads in the 1870s, their contemporaries singled out one above all others: their autocratic policy as to the rate—that is, the price they charged for carrying people and freight. The tug of war between private greed and public interest was, during the 1870s, transformed into a stubborn struggle over the rate, and that struggle was to persist for the next fifty years.

Much time had passed since the first railroads had been chartered, and in that time much had been forgotten about the special character of the railroads. For example, it had been forgotten that the railroads were public highways; that the capitalists who had organized railroad corporations had been chartered to do so by the various states; that these capitalists had been authorized by the states to levy a tax (in the form of freight rates or passenger fares) upon the users of the railed highways; and that this tax, like all taxes, was to be levied with absolute and exact and impartial justice upon one and all alike.

For their part, the men who controlled the railroads looked upon the rate either as a useful device by which they might enrich themselves or as an invaluable weapon in the wars they constantly waged against their competitors. In their hands the rate was arbitrary, it was often exorbitant, it was always discriminatory, it was never fair, it was wholly capricious, and it was utterly lacking in logic. To provoke an Iowa farmer into a blind fury, to make a New York merchant or manufacturer hop with rage, you had only to defend the rate. Nor should this astonish, for as the Hon. William M. Acworth, a British authority on transportation, said: "In America the railroad rate is a matter of life and death."

The free pass was a pettier but even more infuriating evil. Why should some citizens ride free, whilst the others had to pay? The fact that those who rode deadhead were the politicians and the newspaper editors and the legislators and the judges served only to confirm the general suspicion of an invisible government, of the control exerted by the railroads over public officials and public opinion.

The fierce and widespread hatred of the railroads led inevitably to organization and angry opposition. The farmers were the first to rebel, and they made a great clatter. Before long the railroad workers were also up in arms, and they truly terrified the magnates. At last the businessmen closed ranks, and they actually managed to force some lasting changes.

It may be too much to say that the railroad promoters and their agents deliberately and systematically swindled the farmers, in the years after the Civil War, but the farmers said it— *sforzando* and *fortissimo*.

In the upper Mississippi valley nearly every farmer could recall a visit from a friendly railroad agent: if the farmer would buy stock in the new road, the agent had said, talking easily and smiling, he would not only get regular dividends but also have the assurance of cheap freight rates for his produce. The farmer had cut open his mattress and brought out his savings; he had gone to his bank and mortgaged his farm; in exchange he had been given some stock certificates printed on stiff crinkly paper; and, sure enough, the railroad had come and everything had been hotsy-totsy. But sooner or later—it was the same story with every road across the whole wide valley—

after some perplexing quarrel back east, some confusion on Wall Street about which he knew nothing, the farmer had waked up to find that his nice crinkly certificates were worthless, and suddenly the freight agent was demanding extravagant sums to ship his crops to market, and before long his banker was sending him chilly notes about payments due on his mortgage, and what could he do?

Other farmers had been enticed by agents of the railroads to come from Scandinavia, from Germany, from as far away as the Crimea, to settle in Kansas or Minnesota or the Dakota territory. These unfortunates had been freighted west from New York or Boston like cattle,* under conditions so appalling that by 1873 a bill for the prevention of cruelty to railroad passengers had actually been offered in Congress. On their arrival at their homesites on the prairie—that is, on the small slices of land that had been carved from the vast tracts given to the railroad company by Congress, subsequently to be sold by railroad agents—they were given free seed that turned out to be foul with quackgrass and cockle, or they were sold seed in the spring to be repaid in the fall at ten per cent interest. What could they do?

Whatever they did, they were confronted by the rate in one or another of its more fiendish refinements. In Iowa there was the Iowa Pool, which served to keep the rate at a feverish height. But everywhere, and even more exasperating, was the scheme apparently devised for the particular torment of farmers, by which it cost more to send freight a short distance than to send it a long distance.

Does it make sense, that freight rates have no correlation to the distance covered? Of course not; nor did it make sense to the farmers, back in the 1870s and 1880s. But it made a great deal of sense to the railroad freight agents; and so there developed the celebrated long-and-short-haul controversy,

---

*According to a congressional inquiry, the immigrant lived "upon the hard benches of springless cars for many days at his own expense, very often without fire or water, owing to neglect of employees, who care nothing for the comforts or necessities of foreigners."

which flared and sputtered for years. For example, at least seven railroads (the Chicago & North Western, the Rock Island, the Burlington, the Wabash, the Illinois Central, the Missouri Pacific, and the Chicago, Milwaukee & St. Paul) could haul freight east from Omaha. Each of the seven curved through countryside in which each had, speaking relatively, a monopoly, until it approached another great terminus like Kansas City or Chicago. At the terminus, then, competition was fierce and the scramble for business drove the freight rate down under the table; but in between the junctions each railroad exacted, to use the classic phrase, "whatever the traffic would bear." The practical effect of this long-and-short-haul scheme was to drive all commerce and industry into the terminal cities and so create the hideous urban sprawl that now afflicts the republic. But how could the farmer move to the city? He was stuck. And so he was soaked the more heavily, in order that the railroad companies might maintain their dividends.

Then came the winter when the farmer found that it was cheaper to burn his fifteen-cent corn than to buy fuel, since he could not afford to pay the rate to have his corn hauled east, where it was fetching a dollar a bushel. That was the winter of his despair, but there was, ready to his hand, an organization. It was called the Patrons of Husbandry, and it came complete with all the mystification so beloved of American joiners—a sign, a grip, a password, an oath, degrees of ascent toward the summit of the order, and an appropriately vague purpose that permitted its members to move in any direction desired. Its congregations were called granges, whence the inevitable nickname for its members.

The Grangers meant business. They studied politics and political pressure. Their candidates were elected to serve in county courthouses and state legislatures. They began to use their muscle. As early as April, 1871, they forced the state of Illinois to authorize a Railroad and Warehouse Commission "to establish maximum freight and passenger rates and prohibit discrimination." Thanks to this early success, granges sprang up all over the upper Mississippi valley. The Panic of 1873 and the consequent hard times were like manure on a bed of nettles. By 1874 there were more than twenty thousand granges that claimed a total membership of more than one and one half million angry farmers. It became their admirable custom to call Granger conventions in state capitals while the legislature was sitting. In Missouri, in Wisconsin, in Minnesota, in Iowa, in Kansas, in Nebraska, in Montana, in Idaho, in Oregon, laws were whooped through lickety-split: laws forbidding free passes to public officials, laws stipulating that passengers need pay no more than two and one half cents a mile, laws prohibiting the long-and-short-haul abuse, laws enacting schedules of freight rates.

The railroad magnates screamed and leaped about as though jabbed by pitchforks. The Grangers, they cried, were led by demagogues—"Communists," insisted Collis P. Huntington—and had mounted a savage assault upon the sacred rights of property. The editors of newspapers controlled by the railroads keened even more shrilly.* Earlier these editors had giggled at the hayseeds, but now they began to view with alarm. "The Grange," the editor of The New York Tribune warned, "menaced the political equilibrium of the most steadfast States."

The Grangers were unimpressed by these complaints. The law they had pushed through in Iowa made all railroad officers and employees who were convicted of violations liable to fines and terms in jail; it also set up a fund of ten thousand dollars to defray the legal expenses of any citizen who chose to sue for damages under the act. Here were the ground rules for a splendid new game: the Iowa farmers clustered around a depot, climbed on a train, paid the legal minimum, were tossed off the train at the next depot in default of the fare required

---

*Tom Scott of the Pennsylvania owned, for example, The New York World; he sold it to Gould (or to Sage and Gould) in 1880. At this time Gould also dominated the policy of The New York Tribune and, by virtue of the shares he owned in Western Union, could exercise considerable influence on the Associated Press.

by the company, sued for damages, and announced that they would press their suit to the Supreme Court of the United States and sue, as well, to have trainman, conductor, passenger agent, division superintendent, and president of the road fined and jugged for indignities unnameable.

The Potter Act, passed by the legislature of Wisconsin, vexed the railroad magnates even more grievously, for it not only defined various classifications of freight but also fixed the maximum rates for each. In the view of the magnates, this law was tantamount to expropriation, and so they assembled in Wisconsin a few ancient, rumpsprung locomotives and cars and set them to dawdling along on drastically reduced schedules—only one train a day on some roads, the minimal service necessary to maintain their lucrative postal subsidies.

This arrogant proceeding was only one fusillade in a concerted campaign to abolish the Granger laws. The railroad nabobs flatly disobeyed some of the laws and sought in every imaginable way to evade others. (Here and there a maverick magnate could be found seeking to capitalize on the strong current of hostility to the railroads. John Garrett of the B&O, for example, whose road was put through to Chicago early in 1875, posted bills announcing that the B&O came as "the Grangers' friend," for the B&O was transiently engaged in a rate war with the Pennsylvania.) Drafted in haste and passion, the laws were not always sound, and before long some of them were repealed and others amended. But the fundamental principle—that the state had the right to regulate the railroads—was everywhere retained.

The railroad owners thereupon revised their tactics. For reckless opposition they substituted subtle suasion. They hired press agents. They launched a vast propaganda in newspapers and magazines to demonstrate how calamitous were the woes suffered by the public on account of the unjust and iniquitous Granger legislation. In those states that had established railroad commissions, they addressed themselves to capturing a majority of the commissioners. They also replied to the Granger laws by raising the long-haul rates and by raising rates outside the states committed to Granger ideas.

By 1876 the Granger movement had passed its peak. The farmers were relaxing their collective muscle. They felt better: through co-operatives many of them had built their own grain elevators and so were no longer victimized by the gentry who operated the railroads' elevators with sedulous dishonesty; and the rate wars amongst the eastern trunk lines had cut the cost of shipping grain from Chicago to New York by more than sixty per cent and to Boston by more than seventy per cent. Maybe they could give their barns a lick of paint.

Meantime the litigation over the Granger laws had been creeping with due deliberation from lower court to higher and had at last reached the United States Supreme Court. Counsel for the railroads were cautiously sanguine. They had argued that the charters under which the railroads were operated were contracts, and they had triumphantly pointed to Article I, Section 10, paragraph 1 of the Constitution, where it is written: "No State shall . . . pass any . . . law impairing the obligation of contracts. . . ." Moreover, they had argued that for a state to regulate a privately owned corporation on the ground that its business might involve the public interest was a deprivation of that corporation's property, and they had reminded the Court of the Fourteenth Amendment (one of the so-called Reconstruction Amendments designed to clinch equal rights for the Negro), where it is written: ". . . nor shall any State deprive any person of . . . property without due process of law. . . ." That a corporation was, in legal terms, a person was already well established. Counsel for the railroads also appreciatively eyed the august Justices of the Supreme Court: in 1877 they included such presumably amiable fellows as Noah Swayne, formerly a railroad lawyer associated with Russell Sage and others of the North West Ring; Stephen Field, formerly a lawyer for Collis Huntington and a brother of the David Dudley Field who had been Jay Gould's lawyer during the Erie War; William Strong, who had been a railroad lawyer in Pennsylvania and who could be depended upon to interpret

71

the due-process clause in a fashion friendly to the railroads; and Joseph P. Bradley, who was so commonly known to be in Tom Scott's hip pocket that charges to that effect had persistently been published in The New York Sun. There, so it seemed to counsel for the railroads, were four sure-pop votes, and the necessary fifth should not be too difficult to come by.

The decision of the Supreme Court was handed down on Thursday, March 1, 1877, and the timing of it was exceedingly interesting. If the Justices of the Court had wanted to keep their opinion as secret as possible they could have chosen no better time to announce it, for up on Capitol Hill on that same Thursday the most stupendous swindle in American political history was in the works and nothing else could conceivably have claimed the attention of any citizen who cared about his vote and the way he had cast it.

On that Thursday, only three days remained of President Grant's second administration, but whether his successor would be the Republican, Rutherford B. Hayes, or the Democrat, Samuel J. Tilden, had still not been decided. To many observers it seemed that the country was closer to armed insurrection even than in 1860. Abram Hewitt, who had been Tilden's campaign manager in 1876, noted in his diary: "Business was arrested, the wheels of industry ceased to move, and it seemed as if the terrors of civil war were again to be renewed." Hewitt claimed that an army had been mustered in fifteen states and stood ready to move on Washington to force the inauguration of Tilden. In the House of Representatives, which was controlled by the Democrats, Tilden's supporters were determined to use every parliamentary tactic to delay an electoral count that was, they were convinced, dishonest. But a deal had been struck between northern Republicans and southern Democrats, and it was only a matter of time before the theft of the Presidency would be consummated.

The terms of the deal were sufficiently well known. They had been published in The Cincinnati Enquirer on February 14 and republished in The Memphis Avalanche: "As an inducement to secure these [southern Democratic] votes [to elect the

72

Republican, Hayes], the guarantees to the South are: First, one or two cabinet places; second, the control of their own State Governments; third, a guaranteed policy on the part of the Republicans of liberal appropriations for Southern internal improvements; fourth, the passage of the Texas Pacific Railroad Bill." Of these guarantees, the fourth was crucial to the success of the scheme.

As noted earlier, the Texas & Pacific Railroad was Tom Scott's darling, his pet, his own precious lambkin, but to build it he needed a federal subsidy. From the time of the Crédit Mobilier scandals on, however, a railroad subsidy had been anathema north of the Potomac. Scott had been forced to look south. For three years, with the able assistance of General Grenville Dodge, Scott had patiently stalked southern legislators in every canebrake and piney woods, through every bayou and hog wallow from the Virginia tidewater to the Mexican border. By the end of 1876, following the disputed Hayes-Tilden election, a substantial bloc of southern congressmen was snugly posited in Scott's carpetbag.

Scott had not found it easy to collar those congressmen. At every step he had been opposed by Collis P. Huntington, who knew precisely what Scott was up to and who was determined to block his way. Scott's lobbyists had argued that Scott was a plumed knight who sought to end the wicked monopoly of Huntington's Central Pacific and Southern Pacific, and they were right; Huntington's lobbyists had retorted that, if a southern railroad to the west coast were deemed desirable, Huntington was a canny fellow who could get it built without its costing the U. S. Treasury one penny, and they were right, too. Late in December, 1876, however, Scott and Huntington had met and composed their differences: their puissant lobbies, joined by that of Jay Gould of the Union Pacific, began cooperating to jam through the Congress a bill that would oblige the federal government to fork over $89,470,000, in return for which the Texas & Pacific and the Southern Pacific would give the Secretary of the Treasury their bonds, to be paid in gold, after fifty years, with five per cent interest—an aggregate interest of $223,675,000. Such a heist, if it could be brought off, would be the biggest score ever made against the government. The security proposed for this enormous loan was, to say the least, dubious; it consisted of bits and pieces of unconnected roads and the proceeds from the sale of the least valuable parcels of public lands already turned over to the railroads.

Nevertheless, there was the basis for an elegant deal. Scott wanted money; he commanded southern Democratic votes. The Republicans wanted votes to hijack the election; they could always find money somehow, in some fold of the public purse. The southern Democrats wanted a railroad to the west, with branch lines raying east from Dallas to Baton Rouge, and Vicksburg, and Memphis; Scott would build it. To hell with the public interest, the public money, and the popular and electoral vote: let's make a deal.

On January 14, 1877, Scott met in Washington with one of Hayes's lieutenants and they had "a most satisfying talk." When he agreed to marshal his loyal southern Democrats back of Hayes, did Scott feel a pang of regret, as when one plunges a knife in the back of an old friend? Perhaps: for Tilden was Scott's friend and for years had been the Pennsylvania Railroad's lawyer. But business comes first: a railroad king cannot afford such luxuries as loyalty or honor. "Scott's whole powerful machinery will be set in motion at once," one Hayes agent wrote exultantly to another, "& I am sure you will be able to detect the influence of it in *votes* within ten days." Later the same man wrote that Scott had "the *very greatest confidence*" that he would be able to rally the southern Democrats back of Hayes. Still later, after weeks of alarums and excursions and tense political infighting, when Hayes's election seemed all but assured, the same man acknowledged that there could have been no victory without Scott. One of Tilden's advisers angrily agreed. "There never was any intention of inaugurating Tilden," this man wrote later. "The House was controlled from the start by Tom Scott & Jay Gould."

And so, on Thursday, March 1, the House was called to

74

order at 10 A.M. and sat for eighteen hours in a session said
to have been "the stormiest ever witnessed." During that time
the business of the House was conducted quite as much by
the crowds that packed the galleries and by the railroad lobbyists who jammed the floor of the chamber as by the honorable
members themselves. At about 4 A.M. of Friday, March 2, Rutherford Hayes was declared the winner in the electoral count,
by a majority of one vote. The job had been done.*

In the circumstances, it is not astonishing that the decision
of the Supreme Court in the Granger cases failed to provoke a
storm of abuse in those newspapers controlled by the railroad
interests. But the railroad magnates were very disagreeably
jolted by that decision: it sustained the Granger laws in every
major particular, and by a vote of seven to two.†

Indeed, the Justices went further: they held that a state
could regulate interstate as well as intrastate commerce, at
least until the Congress had acted. (This opinion was later
reversed.)

After a week or so, the editor of The Railway World, a
trade publication, had sufficiently recovered his wits to bewail
what he described as "the most important, and, in some respects, the most unfortunate decision ever made by an American court of last resort."

The decision was, without question, an important one. It
clinched, once and for all, the right of the people, acting
through their elected officials and under, if necessary, the
police power, to regulate the rates of the railroads. There was
nothing novel in the rule, although it seemed so at the time.
The right of the people was in the common law, it was in the
early railroad charters; it had been almost strangled to death,
but it had never died. The decision of the Supreme Court
plucked it from the morgue and started it to breathing again.

*For this hasty account of the Compromise of 1877 I have drawn
heavily on C. Vann Woodward's admirable study, Reunion and Reaction.
†The principal cases were: Munn v. Illinois, 94 U.S. 114; Peik v. the
Chicago and North Western Railway Company, 94 U.S. 164; and the
Chicago, Burlington & Quincy Railway Company v. Cutts, 94 U.S. 155.

Railroad management now faced a painful problem. The difficulty was with the flimsy rate structure, more fragile than any greenhouse. To lower it here required raising it there, for a general collapse would crush those delicate annuals, the eight-per-cent dividends. In the present instance, the rate having been endangered in the midwest, every right-thinking railroad magnate promptly concluded that it would have to go up along the Atlantic seaboard.

The presidents of the four eastern trunk lines waited only three days. On Monday, March 4, William H. Vanderbilt of the New York Central, Hugh Jewett of the Erie, John Garrett of the B&O, and Tom Scott of the Pennsylvania met in conference in New York City and at once agreed to boost the rate on all westbound freight by fifty per cent.

Now all hands were in a cheerful frame of mind. Whatever they stood to lose because of the perfidy of the midwestern farmers they could pick up by gouging the eastern merchants and manufacturers. They plunged into a discussion of their competitive difficulties "in a spirit of candor and justice," as Garrett noted in a letter to Junius S. Morgan, his London banker. Garrett and Scott, so often in the past at each other's throats, "joined cordially and heartily" in the task of convincing Vanderbilt and Jewett that they should pull together, and Vanderbilt showed "a sincere . . . cooperative spirit." Garrett had good reason to enthuse over the amiability of the conference, for the B&O had a floating debt of more than eight million dollars; much depended on his ability to convince Junius Morgan of the viability of a bond issue soon to be offered in London. "The great principle upon which we all joined to act," he assured Morgan, "was to earn more and to spend less."

Elated by their five-day feast of reason and flow of soul, the four presidents conferred further in April and in May. By June 8, after "a very harmonious meeting," the four members of the entente appended their signatures to a grand treaty by which all freight traffic west from New York was to be pooled and divided: thirty-three per cent each to the New York

Central and the Erie, twenty-five per cent to the Pennsylvania, and nine per cent to the B&O. Banzai! Rate wars were a thing of the past.

Or were they? After all, this treaty was not the first of its kind. Less than three years before, the presidents of these same four railroads had met in the benign ambiance of Saratoga Springs, New York, and there, whilst the thoroughbreds were racing, they had concluded the first in a series of five solemn covenants designed to end rate wars forever. Each had been founded upon the pledged word of the four railroad presidents, and each had therefore proved worthless. What made this treaty different from all previous treaties? The arrival on the scene of Albert Fink, a cop.

Fink was a German-born engineer and economist who had for many years toiled for the Louisville & Nashville Railroad. In 1875 Fink had engaged to operate a pool of southern railroads and had done such a good job that in May, 1877, he was hired to do the same for the New York Trunk Line Association. His advent, complete with a staff of gumshoes, was official acknowledgment that the word of a railroad president was not to be trusted.

Whilst they were still exhilarated by their new-found ability to get along with each other, the four presidents (in common with the presidents of a great many other railroads) agreed to slash their workers' wages by ten per cent.*

In June, 1877, conductors, who had the ultimate responsibility for the safety and efficiency of their trains, were paid about three dollars a day for a twelve-hour day. Locomotive engineers, those glamorous fellows, upon whose split-second judgment so often depended the lives of dozens of passengers, were paid about the same amount. Firemen were paid rather less than two dollars for their twelve hours.

Brakemen had by all odds the most dangerous job. They had to race along the narrow catwalk atop the swaying cars to spin

*Tom Scott subsequently denied, under oath, that there had been any collusion in the decision to cut wages. Babies are also delivered by storks, and chimneys swing down on hinges to let the stars pass by.

the brake wheels on each car, a particularly zestful task in sleety weather. They had to stand between two cars being coupled so that they might steer link into socket and then let fall the pin that joined them, and this was tricky work, for in that instant when the two cars came together a man could lose a finger, a hand, or a life, and so the brakeman with ten fingers was generally recognized as a new man on the job. The slaughter of brakemen was fearful: hundreds killed and thousands maimed every year, during the 1870s, with no compensation for death or injuries and insurance rates priced out of sight. There were, of course, safety devices—the Janney automatic coupler was patented in 1868 and perfected in 1873; the Westinghouse air brake was patented in 1869—but they cost money and brakemen cost nothing. The Rev. Dr. Lyman Abbott made this point in a piece he wrote for Harper's Magazine in 1874: "So long as brakes cost more than brakemen," Dr. Abbott wrote, "we may expect the present sacrificial method of car coupling to be continued." For their work, brakemen averaged one dollar and seventy-five cents a day—maybe five hundred dollars a year.*

In short, the trainmen earned a wage that ranged from three hundred and thirty dollars a year for the lowliest brakeman to maybe eleven hundred dollars a year for the lordliest conductor.

But in the late spring of 1877, because of a decision reached by four men whose annual income ranged from the forty thousand dollars paid to Hugh Jewett, receiver of the Erie, to the eight million dollars that flooded in upon William Henry Vanderbilt, the wages of thousands of these trainmen were cut ten per cent.

It would not be accurate to suggest that the decision was entirely based on greed. The motives of the four men were various and complex, as were the motives of the dozens of railroad presidents who followed their lead.

Tom Scott, for example, had no obvious reason to cut his

*In 1877 the Pennsylvania was one of the very few companies to have installed both the Janney coupler and the Westinghouse air brake.

workers' wages. To be sure, the Pennsylvania's dividends had sagged from ten to six per cent since 1873; but in 1876 the road had earned more than enough to pay eight per cent, and its revenues for the first five months of 1877 were substantially higher than in 1876. But Scott believed the Pennsylvania needed still more cash, because he was locked in a mighty struggle with John D. Rockefeller, testing who should control the transportation of petroleum. The Pennsylvania had a subsidiary, the Empire Transportation Company, that operated five hundred miles of pipelines, owned a thousand tank cars, and had even presumed to buy an interest in two refineries, one in Philadelphia and the other in New York. As soon as he heard about these refineries, Rockefeller complained to Scott and to his young third vice-president, Alexander Cassatt, who was in charge of freight traffic. Such competition, Rockefeller insisted, was unfair: *he* was the refiner, *they* were the transporters: to each his own. But Rockefeller already controlled more pipeline than did the Pennsylvania. Scott and Cassatt knew it and feared that, if Rockefeller were not checked, he would soon dominate the transportation of oil as he already did the refining of it. In the fight that followed, Rockefeller cancelled all Standard Oil shipments on the Pennsylvania; in desperation the Pennsylvania had to give the independent refiners huge rebates ("We carried oil to New York," Cassatt later testified, "at eight cents less than nothing"); and within three months the Pennsylvania had absorbed a loss of more than one million dollars.

And so, on June 1, twenty thousand employees of the Pennsylvania found their pay sliced ten per cent.

Would they strike? Every railroad president in the land waited to see; and company spies watched, too, in every yard and roundhouse. The trainmen met, they grumbled and cursed, but the only militant action came from a hundred Irish longshoremen working on the Pennsylvania's piers in the New York harbor. By Scott's ukase, their pay had been cut to thirteen and one half cents an hour. They struck, but they settled a few

79

days later at fourteen cents.

The Pennsylvania's trainmen kept the trains running.* And so, much cheered, the president of the Lehigh Valley announced a similar wage cut, and the next day the president of the Lackawanna followed suit, and before long here came the presidents of the New York Central and the Michigan Central and the Chicago & North Western and the Rock Island and the Lake Shore and the Bee Line and the Union Pacific and the Pittsburgh, Fort Wayne & Chicago and the Louisville & Nashville and the Vandalia and the Indianapolis & St. Louis and two or three dozen others, and quite spontaneously, without having exchanged a word with each other, they all cut the wages of their employees by ten per cent.

Still no strike.

There was talk of a strike on the Erie, when Jewett announced a ten-per-cent wage cut to take effect July 1, but Governor Lucius Robinson of New York, who chanced also to be one of the Erie's board of directors, thoughtfully sent detachments of the state militia to march up and down the streets of Rochester and Buffalo, and the talk died away.

More companies—among them the Northern Pacific, the Central Pacific, the Burlington, the Long Island, and the B&O —announced the same wage cut, to take effect July 16.

The B&O was the last of the four big eastern trunk lines— traditionally the bell cows of the industry—to announce a cut.

*At this time, the railroad brotherhoods were weak and docile. The Brotherhood of Locomotive Engineers, organized in 1863, had won strikes during the winter of 1876–1877 against the Jersey Central, the Grand Trunk, and the Boston & Maine but had been almost demolished in April by a masterful strikebreaker, Franklin Gowen, the president of the Philadelphia & Reading, the man who in 1875 had utterly destroyed an organization of anthracite miners called the Workingmen's Benevolent Association. There were also the Order of Railway Conductors, organized in 1868, and the Brotherhood of Locomotive Firemen and Enginemen, organized in 1873, but in 1877 these were only fraternal groups, not trade unions.

Finally, there was an industrial Trainmen's Union, haphazardly organized in the evening of Saturday, June 2, 1877, at Dietrich's Hall in Allegheny, which is now a part of Pittsburgh. This union was short-lived but effective.

80

President John Garrett's caution was understandable. Despite the earnest advice of his bankers, Junius Morgan in London and John Pierpont Morgan in New York, Garrett had insisted on maintaining his dividends at ten per cent, in total disregard of his floating debt of eight million dollars. Rather than reduce dividends, Garrett preferred to slash wages. The cut of July 16 was the second such within eight months. For the trainmen on the B&O it was too much. They struck.

So was touched off the first nationwide strike—and the bloodiest—in our history. It began in Martinsburg, West Virginia, a division point on the B&O, quickly spread to Wheeling, and then crackled, like a string of firecrackers, through Maryland from Cumberland to Baltimore, through Pennsylvania from Pittsburgh to Harrisburg and Reading, through New York from Buffalo to Albany, throughout the midwestern states, and on as far as San Francisco, shutting down one railroad after another. At this time, the land was crisscrossed by perhaps seventy-five thousand miles of railroad track; of these, at least fifty thousand were directly affected by the strike. For seven to ten days, most freight trains and a few passenger trains were stopped dead.*

The presidents of the trunk lines, confronted by this extraordinary defiance, reacted characteristically. John Garrett denounced the strike as an "insurrection" and wired President Hayes, demanding that he "suppress" it. All at once the B&O was, in Garrett's view, transformed from a private corporation into a "great national highway [that] can only be restored for public use by the interposition of the U. S. forces." Grand words. Translated, they meant that Garrett would not be satisfied unless the President sent the army to protect the B&O's dividends. (Before long Hayes did order federal troops to the scene of the "insurrection." The soldiers arrived via the B&O, and the railroad later billed the federal government and collected from the public purse for the cost of their transportation.) Tom Scott also fired off a series of petulant telegrams to

*The most careful and most detailed study of the strike is Robert V. Bruce's *1877: Year of Violence;* Indianapolis, 1959.

81

the President and had his office boys, the governor of Pennsylvania and the mayor of Philadelphia, do likewise. The burden of Scott's demand was that, since the railroads were engaged in interstate commerce, the federal government was obliged to keep them running—a curious argument for Scott to advance, since it was so obviously double-edged, but the occasion called for illogical argument. Vanderbilt contented himself with issuing foot-in-the-mouth statements to the press. First he denied that his loyal trainmen were on strike. Later he insisted that any strikers were only malcontents seeking jobs for which they were not fitted. Finally he said: "Our men feel that, although I"—a deprecatory cough—"may have my millions and they the rewards of their daily toil, still we are about equal in the end. If they suffer I suffer, and if I suffer they cannot escape."

A remarkable aspect of the strike was the warm and widespread sympathy for the strikers. Nearly everybody, it seemed, hated the railway companies, and the strike provided a splendid opportunity to vent the hatred. In Martinsburg, when the governor ordered the local militia to break the strike, none of them had his heart in the job, and back they all marched to shuck off their uniforms. When the militia was mustered against the strikers in the bigger cities, crowds gathered to stone them or massed in the streets to block their way. Since no frightened, ill-disciplined troop of armed men can confront an angry crowd without firing their guns, before long blood ran in the streets of Baltimore, and then of Pittsburgh, and then of Reading and Buffalo and Chicago, and scores of persons were killed. Antirailroad fury reached its height in Pittsburgh. There more than a hundred locomotives and more than two thousand cars were destroyed, the Union Depot and six dozen other buildings were burned, and the coroner counted twenty-four dead.

The strike itself and the violence it bred were alike unorganized, spontaneous, and leaderless, but by Monday, July 23, the strike having within a week spread through Maryland, Pennsylvania, New York, Ohio, Indiana, Illinois, Kentucky,

Missouri, and Iowa, the railroad magnates had figured out who was responsible. It was the Communists. Suddenly the newspapers discovered a plot, a conspiracy, a Communist menace, "unlawful and revolutionary," shrilled the editor of The National Republican, and also "anti-American." The editor of The Philadelphia Bulletin blamed "this present rebellion of the Railroad Communists" on the fact that Tom Scott had not yet been given a subsidy for his Texas & Pacific and so had been unable to spread prosperity abroad. And Jay Gould gloated over what he fancied was "a great social revolution, which cannot be arrested until it has led to the destruction of the republican form of government in this country and the establishment of a monarchy."*

If the strike had been intelligently planned and forcefully led, it would surely have had more tangible results. As it was, the strikers forced several roads—among them the Bee Line, the Missouri Pacific, the Chicago & North Western, the Louisville & Nashville, and the Santa Fe—to rescind their wage cuts; several other roads—among them the Union Pacific, the Central Pacific, and the Long Island—averted a strike only by nimble cancellation of their announced wage cuts. These successes were, however, exceptional. On too many lines, the most militant of the strikers were fired and jailed, and the others counted themselves lucky to get their jobs back at their miserable wages. By the end of July the trains were all running again. But labor had learned its vincible strength; now all that was needed was to learn how to use it.

Had the railroad magnates learned anything? Not much. There was talk of company insurance plans, company pension plans, and the need for improving company morale, but it was only talk; the action was confined to the beefing up of company

*In 1877 Marxist socialism was represented in the United States by something called the Workingmen's Party, which had about four thousand members, most of whom disagreed violently with each other on every conceivable question of strategy or tactics. So far from being responsible for the strike, they seem to have been taken completely by surprise and to have spent their energies in futile efforts to catch up with it.

espionage systems, company black lists, and company police forces, and to the enactment of legislation in the several states to strengthen the National Guard and to build armories so that mobs might be more efficiently chopped up. On behalf of the Pennsylvania, for example, Tom Scott authorized the hiring of one hundred company cops, with a second hundred to be held on inactive reserve. Scott, the strikers' most intransigent opponent, suffered most of all from the strike. The Pennsylvania had lost property valued at two and one half million dollars; the company's shareholders lost their August and November dividends. Further, Scott could no longer sustain his Empire Transportation Company in its fight against Rockefeller: in October he and Cassatt signed the necessary papers and another threat to the Standard Oil monopoly had been wiped out. Finally, all Scott's hopes of wringing a subsidy for his Texas & Pacific from the Congress were smashed. President Hayes was disenchanted by the oligopoly of the railroads as early as August; by December he was ready to break the bargain by which he had won the "election" of 1877: he announced his "grave doubt" of the wisdom of granting any aid whatsoever to the Texas & Pacific, and he summoned up memories of the Crédit Mobilier.

The federal government had learned something else, too. On August 18, John Sherman, the Secretary of the Treasury, urged regulation of the railroads in a speech that was said to reflect the policy of the Hayes administration.

New strength had been recruited at the short end of the rope, in the persistent tug of war between private greed and public interest.

The focus of the struggle now shifted east, and most particularly to New York City, the commercial capital of the nation. Now came the merchants and manufacturers, the most formidable adversaries yet to challenge the railroad kings and their arbitrary manipulation of the rate.

Businessmen (and especially New York jobbers and wholesalers) had excellent grounds for cursing the railroad magnates and wishing them lodgment in the hottest latitudes of Hell. For one thing, there was the trunk-line agreement of 1877 by which, it will be recalled, the rate on westbound freight had been raised fifty per cent. For another, there was what was called the port differential: freight charges to or from New York merchants were ten per cent higher than in Philadelphia and thirteen percent higher than in Baltimore. In theory, the differential was based on mileage from midwestern cities, but the New York merchants were convinced it was a cunning scheme to divert traffic away from New York and a denial of the natural advantages of New York's harbor. Because they had cravenly agreed to the concept of a port differential, Vanderbilt of the Central and Jewett of the Erie were both denounced as traitors to their commercial community.

But the most anguished howl was raised over the rebate, the device by which, contrary to law, equity, and every canon of honest business, favored shippers got lower rates from the railroads than their competitors. (They paid the published tariff but were secretly rebated part of what they had paid.) Favoritism, of course, was in direct ratio to size; and so the big shipper got bigger and so the small shipper was forced out of business or gobbled up. On this score the blackest suspicion attached to the Standard Oil Company, but only because the Standard was the biggest of all and growing bigger every day. Suspicion attached to any big corporation in any industry; to any corporation, big or small, in which a railroad magnate was rumored to have an interest; to any corporation, however infinitesimal, in which a magnate's relative or in-law, however far removed, was rumored, on evidence no matter how shaky, to have an interest. (The suspicion, however faint, inevitably turned out to have been justified.)

To combat these inequities, a few New York businessmen organized an assemblage called the American Cheap Transportation Association, which gradually gathered strength and by 1877 had been transformed into the New York Board of Trade, solid, conservative, and truculent.

Early in 1878 the members of the New York Chamber of

Commerce joined the fight, and these were the most prestigious fat cats on the American commercial scene, but no sooner had they launched a decorous campaign against the railroads than they were savagely counterattacked and charged with being Communists. Their correct and proper agitprop was denounced by spokesmen for the railroads as "a communistic movement against capital invested in railroads."

After that it followed as the night the day that a committee of the New York state legislature (the Hepburn committee) was authorized to inquire into the affairs of the two New York railroads, the Central and the Erie. In April, 1879, Vanderbilt of the Central and Jewett of the Erie jointly and indignantly denied the existence of a single special contract authorizing any rebate by their roads. The committee kept digging for the truth. (The editor of The Journal of Commerce noted: "It is pulled out of them as with a corkscrew, day after day.") By July the committee had established that, in the first six months of 1879, the Central alone had made more than six thousand contracts involving rebates. Fifty per cent of the Central's local traffic, the freight agent testified, was carried at discriminatory rates.

Had Vanderbilt lied? Or was he simply ignorant of the facts? He professed ignorance. He didn't know, he said, whether the Central's traffic was up or down since the year before; didn't know how much of it was local, how much trunk; didn't know operating costs; didn't know how much was paid his road by Standard Oil; didn't know why some got special rates and others didn't; didn't know, didn't know. . . .

The Hepburn committee's counsel, Simon Sterne, epitomized the matter neatly. "The railway charge," said Sterne, "is so important an element in the price of every commodity that is carried from a distance in the United States and intended for export, that it is within the power of our railway magnates to become partners in every special line of occupation, and it is this power to destroy and to build up which no community can allow to roam and exercise itself unchecked, which must be restrained, curbed and rendered subservient to the general

86

public weal through the instrumentality of wise legislation rigidly enforced."

Vanderbilt was now badly rattled. He had been quoted as saying that he owned eighty-seven per cent of the Central's stock, which would have meant about 778,000 of the 894,280 shares outstanding (a better guess is that he owned some 550,000 shares, worth about seventy million dollars); and the Hepburn committee had established, among other things, that more than fifty per cent of the Central's stock was water. Those celebrated eight-per-cent dividends, then, were being paid on grossly fictitious stock. Who was making Vanderbilt rich? Who but the New York businessmen, obliged by Vanderbilt to pay exorbitant rates on their freight?

Other railroad kings could protest that their dividends were the sole support of widows and orphans. Not Vanderbilt. The rumor was spread abroad that the state legislature was considering the advisability of repealing the Consolidation Act of 1869 by which all the Central's watered stock had been declared legal. It was too dreadful to contemplate. In November, 1879, Vanderbilt entered into negotiations with J. P. Morgan. Late that month it was announced that Morgan had formed a syndicate to buy 250,000 of Vanderbilt's shares for thirty million dollars.

As one condition of the transaction, Morgan took a seat on the Central's board of directors. It was not at once evident, but an era had ended. The railroad king was dead: the investment banker had unthroned him.

87

# 5

J. P. Morgan takes over. "The public be damned." Peace between the New York Central and the Pennsylvania. A federal commission to regulate the railroads. ReMorganization and the "community of interest." Morgan's attempts to stop the rate wars.

IN NOVEMBER, 1879, when the Gilded Age was in its late autumnal splendor, it was meet for a Vanderbilt to seek the help of a Morgan. The epoch of the buccaneers was fading, and so William Henry Vanderbilt, a most reluctant buccaneer, weary of the struggle to protect his domain in the rate wars with the other trunk lines and from the raids by Jay Gould and his Wabash Railroad in the west, turned naturally to J. Pierpont Morgan, who at forty-two was already the nation's prepotent financier. For the sake of the ragged and demoralized railroad industry, if not of the much abused public interest, Morgan could not have come upon the scene at a better time. But to impose his will on the obstinate oligarchs Morgan would have to wait for circumstances to present him with the proper moment.

To a banker like Morgan, the chief flaw in the railroad industry was that the promoters who had it in charge had grossly overbuilt it; by 1880, according to John Moody, "they had built twice as much railroad as the country could employ, and issued four times the securities it could pay interest on." Except on the Pacific coast, where Collis Huntington still contrived to discourage would-be trespassers, every profitable railroad was a target for freebooters, who built competing and parallel roads, slashed rates, and sought to snatch all the available traffic; as a result, instead of one profitable road there were two or three roads headed straight for receivership or bankruptcy, while one or more gangs of speculators scurried off with the loot they had accumulated in the course of laying their unnecessary tracks. Poor's Manual estimated that, in the three years 1881–1883, more than one billion dollars had been stolen so from the investing public.

Vanderbilt was easily the favorite target for the sharpshooters. Not only was he the plumpest of potential pigeons, but he was also notoriously reluctant to mix in a knock-down-and-drag-out brawl. The first gang to take aim on him built the New York, Chicago & St. Louis, better known as the Nickel Plate, a railroad that ran between Buffalo and Chicago alongside Vanderbilt's Lake Shore & Michigan, so close to it over much of the way that the trainmen on the two roads could almost talk to each other. The promoters of the Nickel Plate, which was ruinously overcapitalized, launched a rate war with their first train, in October, 1882. Later that month Vanderbilt personally inspected the hateful new competition from his private car. The reporters who met him in Chicago found him in an ugly mood.

The Nickel Plate was poorly built, he said; it could not last.

What, he was asked, about the pool of freight traffic, in which all the trunk lines shared?

"I don't like that expression, 'pool,'" Vanderbilt said; "that is a common construction applied by the people to a combination which the leading roads have entered into to keep rates at a point where they will pay dividends to the stockholders."

But surely the public had a lively interest in the cost of—

"The roads are not run for the benefit of the 'dear public.' That cry is all nonsense."

What about having the rates controlled by commissioners?

"I consider that it is an excellent thing to have the rates controlled by commissioners who are selected by the roads, but I don't believe in those State Railroad Commissioners. They are usually ignorant persons, who have to be bought up by the railroads, if any legislation favorable to the road is desired."

What about the Central's crack passenger limited, between New York and Chicago: was it profitable?

"No; not a bit of it. We only run it because we are forced to do so by the action of the Pennsylvania. . . We would abandon it if it was not for our competitor keeping its train on."

But don't you run it for the public benefit?

"The public be damned," said William Henry Vanderbilt, and with four words won for himself a measure of fame more lasting than his millions would ever confer upon him. "The public be damned! What does the public care for the railroads except to get as much out of them for as small a consideration as possible?"

Vanderbilt's temper was not improved when he found that his—as he considered—quite temperate remarks had provoked press and pulpit to join in savaging him. Worse yet, there remained the problem of the Nickel Plate. In December he irritably paid out $6,527,000 to buy control of the accursed road and its monstrous fixed obligations; only after he had done so would he discover that, if he had waited another six weeks, he could have picked it up on his own terms.

No sooner had Vanderbilt digested this disagreeable information than he was beset by a second gang of sharpshooters, who began building the New York, West Shore & Buffalo, a road that exactly and closely paralleled the Central itself north to Albany and west to Buffalo and at once took on the aspects of another exercise in blackmail. Vanderbilt chose to believe that this gang was backed by his most powerful rival, the Pennsylvania, and in his dull, stubborn way he concluded that the time had come to fight back and, so he hoped, utterly to bankrupt his enemies. To combat the West Shore he slashed the Central's rates to the bone and into it. To teach the Pennsylvania an enduring lesson he projected a new road, the South Pennsylvania, that would with a vengeance destroy the Pennsylvania's monopoly of business from the steel mills of Pittsburgh. As allies in this venture he enlisted a few well-heeled

90

capitalists—Andrew Carnegie, Henry C. Frick, William Rockefeller, among others—and Franklin Gowen, the president of the Philadelphia & Reading, a railroad that had got rich as a carrier of anthracite coal.

Early in 1885, then, there were six trunk lines competing for the traffic between Chicago and the Atlantic seaports, and a seventh, Vanderbilt's South Pennsylvania, was building. Although this traffic was the heaviest in the country, three roads could easily have handled it all, and so the rates were splintered: passengers traveled between New York and Chicago at a fare of one dollar, and grain was carried from Chicago for half the cost.

The moment had come for Pierpont Morgan's Draconian measures. In fact, he was forced to intervene, for he was personally involved with the bitterest disputants, the managements of the Pennsylvania and the New York Central. As a partner in Drexel, Morgan & Company he was fiscal agent for the Pennsylvania; as a partner in J. S. Morgan & Company of London he had sold huge blocks of New York Central stock to English investors, at the same time assuring them that their annual return would be at least eight per cent for at least five years. But the rate war and the appalling competition had sliced the Central's dividend in half and so had put Morgan's personal reputation in jeopardy.

On a summer day Morgan invited George Roberts, who had succeeded Tom Scott as president of the Pennsylvania, Frank Thomson, the first vice-president, and Chauncey Depew, the president of the New York Central, to an all-day conference aboard his yacht, the Corsair, and outlined his proposal: the Central to lease a reorganized West Shore, the Pennsylvania to take over a reorganized South Pennsylvania, and both to profit from higher rates.

So began a most curious cruise, the Corsair steaming slowly up and down the Hudson River and out across the bay, back and forth between Sandy Hook and West Point, while Morgan concentrated on persuading his guests to approve his scheme. Depew soon agreed, but Roberts was adamantine in opposition.

He had to be shown that the South Pennsylvania, in the wrong hands, would hurt the Pennsylvania as badly as the West Shore had already hurt the New York Central. "That's right," Morgan growled; "can't you see it? In the end you would have to control the other road." But, Roberts objected, even if he wanted to buy the South Pennsylvania, which he most certainly did not, the state constitution had been amended to provide that a railroad company could not control a competing road. Morgan snorted. Laws, constitutions—they could always be evaded, one way or another; indeed, what were lawyers for, if not to show how a thing could be done that needed doing? Still Roberts brooded, nursing his grievance that certain rich capitalists were blackmailing his company and that now he was being obliged to submit, to co-operate, to extricate them from their own duplicity. "Oh, no," snapped Morgan. "They'll not get out whole."

The black-hulled Corsair steamed back and forth. The four men gathered together fell silent. Morgan puffed on his black cigar. At length Roberts sighed. "All right," he said, "I agree." Morgan, the master, lifted his hand, and the Corsair turned to steam to its mooring.

The childish squabble had been settled, but some still sulked and some wept angry tears. For one thing, the Pennsylvania's officers suddenly decided to shift their financial business from Drexel, Morgan & Company to Kuhn, Loeb & Company; it seems unlikely that this decision was wholeheartedly endorsed by either Drexel or Morgan. For another thing, Franklin Gowen and the management of the Reading at once whimpered that Vanderbilt had betrayed them. Gone were their dreams of challenging the Pennsylvania; instead there was only a substantial debt, incurred for terminal connections with a railroad that would never be built; the Reading's deficit in 1885 would be more than four and one-half million dollars, and what would become of the Reading? What would become of the vast coal fields and the iron mines owned by the Reading? Their fate was predictable.

Pierpont Morgan desired "harmonious relations" in the

coal industry as in the railroad industry, "in order that suitable prices may be obtained for coal produced and shipped." He stood ready "to bring about satisfactory arrangements with all the anthracite roads, and also the trunk lines, which shall secure to the Philadelphia & Reading Railroad Company, when reorganized, its just share of the business at remunerative rates." This pledge, duly published in The Railway World, would seem to have been Morgan's way of suggesting that if there were to be a monopoly in the coal industry he, not Franklin Gowen, would make it. After a short, sharp struggle, Morgan once again emerged the master. His syndicate furnished the necessary millions, the interest the Reading paid to its bondholders was severely reduced, its floating debt was wiped out by an assessment on the stockholders, and Morgan himself became one of the five trustees who controlled the road.

Later the presidents of the several roads that carried anthracite were summoned to Morgan's brownstone house on Murray Hill, in New York City. Morgan spoke to them in his blunt, brusque fashion. They nodded and, after a time, they dispersed. Before long the rate for hauling coal had gone up, and so had the cost of it to the consumer.

The Morgan prescription for curing what ailed the railroads was now perfected and could be administered routinely. It consisted of two medications, the first taken internally and the second applied externally.

The first was the bitter pill called reorganization or, as a patent medicine, reMorganization, and its function was drastic: it purged the railroad of its debts and put it once again on a profitable basis. Bonds were refinanced, to ease the burden of fixed charges; stock was assessed to pay off floating debt. The device of stock assessment was particularly useful, for when, through ignorance or confusion or lack of cash, a stockholder failed to pay the assessment on his shares of stock, they reverted to those in charge of the reorganization. In this way Morgan could, and often did, wind up with enough stock of the railroad company to enable him to select management,

93

name directors, dictate policy, and control the road utterly.

The second was a soothing salve called community of interest, which was designed to keep a road profitable by discouraging disastrous rate wars and, wherever possible, eliminating competition entirely. It was to proselyte for his community-of-interest plan that Morgan had called the presidents of the anthracite roads together. Already he was planning to compel harmony by arranging to have a railroad under his control purchase, if possible in friendly fashion, a substantial amount of stock in any competing roads, or by contriving to have men sympathetic to the community of interest elected to the directorate of competing roads.

What Morgan wanted was a sound return for investment capital, which in turn required orderly operation of the railroads, high rates, consolidation, and combination. It is impossible not to admire his audacity, for to achieve these ends he had not only to overbear the most powerful men of his time but he had also to thwart an apparently overwhelming popular demand for regulation of the railroads by the national government.

In terms of the continuing struggle between the greed for private profit and the obligation to serve the public interest, Morgan was, of course, instinctively partisan. ("I owe the public nothing," he once said.) But at his end of the rope, in this tug of war, he found a demoralized crew of mutually hostile incompetents, while from the other end the opposition was, for a wonder, pulling as one man. Morgan was obliged to bully and browbeat his buffle-headed allies into a semblance of unity before they were utterly routed. His mastery of the railroad magnates was a remarkable feat, but in retrospect his circumvention of the popular will seems even more impressive.

That will had, by 1886, decreed that the railroads be harnessed, their discriminatory practices outlawed, and their operation put on a competitive basis. Indeed, the report of a Senate Committee on Interstate Commerce epitomized the popular will. "The paramount evil," the committee declared, "is unjust discrimination between persons, places, [and] commodities," and the bill proposed by the committee prohibited not only the rebate and other discriminatory devices, which were caused by competition, but also the pools, which had been contrived to eliminate competition. The bill also proposed a five-man commission with power to investigate "the rates, financial operations, and methods of management of the carriers" and to require a uniform system of accounting. Bills to regulate interstate commerce had often been hatched in the past, and as often squashed; but this one, despite the mournful howls of the railroad lobbyists and the difficulty of reconciling differences between House and Senate versions of what should be done, was finally approved by the Congress and signed by President Cleveland on February 4, 1887.

On the face of it, hip, hip, hooray! Here was the culmination of decades of struggle against the respectable gangsters who had so persistently robbed the nation; the war was won, the public interest had triumphed, democracy was once again vindicated.

Yet, curiously, nobody took much joy in the new law. For one thing, it did not go far enough: the new Interstate Commerce Commission was given no power to fix rates, and only that power could curb the worst abuses. Nor had the Commission the authority to enforce its own decisions. Another flaw was that the law prescribed competition, but, in the nature of the business, competition was suicidal. Moreover, the law could too easily be flouted: every freight agent knew a dozen surreptitious ways of giving a shipper a rebate, and no one the wiser.

So once again all was in a snarl. The rate wars broke out, as cutthroat as ever, and the railroad presidents fumed and cursed but were impotent to stop them. Charles Francis Adams, who had been actively involved with railroads for twenty years —as a Massachusetts commissioner, then as the arbiter of disputes amongst the trunk lines, and since 1884 as president of the Union Pacific—was well qualified to summarize the state of affairs in 1888:

Stockholders are complaining; directors are bewildered; bankers are frightened. . . . The railroad system, especially in regions west of Chicago, is to-day managed on principles which must inevitably lead to financial disaster. . . . The dishonest methods of rate-cutting, the secret system of rebates, the indirect and hidden payments made to influence the course of traffic resorted to or devised in the last two years are unprecedented in the whole bad record of the past. . . . There is an utter disregard of fundamental ideals of truth, fair play, and fair dealing.

Once again, the situation invited intervention by Pierpont Morgan. When the Baltimore & Ohio slashed its rates, tangled in a rate war with the Pennsylvania, and almost collapsed into bankruptcy, Morgan formed a syndicate that raised the fifteen million dollars needed to put the B&O back on its feet. When the Chesapeake & Ohio unexpectedly slid into receivership, he formed a syndicate that reMorganized it and brought it firmly within his community of interest. Finally, when he learned how competition, rate wars, and pigheaded management were eating away at profits—in 1888, while gross earnings were up three and one half per cent over those of 1887, net earnings were down six per cent—Morgan decided he must bring order to the railroads beyond the Mississippi.

In this presumptuous effort Morgan persisted for nearly three years, accomplishing approximately nothing. On the face of it, the task he had set himself seemed simple enough. All he had to do was to get a group of gentlemen to agree to fix and stick to a set of reasonable rates; since they knew that any alternative would lead to economic disaster, surely they would agree. In fact, however, the task was an impossible one, for none of the gentlemen trusted any other; and few, if any, of them trusted Morgan or the other bankers who were part of Morgan's scheme.

In December, 1888, after a meeting at his house in Murray Hill with men who commanded more than half the railroad mileage in the nation, Morgan announced publicly that he considered "the Western rate wars as practically at an end."

It was as though the distinguished financier had confidently placed his well-shod foot on a banana peel and thereafter described a glorious arc into fatuity, for a week later Jay Gould cut the rate for grain shipments on the Missouri Pacific, and the wars began anew.

Morgan's second conference, in January, 1889, attracted a notable group of western railroad magnates; to lend a tone, the presidents of a half-dozen eastern roads were also on hand.* After two days of wrangling, the magnates gave their gingerly approval to an Interstate Commerce Railway Association and pledged their worthless word of honor to maintain the rate structure. But the presidents of the western roads adjourned "in order," said one of them, "to separate the discussion from the banking interests." Another said: "We did not swallow whole the arrangement evidently prepared for us." Within a month the scheme had collapsed.

But Morgan did not despair. He noted that, aside from wasting their substance in rate wars, the western railroad magnates had joined in costly wars of territorial expansion, contending for control of the traffic from the Pacific northwest. Collis P. Huntington had pushed a subsidiary of his Southern Pacific through the Cascades into Oregon; Henry Villard, backed by German bankers, imagined that he controlled the Northern Pacific and so all the trade with the Orient; the Union Pacific, having laid track north from Wyoming, disputed these claims; and James J. Hill, whose Great Northern was both prudently financed and soundly operated, had already flung his rails over the northern Rockies and now posed a challenge to all rivals. Such wasteful competition, Morgan knew, was sure to bring two or three of these four belligerents, hat in hand, to his

*The western railroads represented were the Burlington, the Rock Island, the Chicago & North Western, the Chicago, Milwaukee & St. Paul, the Chicago, St. Paul & Kansas City (later to be absorbed into the Chicago & Great Western), the Wabash, the Santa Fe, the Missouri Pacific, and the Union Pacific. The eastern roads represented were the four big trunk lines—the Pennsylvania, the New York Central, the Erie, and the B&O—and two anthracite carriers closely identified with Morgan's interests, the Lehigh Valley and the Lackawanna.

door. He could afford to wait.

Meanwhile the value of railroad securities inevitably declined. The magnates blamed each other, their plaints rising in a resentful clamor. They yearned to combine but could not agree how. Perkins of the Burlington wanted long "lines of traffic" reaching unbroken across the continent; Huntington of the Southern Pacific wanted all the roads west of the Mississippi merged under one management; T. B. Blackstone, the president of the prosperous Chicago & Alton, went so far as to recommend that all interstate railroads be nationalized. "If things go on as now," Blackstone warned, "in ten years all the roads will be hopelessly bankrupt."

In December, 1890, Morgan again convened the western presidents and now, besides the original group, there were Stuyvesant Fish of the Illinois Central, Thomas Oakes of the Northern Pacific, Hill of the Great Northern, Huntington of the Southern Pacific, Russell Sage, ostensibly representing the Iowa Central, and the presidents of the Denver & Rio Grande and the Rio Grande Western. This time every important western road was represented. Morgan told them of an agreement he had negotiated between the Pennsylvania and the New York Central "to avoid wasteful rivalry and to establish uniformity of rates between competitive points."* He urged them to sign a similar pact and, when they agreed, Morgan pronounced himself "thoroughly satisfied" and issued a public statement. "Think of it," he said proudly, "all the competitive traffic of the roads west of Chicago and St. Louis in the control of about thirty men. It is the most important agreement made by the railroads in a long time, and it is as strong as could be desired."

Wrong again. Already the most revealing remark uttered at the conference had been reported in the press. "Gentlemen," one of the presidents had said to the others, "I have the utmost

*This was the first of several such treaties between the two systems that controlled a major share of the traffic between the Mississippi and the Atlantic coast. All the treaties were in violation of the Interstate Commerce Act and the Sherman Antitrust Act.

98

respect for you individually, but as railroad presidents I wouldn't trust you with my watch out of sight." He had spoken for all of them, and prophetically, for the men who had gathered around Morgan's table once more proved too willful, too greedy; besides which, in all likelihood it was already too late. Time after time they had been offered their opportunity, as on a golden charger, but invariably they had rejected it. None of the railroad magnates had ever for a moment considered whether his decision might or should benefit the public, and for his part Morgan, quite as stupid, evidently imagined that the public would rejoice to find that the cost of all the traffic west of the Mississippi might be fixed by a cabal of thirty insatiable despots. But the public knew in its bones and painfully felt in its pocketbook how, as the number of railroads diminished, the cost of everything—bricks and boots, bread and beer—climbed steadily higher.

But if in wooing the railroad oligarchs with sweet reason he was a flop, Morgan nevertheless could shrug it off. They were highballing down a one-way track to insolvency. As a banker, he would be able to pick up the pieces he fancied from the wreckage.

*The Panic of 1893: Morgan selects a few railroads for re-Morganization. The Interstate Commerce Commission is gutted. Debs and the American Railway Union. The Pullman strike: Debs jailed and his union crushed.*

THE PANIC OF 1893 and the consequent severe depression took their toll of the railroads, but the melancholy truth of the matter is that many of those roads were bankrupt in fact even before the panic forced them into the courts to be declared bankrupt legally. More than two hundred railway companies failed between 1890 and 1895—nearly sixty thousand miles of track, one third of the nation's total, capitalized at more than two and one half billion dollars—a splendid scrap heap.

Pierpont Morgan went about like a junkman, picking up some pieces, discarding others.

Here was the Hocking Valley (the Cincinnati, Columbus & Hocking Valley Railroad), fraudulently promoted and valuable only as a threat to the rate structure of bigger roads that served the coal fields of West Virginia and southern Ohio. Morgan picked it up, brushed it off, reMorganized it, and tucked it away for profitable sale in the future.

Here was something called the Richmond & West Point Terminal System, which had been methodically looted by a syndicate of southern speculators and New York investment bankers. It comprised four holding companies and more than fifty railroads patched together in a shaky, eighty-five-hundred-mile system that sprawled all over the southeast from Virginia to Louisiana and that had been financed by one hundred and ten different issues of stocks and bonds. It was a mess. The region it served was impoverished, and Morgan professed a low opinion of its prospects. "Niggers," said Morgan, "are lazy, ignorant, and unprogressive; railroad traffic is created only by industrious, intelligent, and ambitious people."* Maybe he believed this; maybe he said it only to get a better bargaining position. In any case, at length he agreed to reMorganize the system. Bonded debt was slashed, some stocks were severely assessed and others ruthlessly wiped out, worthless miles of track were lopped off, potentially profitable main lines were rebuilt, and links to the north and west were financed. One railroad, the Central of Georgia, was amputated, separately reMorganized, and connected with midwestern carriers. There finally emerged the Southern Railway, a seven-thousand-mile system that joined New Orleans and Mobile and Atlanta to St. Louis and Chicago and Washington. (And Morgan got $750,000 in common stock, $100,000 in cash, and control of the system.)

Here was the Santa Fe, another road that had been methodically looted, in this case by the Boston financiers who controlled it and who subsequently falsified its books to conceal, as they hoped, their peculations. On the Santa Fe the fraud reached all the way from its loftiest directors down to its humblest section hands. Payroll swindles on just one division, the one between Chicago and Topeka, amounted to seventeen thousand dollars a month; during 1891 and 1892, illegal payment of rebates amounted to almost four million dollars. The Santa Fe was owed three hundred thousand dollars by the Union Pacific and the Southern Pacific, but the debt could not be collected in court since it had accrued from an illegal pool of traffic shared with those roads. Falsification of the Santa Fe's books over a three-year period amounted to more than ten million dollars. (But the directors were charged with no crimes; all was serene on Beacon Street; their well-bred sons

*The quotation is from John Moody in *The Railroad Builders*, Yale University Press, 1920, pp. 188-189.

proceeded through Harvard to take their places in offices on State Street.) Even if Morgan had been asked to pluck the Santa Fe from the scrap heap he would have refused, for its tracks curved through the southwest, a land Morgan dismissed as a desert waste.

Here was the Baltimore & Ohio, which Morgan yearned to bring within his community of interest, since over the years its management had so often and so aggressively tangled in rate wars with the Pennsylvania and the other eastern trunk lines. Once before Morgan had tried to get his hands on the B&O. In 1887 his man Samuel Spencer had been elected president, had found twenty-four million dollars' worth of fictitious assets on the B&O's balance sheet, and had, so to say, corrected the error; but the Garretts, who for generations had controlled the B&O, had ungratefully given Spencer the boot. This time Morgan was not allowed near the road. The Garretts still feared his harsh methods. They turned instead to Kuhn, Loeb & Company and to Speyer & Company, who presently learned, by examining the B&O's books, that the shareholders had been defrauded of still another twenty-two million dollars. After reorganizing the road, the kindly bankers sold forty per cent of its stock to its chief competitor, the Pennsylvania, for about forty million dollars. Officers of the Pennsylvania promptly took over as officers and directors of the B&O, smoothly transforming a rival into a slave.

Here was the Erie, back in receivership for the fourth time in forty years and still struggling to recover from the depredations of Drew, Gould, Fisk, and Jewett. Since many of its unhappy bondholders were Morgan's clients in England, he decided he must, for a price (five hundred thousand dollars and expenses), undertake once again to reorganize it. But the owner of a few hundred thousand dollars' worth of Erie bonds was Edward H. Harriman, now forty-six years old and the active operating head of the Illinois Central, and Harriman objected to the way Morgan proposed to reduce the value of his bonds. Harriman was asked, "Whom do you represent?" "Myself," he retorted, and he fought so hard that the reorganization had to be revised. It was not the first time that Harriman had opposed Morgan, and so Morgan's hatred of Harriman grew hotter. (But Morgan took control of the Erie.)

Here was the Philadelphia & Reading, a road prised from Morgan's grip a few years before by a group of Philadelphia financiers and controlled in 1893 by one Arthur Alexander McLeod, who dared the wrath of Jupiter Morgan by presuming to construct a monopoly in the Pennsylvania coalfields and to try to create a trunk line that would threaten the profits not only of the Pennsylvania but also of the New York Central. Contumacy, perfidy, apostasy! Morgan was fiscal agent for the Reading and consequently able to influence if not dictate its corporate policy; but McLeod said, loudly enough to be overheard, "I would rather run a peanut stand than be dictated to by J. P. Morgan," after which it was only a matter of time before McLeod would be pricing the available peanut stands. McLeod attempted to invade New England, a region that Morgan regarded as his personal fief; McLeod's policy of expansion obliged him to borrow huge sums at high interest and then to try to sell bonds. Swiftly and easily Morgan drove the price of the Reading's stock down, sent the road into bankruptcy, forced rejection of McLeod as receiver, blocked the Reading from New England, reorganized it, and secured its control under a voting trust. Its new president, George F. Baer, was of course Morgan's man.*

Here was the Union Pacific, an unusual hunk of scrap for the reason that several junk dealers, among them the federal government, were loudly disputing as to who owned it and what should be done with it. Attracted by the clamor, Morgan

*As president of the Reading, which owned many large coal fields in Pennsylvania, Baer was also the chief spokesman for the mine owners. In this capacity, he won himself celebrity of a sort when, a few years later, the United Mine Workers struck for recognition of their union and a raise in their pay, which averaged five hundred and sixty dollars a year. Baer said: "The rights and interests of the laboring man will be protected and cared for—not by the labor agitators, but by the Christian men to whom God in His infinite wisdom has given control of the property interests of this country."

strolled over to listen, and before long he was trying to yank it away from the others so that he might reMorganize it. Now reMorganization routinely required, as part of the price for making a failed railroad profitable, that its bondholders agree to take a smaller return on their investment than they had been promised. But since the Union Pacific was one of the roads built with the considerable assistance of cash loaned from the public purse, the government was its biggest bondholder. In the past the government had never been an exigent creditor. One friendly Congress after another had agreed to postpone payment of interest on the bonds; in consequence the debt was already so huge in January, 1888, that President Cleveland had remarked: "No one, I think, expects that these railroad companies will be able to pay their immense indebtedness to the Government at its maturity." At maturity, it was estimated the Union Pacific would owe

| | |
|---|---|
| In principal | $33,539,512 |
| In interest, for thirty years | 36,944,300 |
| In all | $70,483,812 |

In 1892 the men who managed it were Jay Gould and Russell Sage. Neither of them dreamed that the debt would be paid; as directors of the Union Pacific they had put away less than ten million dollars against the day when the debt would fall due, while they had earlier lined their pockets with at least twenty millions by purchasing certain subsidiary roads and selling them to the Union Pacific at a fat profit. Morgan also assumed that the debt could at least be sharply reduced. But the Congress, under public pressure in 1894, suddenly got its back up and demanded payment in full. At this point Morgan made the mistake of his life. He tossed the Union Pacific back on the junk heap and turned away, leaving it to be reorganized by the one man, Harriman, who might be able to outwit him.

The only other considerable hunk of scrap on the heap was the Northern Pacific. Its promoters had been more concerned with looting the public lands than with building an efficient railroad; its financiers had got rich while burdening it with a

104

monstrous debt structure. So long as it was the only road to the northwest, the Northern Pacific could totter along, but from the moment James J. Hill's Great Northern reached the west coast it was doomed. Its operating costs and its fixed charges were alike fifty per cent higher than those of Hill's road. In 1893, when Hill cut his rates, he gave it the coup de grâce. The Northern Pacific went bust, and presently Morgan engaged to revive it. His first plan involved a simple consolidation. The Great Northern would acquire the Northern Pacific, guaranteeing the interest on a new bond issue in return for half of a new stock issue. While simple, this consolidation was also illegal, since it created a monopoly; it proved too much for the Supreme Court to swallow. Morgan shrugged and devised a new plan. If the Great Northern could not own the Northern Pacific, there was no law against the two roads being owned by the same individuals. By the terms of the new reMorganization, the owners of Northern Pacific common stock were assessed fifteen dollars a share; when a great number of stockholders refused to pay, some three hundred thousand shares fell into Morgan's hands, and he promptly sold most of them (worth, at par, nearly twenty-six million dollars) to Hill and one of Hill's partners for $4,133,456—or sixteen dollars a share. All quite legal, and immensely profitable. The two parallel and competing roads were, as Hill assured Morgan, "together as nearly as possible in general policy [since] a controlling interest in both companies [is held] by the same parties." Then Morgan picked up his phone and hired one Charles S. Mellen to be president of the Northern Pacific, in this fashion:

MORGAN: Is that you, Mr. Mellen?
MELLEN: Yes.
MORGAN: Anybody hear what we say?
MELLEN: No.
MORGAN: Will you take the Northern Pacific?
MELLEN: Yes.
MORGAN: Will you leave it all to me?
MELLEN: Yes.

105

At least for Mr. Mellen, this was easier than floating up in a balloon, and a great deal more secure.*

These reorganizations, consolidations, and combinations—and dozens of others worked out in the 1890s—were transacted without reference to the Interstate Commerce Commission and without regard for the public interest. If any of them chanced to serve the public interest, it was only by accident. The men who controlled the railroads persisted in considering those roads their private property, to be operated primarily for their private profit and, whenever convenient, for the profit of their stockholders. Government regulation was a joke. The statute of 1887, which the public had fancied would oblige the railroads to be competitive, was sedulously flouted. As for the Commission, its powers and functions were duly scrutinized by judges who, prior to their appointment to the bench, had proved their skill as attorneys either for the railroads or for the trusts that had grown powerful thanks to the illegal rebate of railroad rates; one by one the Commission's powers were emasculated by the courts, one by one its functions were abolished. After President Cleveland appointed Melville Fuller, a wealthy railroad lawyer, to be Chief Justice, the Supreme Court was especially inimical to the Commission. The most damaging decision came in the maximum rate case (160 U.S. 479), by which the Commission was forbidden to substitute a new rate for one that had been declared unreasonable. Justice Harlan gave it as his opinion that the Commission was "a useless body for all practical purposes," and in 1897 the commissioners agreed, stating in their annual report: "Under the law as now interpreted, there is today and there can be no effective regulation of interstate carriers." They blamed the failure of regulation on the gross dishonesty of the railroad managers, a malignancy with which they were unable to cope.

*This dialogue was later recalled by Mellen during the course of an investigation by the Interstate Commerce Commission into his affairs and those of Morgan. It was reported in The New York Times on May 20, 1914.

The impotence of the Commission had been manifest as early as 1890, but the railroad magnates had nevertheless squealed like pigs in a meatworks whenever they thought of it. In 1892, after Cleveland had been re-elected to the presidency, Charles Perkins, the president of the Burlington, devoutly prayed that the new administration might scuttle the Commission. This was stupid, and Richard S. Olney, who was the Burlington's corporation counsel and a director of two other railroads, explained why in a letter he wrote to Perkins:

> The Commission [Olney wrote], as its functions have now been limited by the courts, is, or can be made, of great use to the railroads. It satisfies the popular clamor for a government supervision of railroads, at the same time that that supervision is almost entirely minimal. . . . The part of wisdom is not to destroy the Commission, but to utilize it.

In February, 1893, this same Richard Olney was invited to serve in Cleveland's cabinet as Attorney General. He wrote again to Perkins, wondering if it would be "to the true interest" of the Burlington for him to accept the appointment. Evidently Perkins saw some advantage, for Olney took the job.*

Indeed, there was much that Olney could do, as Attorney General, that was "to the true interest" not only of the Burlington but of the entire railroad industry. He was, perhaps, most helpful in dealing with those of their workingmen who were driven to strike. The considerate Olney proved himself a superlative strikebreaker. In the chain of circumstance that lay ready to Olney's hand, the first link was a strike on the Northern Pacific.

After the Northern Pacific failed in August, 1893, its receivers twice cut wages, the second reduction slicing pay envelopes as much as thirty per cent. At once a strike was organized, but Judge James Jenkins of the U. S. circuit court granted an

---

*Cleveland, who had himself been a lawyer for three railroads and also for the Standard Oil Company before being elected to public office, spent the years between his two terms as President in the law firm headed by Francis Lynde Stetson, who was Pierpont Morgan's chief counsel and generally referred to as Morgan's attorney general.

injunction prohibiting the men "from combining or conspiring to quit" work and forbidding them to urge others to quit. This procedure was denounced by the Judiciary Committee of the House of Representatives as "an abuse of judicial power" and "an invasion of the rights of American citizens," but Judge Jenkins's order was unheld by the Supreme Court and the strike was smashed.

None of this had escaped the attention of James J. Hill. Despite the enviable prosperity of his Great Northern, Hill ordered a general wage cut for his nine thousand employees in August, 1893; he ordered a second cut in January, 1894; he ordered a third cut in March. After each of these reductions Hill paused, alert and watchful. There was one new factor to which he had to be sensitively responsive, one intangible, one cause for concern—something called the American Railway Union.

The A.R.U. was unique in the American labor movement. Its leader—its indomitable heart and spirit—was Eugene Victor Debs, who, as secretary-treasurer of the Brotherhood of Locomotive Firemen, had zealously spread the gospel of industrial unionism in the railroad industry. In 1889 Debs had helped to build a federation of the brotherhoods; he had grieved in 1891 when the federation was splintered by craft jealousies; and in August, 1893, he had plunged into the organization of one big union for all railroad workers—the American Railway Union. His success was phenomenal. Section hands, switchmen, brakemen, roundhouse workers, even firemen, engineers, and a few conductors signed on as members of A.R.U. lodges; they flocked in by the hundreds, by the thousands; in January, 1894, a half-dozen western railroads—including the Union Pacific, the Santa Fe, and the Denver & Rio Grande—were solidly organized from one end to the other. Debs had said: "The strike is the weapon of the oppressed, of men capable of appreciating justice and having the courage to resist wrong and contend for principle." When Hill slashed wages for the third time, Debs was ready. On April 13 the members of his A.R.U. struck the Great Northern and stopped its trains dead on their tracks.

108

Now here came Richard Olney to direct that great signs be posted along the Great Northern's right-of-way, from Minneapolis to Puget Sound, warning that any hindrance of the United States mails would be punished by a fine of ten thousand dollars and a two-year term in prison. These monitory placards, signed by one of Olney's assistant attorneys general, alarmed nobody; Debs had already instructed A.R.U. members to move the mails, but only the mails; and so the federal government was left with nothing to do. Before long, to the consternation of the men who traveled about the country in their private railroad cars, Hill capitulated, the strike was over, and the A.R.U. had amazingly won a pay raise amounting to one hundred and forty-six thousand dollars a month.

The union, grown the biggest in the country, was jubilant. Debs spoke exultantly of one union for all workingmen, so strong that no trust would dare rob them of their rights. While the A.R.U. was still suffused with this happy glow of triumph, the union was approached by a delegation of workers from the Pullman Palace Car Company, who begged for help.

The Pullman Company was a peculiar phenomenon: it manufactured railway equipment, and it monopolized the operation of sleeping cars, which it leased to every railroad company in the nation. Manufactory and monopoly were alike exceedingly profitable: from 1872 onwards the company had paid regular annual dividends ranging from eight to twelve per cent of a steadily expanding capitalization and had also managed to put away a reserve fund amounting in 1893 to twenty-five million dollars. George Pullman nevertheless seized upon the Panic of 1893 to exploit his workers even more than he had in the past. He had built a "model" company town outside Chicago and modestly christened it Pullman; here the men who built his railway cars lived in ugly little cottages, crowded close together, for which the rent, the gas rate, and the water rate were as much as twenty-five per cent higher than in the neighboring suburbs. In August, 1893, Pullman laid off most of his factory workers and then began slowly to rehire them at wages cut by twenty-five per cent; but their rents and rates

109

remained the same. When the workers elected a committee to discuss the matter with Pullman, he fired three of the committee. "We have nothing to arbitrate," Pullman said, and later he said: "The workers have nothing to do with the amount of wages they shall receive; that is solely the business of the company." This was the picture:

|  | Dividends | Wages |
| --- | --- | --- |
| For the year ending July 31, 1893 | $2,520,000 | $7,223,719.51 |
| For the year ending July 31, 1894 | $2,880,000 | $4,471,701.39 |

The workers in Pullman earned, in 1893, on the average, $613.86. Their biweekly checks early in 1894 amounted (after deductions for rent, gas, and water) sometimes to four cents, sometimes to as much as one dollar. On May 11, in despair, they struck. In June they appealed to Eugene Debs and the A.R.U. for help, and on June 26 they got it. The members of the A.R.U. on that day refused to handle the cars of the Pullman Company.

In those days Chicago was the junction for two dozen railroads, and their operators, united in a General Managers Association, announced that they would respect their contracts with the Pullman Company. The officers of the brotherhoods refused to support the strikers. Strikebreakers were hired. Newspapers, especially in Chicago, set up a shrill chorus of protest against the strike and especially against Debs. Nevertheless, one hundred and twenty-five thousand A.R.U. members stood solid, the railroads were tied up, and by July 1 Debs was confident of victory. "Their properties were paralyzed," he said later, of the General Managers Association, "and they were unable to operate their trains." He insisted that "no sign of violence or disorder" had appeared.

But in Washington Richard Olney, the Attorney General of the United States, had also been at work. Olney appointed as his special federal attorney in Chicago one Edwin Walker, who was also an attorney for the Chicago, Milwaukee & St. Paul Railroad; he sent Walker a message: "I feel that the true way of dealing with the matter is by a force which is overwhelming and prevents any attempt at resistance." An injunction against any support of the Pullman strike was issued by two federal judges. Finally, President Cleveland ordered federal troops to Chicago. When Governor Altgeld of Illinois and Mayor Hopkins of Chicago at once protested that they had sought no federal intervention and needed none, Cleveland had a splendid demagogic retort ready: "If it takes the entire army and navy of the United States to deliver a postal card in Chicago, that card will be delivered." With the troops came violence, rioting, death for twelve men, and wholesale arrests of union leaders. By July 19 the strike was broken, Debs was in jail, and the biggest union in the country had been smashed. Cleveland declared he had acted under the authority of the Interstate Commerce Act. This was too much for even the editor of The Bankers' Magazine, who observed that the President had "perverted" the Act "to protect those whom the government notoriously has never compelled to obey it, nor punished for breaking it."

No matter: it had been demonstrated once again that the men who controlled the railroads were the masters of the republic, arrogant and shameless as they had been for fifty years.

# 7

---

*More consolidation. The six great railroad systems. Edward H. Harriman in control of the Union Pacific and the Southern Pacific. Harriman and the Standard Oil vs. Hill and Morgan: the Panic of 1901. The Northern Securities Company dissolved. Harriman triumphant.*

---

CONSOLIDATION, COMBINATION, COMMUNITY OF INTEREST—in these lay the triumph of the private interest over the public interest. As the century turned, the two forces still tugged and hauled back and forth, but Pierpont Morgan, having finally got his cohorts to pull in unison, found himself in command. He had bent the law to his bidding, whatever opposition was afforded by labor had been destroyed, competition was at a minimum, the rate was everywhere high and moving higher. The government, a cat's-paw of the private interest, would do no more than describe the defeat of the public interest in official reports. Thus, early in 1902, there appeared the Final Report of the Industrial Commission, in which it was stated that most of the profitable railroad mileage was controlled by six groups, to wit:

1. The Vanderbilt group: 19,517 miles.

Here were included the New York Central system, the Boston & Albany, held after 1900 under a ninety-nine year lease, the Delaware, Lackawanna & Western, and the Chicago & North Western.

2. The Morgan group: 19,073 miles.

Here were included the Southern, the Central of Georgia, the Atlantic Coast Line, the Reading, the Lehigh Valley, the Erie, the Central of New Jersey, and a few smaller southern roads.

3. The Harriman group: 20,245 miles.

Here were included the Illinois Central, the Union Pacific, the Oregon Railroad & Navigation Company, the Oregon Short Line, the Chicago & Alton, the Southern Pacific, and a couple of smaller roads.

4. The Pennsylvania group: 18,220 miles.

Here were included the Pennsylvania system, the Chesapeake & Ohio, the Baltimore & Ohio, the Norfolk & Western, the Long Island, and a couple of smaller but strategic roads.

5. The Gould group: 16,074 miles.

Here were included the Wabash, the Missouri Pacific, the Texas & Pacific, the Denver & Rio Grande, the Rio Grande Western, the Missouri, Kansas & Texas (better known as the Katy), and two other long, sprawling, southwestern roads.

6. The Hill group: 10,373 miles.

Here were included only the Great Northern and the Northern Pacific.

The report of the Industrial Commission also referred to a Belmont group, based on the Louisville & Nashville (4,430 miles) and to a list of ten so-called "independent" roads that ranged in size from the Chicago & Great Western (1,023 miles) to the Santa Fe (7,808 miles) and the Burlington (8,070 miles).

Unhappily, this table in the report to the Congress was in part misleading, in part mistaken, and in part obsolete. It failed to reflect the pace and the extent of the process of consolidation; it revealed the government's ignorance of how successful was Pierpont Morgan's overruling strategy; it reads

113

as if it had been compiled by someone listening to the ill-informed gossip in a Wall Street barbershop.

Among the eastern roads, the situation was far more complex than indicated by the report, and competition of much less consequence.* The Gould group, despite its impressive ramifications, was a poor thing, already condemned to impotence; contrariwise, the Harriman group already bestraddled the wide continent like a colossus. The most egregious blunder in the report, however, had to do with the Hill group, which in 1901 had bought control of the Burlington and had thereby nearly doubled its mileage and its net profit. Since this acquisition and its repercussions directly affected railroad strategy all over the country in the next decade and eventually led to the collapse of the community-of-interest scheme, it deserves more than passing attention.

The purchase had been consummated by the Great Northern and the Northern Pacific primarily to give the two roads access to the great railroad junction at Chicago, but Hill had perceived other advantages. The Burlington reached down the Mississippi to St. Louis, giving him access to the westbound cotton trade; it reached across the plains to Denver, giving him a market for his eastbound lumber; moreover, the Burlington might well be extended to the Pacific and thus, by outflanking Harriman's Union Pacific, enable him to monopolize the flow of transcontinental freight. Hill's partner and banker, Pierpont Morgan, after this strategy had been explained to him, was delighted, for he envisioned a triumph over the rival whom he was used contemptuously to dismiss as "that little fellow Harriman."

*The Chesapeake & Ohio was jointly controlled by the Pennsylvania and the New York Central; the same two roads, through subsidiaries, shared control of the Reading, which in turn controlled the Central of New Jersey; blocks of stock of the Lehigh Valley were held by the Erie, the Lackawanna, the Central of New Jersey, and a New York Central subsidiary; control of the Hocking Valley had similarly been distributed. This intricate web had been most deliberately spun by Pierpont Morgan so that no ambitious tycoon might be tempted to start another rate war.

In fact, the whole heavily industrialized area north of the Ohio River and west of the Mississippi was dominated by the alliance of the Pennsylvania and the New York Central.

114

To be sure, Edward H. Harriman was a little fellow—physically short and slight, nervous and laconic, even mousy behind his gold-rimmed spectacles and his drooping, stringy mustache, a man of nowhere near the commanding presence of a Pierpont Morgan—but he was incontestably the most brilliant railroad executive in American history, shrewder than Gould or Sage, better informed about railroad operation than Huntington or Hill, more imaginative by far than Morgan or any of the Vanderbilts. He was also ruthless in competition and utterly without conscience as to the general welfare.

Harriman had learned the railroad business as a young and ambitious director of the Illinois Central, at a time when that road was largely owned by such old New York families as the Astors, the Cuttings, the Fishes, and the Goelets, all, in the elegant phrase of a later generation, good contacts. He formed other important connections: with old August Belmont, with young George Gould, with the Vanderbilts. Twice, in minor railroad squabbles, he crossed swords with Morgan himself; each time he scored his point. He was, however, still unknown outside Wall Street when in 1895 he boldly undertook to reorganize the Union Pacific.*

In this venture, Harriman was allied with two formidable financiers: Jacob Schiff, the senior partner of Kuhn, Loeb & Company, and James Stillman, the president of the National City Bank, which was already winning a reputation as the bank of the Standard Oil Company. Backed by these nearly inexhaustible resources, Harriman, in less than four years, encompassed miracles.

He spent millions of dollars to shorten, straighten, double-track, and reduce the grades of the Union Pacific, a virtuous

*On January 1, 1898, a new Union Pacific Railroad Company was formed and its officers agreed to pay $74,591,046 to the United States (the full principal and interest to October 1, 1897, on the old government bonds), but only after many maladroit efforts to squirm out from under the obligation. The money was raised by peddling bonds worth eighty-five million dollars and by assessing the stockholders fifteen dollars a share. Before very long Harriman was the railroad's chief executive officer.

115

task for which he was providentially rewarded when the semi-arid western states, as yet unirrigated, were favored with an unusually abundant rainfall and a sudden prosperity. The Union Pacific's gross earnings soared. By another stroke of luck the Spanish-American War and the consequent annexation of the Philippines gave the road another great rush of business. With operating expenses down and revenues up, Harriman was able to declare dividends.

When he issued stock of the Union Pacific worth thirty-two million dollars, he at once found buyers. This new money went to purchase the Oregon Short Line and the Oregon Railroad & Navigation Company, roads that extended his system into the Pacific northwest and gave him muscle in the struggle for commerce with the Orient.

Together with Schiff, Stillman, and his friend George Gould, Harriman next formed a dog-in-the-manger syndicate to buy the prosperous Chicago & Alton and proceeded, with all the familiar techniques of fraud and financial unscrupulosity, to loot its treasury.*

Now more amply armed than ever with cash, credit, and the confidence of his associates, in the spring of 1900 Harriman directed his covetous gaze on the Burlington, just as, some months later, would Hill. When the directors of the Burlington rebuffed Harriman's offer for the road, he turned again to Schiff, Stillman, and Gould; the syndicate began secretly to buy shares in the open market. It was slow going, for the stock was closely held. By the end of July the four men had paid out ten million dollars but owned less than eight per cent of the outstanding shares. Suddenly Harriman's attention was distracted from the Burlington by a vision of empire: Collis P. Huntington had died and control of the Southern Pacific lay

*The Alton, a road that ran from Chicago to St. Louis and then west to Kansas City, had for many years paid an average annual dividend of eight per cent. The curious can find the morbid details of its rape in two government reports: 12 I.C.C. 277 and 12 I.C.C. 340. A defense of Harriman's financiering can be found at pp. 228–310 of vol. II of George Kennan's biography of Harriman.

ready to the grasp of whoever might seize it.

Hastily the directors of the Union Pacific were convened to authorize an issue of bonds worth one hundred million dollars, while as hastily the directors of the Oregon Short Line voted an issue worth forty-five million. Since the bonds were convertible, both issues were quickly subscribed and the cash put at Harriman's disposal. He needed less than fifty million to tuck the Southern Pacific under his arm. As none knew better than he, at one stroke he had cataclysmically transformed the flow of transcontinental traffic.

Over the years the flow of that traffic to California had gradually carved out four channels that marked the way of four distinct, fiercely competitive, transcontinental railway systems. These were: first, the Sunset Route of the Southern Pacific, comprising a railroad from Portland and San Francisco to New Orleans, in conjunction with the system's steamship lines from New Orleans to the Atlantic seaports; second, the Union Pacific from Omaha to Ogden, Utah, in conjunction with the Central Pacific to San Francisco; third, the Gould system, a continuous line from Toledo to Ogden, likewise in conjunction with the Central Pacific to San Francisco; and, fourth, the Santa Fe, which owned its own road from Chicago to Los Angeles and San Francisco.*

But when Harriman took control of the Southern Pacific, he took control as well of its subsidiary, the Central Pacific, the link between Odgen, Utah, and San Francisco. He not only collared the profitable Sunset Route, he also canceled all traffic agreements made by the Central Pacific with his old friend George Gould. Alas, poor Gould! Harriman had known him well, and used him, too, as expediency had suggested. It was a pity. Thanks to his traffic agreements, Gould had formerly

---

*A fifth route was provided by a steamship line from San Francisco to Panama, a railroad across the Isthmus, and another steamship line from Colon to New York; but the way was slow and infrequently used. Early in 1901 a new railroad, the San Pedro, Los Angeles & Salt Lake City promised (or threatened) to provide still a sixth route. But in January, 1901, nearly all transcontinental traffic to and from California moved over the four routes just described.

been able to haul westbound freight to the Pacific slope, but all at once he found that his rails ended abruptly at Ogden. The eastbound traffic that the Southern Pacific had formerly divided between the Union Pacific and the Gould system was now entirely consigned to the Union Pacific.*

Now Harriman, who had faced three contentious rivals, had to cope with only one, the Santa Fe. By rights he should have rejoiced, and he would have, too, save only that he was prey to some sinister suspicions.

For one, there was this new railroad, the San Pedro, Los Angeles & Salt Lake City. Ostensibly it was financed by William A. Clark, the copper tycoon of Butte, Montana, who had recently bought a seat in the United States Senate by bribing thirty-five members of the Montana legislature with $431,000. But Harriman wondered. Was Clark mixed up somehow with Hill? Might the San Pedro be Hill's cunning scheme to snatch the traffic of southern California? In any event, Harriman had to block the San Pedro. Its engineers planned to lay tracks through a long narrow canyon in the southern tip of Nevada; here Harriman dispatched his well-armed construction gangs; here, on the banks of a stream called the Meadow Valley Wash, the opposing gangs fought in pitched battle until their commanders were haled into court and a truce formulated by the terms of which Harriman took fifty per cent of the San Pedro for the Union Pacific. Might was once again proved to be right. Another potential competitor had been flummoxed.

But still Harriman suspected Hill was up to some mischief. He made inquiries and, sure enough, he found that Hill and Morgan had secretly been buying the stock of the Burlington. No need to draw Harriman a diagram: he saw instantly how Hill could usurp the markets of Southern Pacific (cotton) and

*Gould's only recourse was to build his own railroad—the Western Pacific—from Salt Lake City to San Francisco. It was not opened to traffic until 1909. The loss of a share in the enormously expanding business from the Pacific coast during this decade, coupled with the costly construction of the new road, led to the collapse of the Gould system in 1911.

Union Pacific (agricultural produce), how Hill could dictate the rate and so monopolize the traffic. In a cold fury Harriman confronted Hill in New York, at the house of George F. Baker, the president of the First National Bank.

These two men, each at the head of a mighty railroad empire, each representative of an awesome agglomeration of capital—Harriman allied with Schiff of Kuhn, Loeb & Company and Stillman of the National City Bank, with William Rockefeller and H. H. Rogers of the Standard Oil Company looming in the background; Hill allied with Pierpont Morgan and George F. Baker, with the powerful resources of the Vanderbilts and the new United States Steel Corporation looming in the background—these two men were headed at full speed on a collision course. It was the inevitable clash of capitalist forces instinctively seeking monopoly, the climactic moment in an epoch of greed.

Harriman's position was the weaker; he sought to bargain; he asked for a one-third interest in the Burlington, offering to pay one third of the purchase price and so establish a joint, comprehensive monopoly of all the western railroad systems. Hill believed his position impregnable. He refused even to bargain.

Harriman's retort was magnificent; it prefigured the high camp of cinema melodrama. "Very well," he said; "it is a hostile act and you must take the consequences."

So was precipitated the last of the splendid, lawless brawls of the railroad kings. It was tainted neither by the naked corruptions of the Erie War nor by the subcutaneous pus of the Crédit Mobilier affair; by 1901 such delinquencies were regarded as vulgar and superfluous; the opposing parties were both so far removed from considerations of legality as to suppose them irrelevant. The law? It was written to punish footpads, cutthroats, union leaders, and other enemies of private property. The bankers and the railroad magnates would do what they had to do and later, at their leisure, they would indicate to the Congress what laws should be passed to legit-

119

imize what they had done. Public policy? It was archaic; let it scramble to catch up with the necessities of industrial commerce.

Hill, after imperturbably acknowledging Harriman's ultimatum, climbed into his private car and was carried west to Seattle, where he began to count the many unhatched eggs of his trade with the Orient. He was sublimely confident, and why not? With Morgan's help he had acquired 96.79 per cent of the stock of the Burlington in exchange for four-per-cent bonds worth $215,154,000; it was held, half by the Great Northern, half by the Northern Pacific, safe from any raid by Harriman. Or so Hill thought.

The purchase of the Burlington was announced on April 20, 1901. On that day Harriman, who dearly loved a fight, was swiftly and silently at work as he had been ever since Hill refused him one third of the Burlington. His stratagem was simple, it was audacious, it was unprecedented, and it was working like a charm. He was buying the Northern Pacific (and with it one half of the Burlington) right in the open market, right from under the noses of James J. Hill and J. P. Morgan & Company. The most delectable aspect of the affair was that he was buying much of the stock from the Hill-Morgan interests themselves, and they none the wiser.

Harriman was prepared to spend eighty million dollars, enough to secure an absolute majority of the capital stock of the Northern Pacific. If he succeeded, he would be master of every railroad to the Pacific coast. (Hill later admitted, "We would not have held the Great Northern a day longer than we could have sold it.")

By the end of April, Harriman's scheme was proceeding admirably. Meanwhile Pierpont Morgan was taking his ease in Aix-les-Bains; carefree; relaxing, so it was rumored, with a lady of the French aristocracy but of no particular discretion. Out in Seattle, Hill took belated notice of the active market in Northern Pacific: Why was its stock so steadily rising? Who was buying, at these high prices? In sudden alarm he ordered a special to speed him east over cleared tracks; even as his

120

private car was being switched about at St. Paul, the Northern Pacific was itself selling Harriman thirteen thousand of its own shares and J. P. Morgan & Company was selling him another ten thousand.

In the afternoon of Friday, May 3, Hill reached New York and went straight to Jacob Schiff at the offices of Kuhn, Loeb & Company. Yes, Schiff told him; he was buying Northern Pacific for Harriman's account.

"But you can't get control. The Great Northern, Morgan, and my friends were recently holding thirty-five to forty million dollars of Northern Pacific stock, and so far as I know none of it has been sold."

"That may be, but we've got a lot of it. . . ."

"It can't be done."

On investigation Hill learned, however, that his friends and Morgan's owned only some 260,000 of the 800,000 shares of common stock outstanding and even less of the 750,000 shares of preferred (which then had voting rights). As may be imagined, Hill was furious. His empire was slipping through his fingers, and where was Morgan? Cuddled and cosseted in Aix-les-Bains! An urgent cable was at once dispatched.

So far, in this struggle of financial and industrial giants, only Hill, Morgan, and their associates had displayed their acumen. Now, with victory in their grasp, it was time for Schiff, Harriman, and *their* able executive assistants to array themselves in dunce caps and motley.

At the close of business on Friday, May 3, Harriman had bought 370,000 shares of Northern Pacific common and 410,000 shares of the preferred. While this holding was an absolute majority of the total voting stock, nonetheless Harriman had the fidgets, for to obtain a majority of the common he still needed at least 30,000 shares.* He never got them. He

*The common was more important, for the preferred could be retired by the directors on January 1, 1902. But the by-laws of the Northern Pacific Company provided that directors were to be elected in October. If this meeting were held, Harriman would be in control. If it were postponed until after January 1, he would need those 30,000 shares of common to exercise control.

waited till Saturday to phone his order to buy the crucial last few thousand shares (in those days the stock exchange was open on Saturday morning) but his order required the approval of Schiff, who was worshiping at his synagogue. After prayer and meditation, Schiff advised against any further purchases.

This timid counsel gave Morgan the chance to redeem his folly. On Monday and Tuesday his traders thronged the floor of the exchange, buying every share of Northern Pacific that was offered, bidding it up from 110 to nearly 150, capturing 150,000 shares, saving control of the company for Morgan, and triggering the most unexpected and one of the severest financial panics the country had ever experienced.

Infected with the virus of greed by the insatiable demands of Morgan's brokers, scores of speculators had contracted to deliver tens of thousands of shares of Northern Pacific; but they had sold what they did not own, they had sold nearly 80,000 shares that did not even exist. Ravenous to cover their contracts, they bid Northern Pacific up to 300, up to 500, and finally, in a last paroxysm of despair, up to 1,000 a share, while every other security on the exchange shuddered and tumbled— U. S. Steel off 22, Chicago, Milwaukee & St. Paul off 31, Santa Fe off 35, Union Pacific off 37—and money vanished along with credit, and the bankers crept in to loan cash at forty to sixty per cent, and humble investors in their uncounted thousands were wiped out.

Too bad. Morgan, confronted by a reporter in Paris, said only, "I owe the public nothing."

But the violent revulsion of public feeling after the wanton panic made it clear even to Morgan that his friends and his enemies must mend their quarrels. (Besides, the country was prosperous; railroad traffic was profitable; why rock even the shabbiest caboose?) He took ship back to New York to preside over a mighty *entente* that was, however, not conspicuously *cordiale;* to form a Northern Securities Company that would hold the stock of the Great Northern and the Northern Pacific, a four-hundred-million dollar monster so big that nobody could buy it; to seat all the contentious factions on its board of directors; to declare, on behalf of the community of interest, that "an understanding has been reached."

Was the understanding legal? Especially to businessmen in Minnesota it seemed a most blatant substitution of monopoly for competition, and they howled.* Before very long, President Theodore Roosevelt, ever responsive to public clamor, instructed his Attorney General, Philander Knox, to proceed against the Northern Securities Company. When Morgan heard of it, he was vexed. He thought it *wrong* for a President to do such a thing; it unsettled the market and upset the financial community; he went straight to Washington, in person, to scold Roosevelt.

"Why," Morgan demanded petulantly, "didn't you let me know of the suit?"

"That is just what we did not want to do."

"If we have done anything wrong, send your man to see my man, and they can fix it up." By this curious command, Morgan meant that President Roosevelt should send Knox to bargain and make a deal with Francis Lynde Stetson, who was Morgan's attorney general.

Roosevelt said: "That can't be done."

Knox told Morgan: "We don't want to fix it up, we want to stop it."

*The Sherman Antitrust Act of 1890 expressly outlawed "every contract, combination . . . or conspiracy in restraint of trade or commerce among the several states" and declared that "every person who shall monopolize, or attempt to monopolize, or combine or conspire with any other person or persons to monopolize any part of the trade or commerce among the several states" was guilty of a misdemeanor and liable to fine and imprisonment. The argument that the Antitrust Act did not apply to railroads was struck down by the Supreme Court in March, 1897 (United States *v.* Trans-Missouri Freight Association, 166 U.S. 290), and again in October, 1898 (United States *v.* Joint Traffic Association, 171 U.S. 505). These decisions prohibited mergers of competing railroads and treaties between them to fix rates.

Morgan, Harriman, Hill, and their associates would seem to have been nerved to defy these explicit interdictions by the remarkable reluctance of three Presidents—Harrison, Cleveland, and McKinley—to direct their Attorneys General to enforce the law.

For Morgan, a great bore. All that costly litigation! The waste of so much time! But meanwhile he could sew a few patches on his fabric of consolidation. Here was the Louisville & Nashville, suddenly in the hands of John W. ("Betcha-a-million") Gates, an impossible person—"a dangerous element," said Morgan, "not a proper man to be in control of that railroad." The road had cost Gates about thirty-seven million dollars in the stock market; he demanded of Morgan at least a seven-million-dollar profit. Morgan acquiesced and in turn sold the road to a trustworthy friend who owned the Atlantic Coast Line. An A.C.L. officer testified later: "We bought the Louisville & Nashville just as you would buy a box of candy. It was wrapped up and delivered to us, and we paid fifty million dollars for it. That was all there was to it." A profit to Morgan of another five or six million dollars. What mattered a few odd pennies? The public would pay, in the end.

During this time of judicial, if not legal, uncertainty, Harriman was also attending duly to the problems of consolidation. He had to face the problem of his one remaining competitor, the Santa Fe, which, under aggressive leadership, was threatening expansion in Arizona and even in the very heart of his empire, at San Francisco. Intolerable! When Santa Fe workmen began building through a canyon into southern Arizona, lo! there on the side of the mountain above them appeared the Arizona Eastern Railroad Company, alias E. H. Harriman, to drill and blast and send tons of rock down upon the carefully graded roadbed of the Santa Fe. When other Santa Fe workmen began to build south from Eureka toward San Francisco (heedlessly slashing through an invaluable stand of redwoods), Harriman at once laid tracks north to block them. These rough-and-tumbles had each reached an interesting pitch of intensity when the Supreme Court quite unintentionally provided Harriman with the means to control the Santa Fe in more peaceful fashion.

In March, 1904, five of the nine justices declared the Northern Securities Company illegal and required its dissolution. This meant that the stock of the Great Northern and the

124

Northern Pacific had to be returned to its owners. Thus Harriman unexpectedly got back securities for which he had paid eighty million dollars but which, in a booming market, he was ultimately able to sell for almost one hundred and sixty million; a nice turn. By September he and a few of his friends—among them the Messrs. Schiff, Stillman, William Rockefeller, H. H. Rogers, and Henry C. Frick—owned enough Santa Fe stock to nominate and elect two directors to the Santa Fe's board. Rates for westbound freight were at once raised. The shippers naturally passed the higher charges on to the consumer; and so every citizen on the Pacific slope paid his tribute to Harriman, a penny, a nickel, a dime, a dollar; and so Harriman's hand stole into every citizen's purse, and so once again were demonstrated the undeniable, if limited, benefits of monopoly.

*Angry public reaction. Deaths on the railroads. Corruption
by the railroads. The evil of the rebate. La Follette of Wisconsin
investigates. The Congress driven to act. The Interstate Commerce Commission suddenly grown more powerful. The Hepburn Act of 1906. Harriman investigated. Morgan under attack.
An era draws to a close.*

IN OPPOSITION to the imperial designs of such as Harriman and
Morgan there was the public and, very gradually heedful of the
public power, there was the government.

The public, confused, demoralized, and disorganized for
more than a generation, had been steadily storing up its wrath,
and by 1905 its mood was one of bitter, explosive resentment.
Whenever the public thought of railroads, its fingers twitched.

In the first place, the railroads were mortally dangerous.
Ten thousand Americans were killed in railroad accidents every
year, and another eighty thousand were seriously injured; yet
very little had been done to impose standards of safety.

In the second place, the railroad companies were more cor-
ruptive than ever. The evil of the free pass had grown monstrous. On the floor of every legislature the railroad lobbyist
was an exceedingly popular and powerful individual, often
sitting at a desk in the front row, always glad to issue a legis-
lator trip passes for his constituents; annual passes were reserved for all persons able to affect legislation, judicial decisions, executive appointments, or public opinion. The traffic
was enormous: free passes handed out by the Pennsylvania, for

example, reduced that road's gross earnings by one million dollars a year. This generosity was repaid with all kinds of amiable laws: laws that either protected the railroads from having to pay any state or local taxes whatsoever or provided that the assessors would be conveniently blind to the value of railroad property; laws permitting the railroads to work their trainmen more than twelve hours a day on passenger trains and more than sixteen hours a day on freight trains; laws that winked at black lists; laws that made a joke of compensation for injuries; laws that outraged public policy and impoverished the public purse. "No single influence," observed the editor of The Philadelphia North American in 1905, "has done so much to poison the very fountains of political life as the railroad free pass."

In the third place, the railroads persisted in paying rebates to their favored shippers, who were invariably their biggest shippers—the Rockefellers (oil), Carnegies (steel), Morgans (coal), Armours (beef), Havemeyers (sugar), and so on. But, as the public had come to realize, when the rate to the big shipper was rebated, the small shipper had to pay the difference so that the railroad might earn its fat profit. In consequence, everyone who bought food, clothes, or shelter—and the price tag on every item included a charge for freight—was being taxed to compensate for that rebate and was thereby inevitably enriching the Rockefellers, Carnegies, Morgans, Armours, Havemeyers, and so on.

Could the Interstate Commerce Commission do nothing? Commissioner Charles A. Prouty, a Yankee Republican from Vermont, thought not. "The railroads own many of our courts and other public bodies," Prouty told a Chicago newspaperman, late in 1904. "Not because they have of necessity bought them by the expenditure of money; they have a different way of doing things. They see to it that the right men, the men of friendly inclinations, are elected. If the Interstate Commerce Commission were worth buying, the railroads would try to buy it," the commissioner added sardonically. "The only reason they have not tried to purchase the Commission is that this body

127

is valueless in its ability to correct railroad abuses."

The public grew angrier; it clenched its fists.

For their part, the railroad magnates denied everything; in particular they denied that they paid a rebate to any shipper, large or small. Great heavens! wasn't there a federal statute on the books that specifically outlawed the rebate? (In fact there was: it had been drafted in the office of A. J. Cassatt, the president of the Pennsylvania, and it bore the name of Stephen B. Elkins, the United States senator from West Virginia, who was also, by a happy chance, a heavy investor in several railroads that served the coal fields south of Pittsburgh.) Early in 1905 a long line of railroad presidents formed before the Senate Committee on Interstate Commerce, of which the chairman was the aforesaid Elkins. His questions and their answers slid into a smooth groove:

> *Q:* Does your company pay rebates?
> *A:* No, sir; rebates have disappeared.
> *Q:* How about discriminations?
> *A:* Discriminations are unknown, sir.

Just so; and Senator Elkins was of course too polite to suggest that he have a look at their books, in order that he might satisfy himself that they spoke sooth. Who was he, a mere owner of railroads, to challenge the sworn word of a railroad president?

But in Wisconsin Governor Robert La Follette was suspicious of any statement made by any railroad official, sworn or not; he set a pack of sharp-eyed accountants to the pursuit of truth across the books of a half-dozen railroads that shared the commerce of his state, after which it was duck soup for him to prove that the officials of all of them were habitual liars. Indeed, some of those officials even signed stipulations admitting that they (a) had secretly and illegally paid rebates totaling more than ten million dollars, (b) had thereby defrauded the state of taxes amounting to more than four hundred thousand dollars, and (c) had lied about the whole thing.

To say that the La Follette investigation provoked the liveliest interest throughout the midwest is nothing. Thereabouts the citizens, if they were not Grangers themselves, were the children of Grangers, and what they had learned about the railroads whilst perched on daddy's knee could not be mentioned in polite company. A low, menacing rumble began to proceed toward Washington from these midwestern states, all traditionally Republican, and under the dome of the Capitol every prudent Republican politician gave ear, attentively and apprehensively.

There followed a series of sharp seismic shocks.

In August, 1905, the Interstate Commerce Commission launched an inquiry into the combination of railroads and private-car companies.*

In December, Roosevelt asked the Congress to legislate "some scheme to secure to . . . the government supervision and regulation of the rates charged by the railroads."

A week later, the Attorney General, in a marked manner, instructed all United States attorneys to prosecute with vigor any and all railroad companies found to be paying rebates.

In January, 1906, Representative William P. Hepburn of Iowa introduced the railroad-rate bill that Roosevelt had asked for. This bill would seem to have been drafted by the Avenging Angel. It outlawed the free pass; it empowered the Interstate Commerce Commission to prescribe and enforce uniform systems of accounts; it gave the Commission jurisdiction over the private-car companies, sleeping-car companies, express companies, terminal railroads, and pipeline companies; it declared the rebate to be a crime punishable by imprisonment; and, most important, it authorized the Commission to fix a maximum reasonable rate.

In February the House of Representatives, after strengthen-

*These companies (there were more than three hundred of them, of which Armour & Company, the big Chicago butcher, controlled more than a dozen) could offer the railroads enough traffic to impose their own rules. They could dictate rates and even require the illegal payment of illegal rebates by illegal contract. All this, in juicy testimony, the Commission spread on the record. (Strictly defined, the private car is one operated by, but not owned by, a railroad.)

129

ing the bill by giving the Commission the absolute right to fix a definite rate, passed it by a vote of 346 to 7 and sent it on to the Senate.

In March, the Congress instructed the Commission "to make an examination . . . of railroad discriminations and monopolies in coal and oil." This was aimed straight at the compact monoply, constructed by Pierpont Morgan, which had enslaved the independent coal operators to a dozen or more railroad companies and in turn fettered those railroad companies to the Pennsylvania and the New York Central. The scandalous graft that had enriched especially some officials of the Pennsylvania, at the expense of the public, spread its stench across the front pages of newspapers throughout April and May.*

In May, the Senate passed the railroad-rate bill, by a vote of 71 to 3, with all the delight of a small boy taking a stiff dose of castor oil.

In June, the differences between the House and Senate versions having been adjusted in committee, the Hepburn bill was signed by Theodore Roosevelt and became law.†

Had an era drawn to a close?

Certainly the enactment of the Hepburn bill transformed the continuing tug of war between private profit and public interest. The shift of strength was at once evident. Especially in the east, the fabric woven by the community of interest began to unravel. The proud Pennsylvania, suddenly grown

---

*One Pennsylvania executive had augmented his salary of $225 a month by grafting $50,000 in cash and $11,000 in securities from various coal companies; another man, a chief clerk for a division of the Pennsylvania, contrived, on a salary that ranged from $30 to $136 a month, to amass more than $75,000 in securities of coal companies. On the Pennsylvania, clearly, the memory of men like Tom Scott remained ever green.

†The House agreed that the Commission should have the right to fix only a maximum rate, not a definite rate; in return the Senate agreed to include a "commodities clause," designed to combat the railroad monopoly of the coal mines, which barred the railroads from carrying any commodity, other than timber or its products, in which they were financially interested. (The railroads got round this clause by forming separate companies, the stock of which was distributed amongst their own stockholders.)

130

timid, took steps to divest itself first of its stock in the Chesapeake & Ohio and next of half its holdings in the Baltimore & Ohio; as a direct consequence, lesser roads all over the region regained a measure of independence. Just as suddenly the Interstate Commerce Commission waxed more powerful and, after years of impotence, showed itself cheerfully disposed to exert its new muscle. There were rumors of a sweeping investigation into the practices of all railroads and, as well, into the secret financial ramifications by which they were reputedly linked together in a half-dozen supersystems. It was as though the cops had at last caught up with the robbers and would now at least be able to keep them under sharp surveillance.

But had an era drawn to a close?

Eras emerge and disappear only in the tidy comprehension of subsequent historians. At the time, in the summer of 1906, at least two men—E. H. Harriman and J. Pierpont Morgan—saw nothing definitive or even very ominous in the turn of events. They had been temporarily thwarted: they would now proceed toward their same monopolistic goals along other paths.

Harriman's course was the more spectacular. His western railroads had, under his hand, become a bank whose coffers were bursting with cash: the one hundred and sixty million dollars he had realized from the sale of his shares in the Northern Securities Company, the enormous revenues from his operation of Southern Pacific and Union Pacific, what was he to do with it all? He could choose from among five advantageous alternatives.

He could extend his own system into undeveloped territory, double-track the main lines, build new terminals, improve his service to shipper and passenger alike.

He could buy his railroads' bonds (held chiefly by the public) and so reduce his corporate indebtedness.

He could lower his railroads' rates and so share with the public his remarkable prosperity.

He could raise his dividends.

He could invest in, and so extend his control over, other profitable railroads.

131

This is a multiple-choice question: which two of these five alternatives did Harriman select?

In August, the directors of the Southern Pacific met and declared a five-per-cent dividend. They then adjourned and reconvened as directors of the Union Pacific and raised *its* dividend from six to ten per cent. The news of this action was concealed from the public for nearly two days, while the directors of the Union Pacific did whatever seemed to them necessary in the circumstances. When news of the dividend was at length announced, the public loyally responded by booting the price of Union Pacific up forty dollars in two sessions of the market.

Meanwhile, and during the next several months, Harriman invested part of his huge surplus of cash as follows:

| | |
|---|---|
| Baltimore & Ohio | $45,466,960 |
| Chicago, Milwaukee & St. Paul | 5,997,750 |
| Chicago & North Western | 5,303,673 |
| Santa Fe | 10,395,000 |
| Illinois Central | 41,442,028 |
| New York Central | 19,634,324 |

With funds of the Illinois Central, Harriman proceeded to purchase the Central of Georgia, which gave him access to the southeast. Through the Union Pacific he and his friends controlled the B&O; they owned about sixteen per cent of the New York Central—more than the Vanderbilts, more than Morgan himself. Since Harriman had also wrested control of the Erie from Morgan, he could justly claim that three of the four eastern trunk lines were managed in sympathy with his wishes. He personally controlled and managed twenty-five thousand miles of railroad and thirty-five thousand miles of steamship lines; his was the decisive vote that controlled another fifty thousand miles of railroad. Never before or since has one man held so much power over the commerce of the nation.

In November, 1906, the Commission launched its promised investigation (In the Matter of Consolidations and Combinations of Carriers, Relations Between Such Carriers, and Community of Interests Therein, Their Rates, Facilities, and Practices, 12 I.C.C. 277) and, in the circumstances, it was scarcely astonishing that Harriman drew most of the commission's attention. He was asked about his future plans: did they include outright purchase of the Santa Fe?

A: If you will let us, I will go and take the Santa Fe tomorrow.
Q: Then it is only the restriction of the law that keeps you from taking it?
A: I would go on as long as I live.
Q: Then after you had gotten through with the Santa Fe and had taken it, you would also take the Northern Pacific and Great Northern, if you could get them?
A: If you would let me.
Q: And your power, which you have, would gradually increase as you took one road after another, so that you might spread not only over the Pacific coast, but spread out over the Atlantic coast?
A: Yes.

Such candor amounted to provocation. The government retorted by bringing suit to dispossess the Union Pacific of the Southern Pacific. President Roosevelt, once again attuned to the public dissatisfaction, clapperclawed Harriman as "an enemy of the republic" who was lost in "deep-seated corruption." Before long, public outrage against Harriman had forced another legal battle, this one to reclaim the immense timberlands in Oregon that had been handed over to the Southern Pacific.*

Whenever before he had been challenged to combat, Harriman had tucked up his sleeves and waded in, full of fire and confidence, but in 1909 he was tired and sick. Death spared

*In fact, the several million acres of virgin timber were given to the Oregon & California, a subsidiary of the Southern Pacific. By the terms of the grant, the lands were to be sold to settlers in 160-acre chunks, at no more than two dollars and fifty cents an acre. Executives of the Southern Pacific found these conditions unprofitable and obedience to them intolerable. They preferred to sell to land speculators and logging companies. State laws? Federal laws? Ridiculous.

133

him the bitterness of his inevitable defeat. In 1910 California elected a governor who had pledged "to drive the Southern Pacific out of the politics of this state." Although this would seem to have been as quixotic a venture as to drive the salt out of the Pacific Ocean, before long the company's influence in Sacramento had wonderfully dwindled, and counties and even towns were brashly levying taxes on the Octopus itself.* In December, 1912, after five years of argument, the Supreme Court ordered the dissolution of the Union Pacific's control of the Southern Pacific. In 1915 the suit over the Oregon timberlands was at last settled when the government reclaimed some three million acres of land, worth an estimated thirty million dollars; other tracts of land, under which lay rich oil deposits, were likewise expropriated. The emperor was dead; the empire crumbled.

Meanwhile Morgan, alone among the railroad masters of the east, had been pushing his monopolistic schemes more impudently and stubbornly than ever, as if unaware that the public temper was set against him. The bailiwick selected for his kindly ministrations was New England; his instrument was the New York, New Haven & Hartford Railroad; from the effects of his policies the road has never completely recovered.

Morgan, who had been elected to the board of the New Haven in 1892, made Charles S. Mellen its president in 1903 just as he had previously made Mellen the president of the Northern Pacific. Later, when the Commission was investigating the collapse of the New Haven, the chief counsel asked Mellen:

Q: Were you Mr. Morgan's man as president of the New Haven?

A: I have been called his office-boy. I was very proud of his confidence. I regard the statement that I was his man as a compliment.

The Morgan-Mellen regime lasted from 1903 to 1912 and was

*The Southern Pacific paid only a little more than four million dollars in local taxes in 1910; by 1926 this figure had quadrupled.

officially characterized as "one of the most glaring instances of maladministration in all the history of American railroading."*
Their aim was complete control of every type of public transportation in New England, or to it, or from it; and to encompass their aim the capitalization of the New Haven was increased from ninety-three million dollars in 1903 to four hundred and seventeen millions in 1912, mostly by issuing bonds, mostly to buy interurban trolley lines and steamship lines, mostly at grossly inflated prices, and always in the teeth of a blizzard of protests by businessmen, shippers, state legislators, investors, passengers, newspaper editors, and public-spirited citizens. One director made a profit of two million seven hundred thousand dollars simply for sequestering some shares of the Boston & Maine at a time when the purchase of that road by the New Haven was inconveniently illegal. Another road, the New York, Westchester & Boston, which was worth maybe twelve million dollars, was acquired by the New Haven for thirty-five million; the directors of the New Haven, who were given no idea of "what they were buying at such a big price," felt themselves obliged to inquire of President Mellen. Poor Mellen later testified as to what happened when he begged Morgan for some elucidation:

MELLEN: Can you give me a few moments?
MORGAN: Certainly.
MELLEN: This note [for the purchase of the small railroad] is not in the form it should be—there should be additional information given.
MORGAN: Did not Mr. [Francis Lynde] Stetson draw that note?
MELLEN: Yes, I suppose so.
MORGAN: Do you think you know more how it ought to be done than he does?

After which Morgan wrathfully took up his stick and his hat and left.

*There were several investigations of the Morgan stewardship of the New Haven; they are summarized in 27 I.C.C. 581 and 31 I.C.C. 15, 31, 41, 85, and 108 and in Senate Documents 543 and 544, 63rd Congress, 2nd session.

For nine wretched years the story of the New Haven was one of reckless disregard of the public and of its investors, one of wholesale bribery, of corporate accounts falsified and unearned dividends declared, of dreadful accidents and unconscionable interruptions of service, of looting and corruption and financial chicanery. Mellen was once indicted for manslaughter and once for criminal restraint of trade. J. P. Morgan & Company were charged with having pocketed "excessive profits" in raising money for the road and were finally forced to withdraw as fiscal agents and to remove their representatives from the board of directors.

In 1914, when he was enduring one of several investigations by the Commission, Mellen grew pensive. "I think the record of the New Haven's transactions," he remarked, "with the elimination of Mr. Morgan, would have been as tame and uneventful, as devoid of interest and incident, as would the record of a herd of cows deprived of the association of a bull." Thus graphically, if unintentionally, Mellen suggested what Morgan did to the New Haven.

By then Pierpont Morgan was dead and gone, and so was the monopoly he had briefly constructed in New England, and so were the supersystems. Each succeeding Congress had tightened the vise of federal regulation, the Commission had been given the power to make rates, and Commissioner Prouty had already announced an ominous new aspect of the public interest:

> The government cannot rightfully grant an increase of railroad rates [said Prouty] until it knows that the money so raised shall be properly expended. That will be when railroads cannot spend money except for railroad purposes, when they cannot buy the securities of other railroads, when they cannot issue securities of their own without the consent of the federal government, and when they cannot put the securities to any use except those specified.

There was now no doubt about it: an era had drawn to a close.

# 9

*The railroads unable to cope with the demands of the War of 1914–1918. The government takes over the railroads. Sabotage by the railroad executives. Should the railroads be nationalized? The railroad companies try to raid the United States treasury.*

THE OUTBREAK OF WAR in Europe found the masters of American railroads sullen and despondent. As always when one segment of humanity sets out to annihilate another segment, the cost of everything—labor, material, and money—was, like the prayers of the faithful, soaring rapidly toward the heavens above; yet the Interstate Commerce Commission, now firmly in the saddle, persisted in refusing requests for big boosts in the rates. The Commissioners argued that vast economies could still be effected in the operation of the railroads; the directors of the railroads countered by reducing the funds needed to maintain their roads and their equipment. Inevitably the nation's system of railroads began to go to pot.

The disruption of international commerce brought a slump in railroad traffic for a few months, but in 1915 and again in 1916 that traffic was enormously swollen when American industry was called on to supply goods to the British and the French. To handle the extraordinary rush of business, the railroads had fewer freight cars in 1916 than they had had in 1914. There had always been seasonal shortages of freight cars, but by 1916 the shortage was chronic and growing steadily worse. Inadequate terminal facilities at the ports along the Atlantic

137

seaboard aggravated the situation. Miles of loaded cars stood on sidings outside those ports; other loaded cars crowded the yards and the terminals. They stood for weeks, waiting to be unloaded. And when at length they were emptied, still they stood in the yards or on the sidings, for there is an unwritten law that no freight car shall be moved until sufficient freight has accumulated to fill it for its return trip.

By the end of February, 1917, one hundred and forty-five thousand empty cars cluttered the eastern terminals.

By the end of March, 1917, there was a shortage, across the nation, of one hundred and forty-five thousand cars.

An interesting coincidence; and because of it mills were shut down, perishable commodities were destroyed, prices went up, and the lack of fuel for public utilities threatened the supply of light, heat, and power. After investigation, the Commission blamed executives of the eastern railroads for the mess.

Meanwhile, the antediluvian policy of the railroad magnates toward their employees had forced the Congress to intervene, in August, 1916, by legislating an eight-hour day for the industry, with increased pay for overtime. The railroad operators refused to obey this law, of course; they challenged its constitutionality and fought it in the courts for months. In March, 1917, the Railroad Brotherhoods, thoroughly out of patience, served notice of a strike unless the law was at once obeyed. The operators sulkily yielded, and later the same day the Supreme Court upheld the law. Another three days, and Samuel Rea, the president of the Pennsylvania, was admitting, in testimony before the Commission, that "the condition of the railroads today presents a menace to the country."

Two weeks later the country was at war.

The principal railroad executives met in Washington on April 11. They were, they said, "stirred by a high sense of their opportunity to be of the greatest service to their country." They selected five of their number to constitute a Railroads' War Board and pledged themselves to "coordinate their operations in a continental railway system, merging . . . all their merely individual and competitive activities . . . to produce a maximum of transportation efficiency."

Brave words, but on balance the Railroads' War Board was a flop. To be sure, the Board somewhat eased the freight-car shortage, but only briefly and only at the expense of the weaker carriers. The powerful roads, giving full play to "their merely individual and competitive activities," grabbed all the traffic they could, even at the risk of ruinously clogging their tracks. The classic instance of such greed came at the aptly named Hog Island, in the Delaware River south of Philadelphia, where a shipyard was hastily flung together that soon became the site of the gamiest frauds of the war to end war. To Hog Island, from as far away as Oregon and Washington, came carloads of pilings, carloads of structural steel, carloads of all kinds of bulky matter, all of them sweetly profitable to the Pennsylvania Railroad and most of them delivered before any facilities had been built to unload them. The terminals in Philadelphia and the sidings for miles back into the countryside were hopelessly jammed. A wistful system of priorities bogged down almost at once, for every freight agent was given a bundle of "preference" tags and he used them as he had traditionally used his sly skill in granting rebates: every shipper got his tag, as a personal favor, and before long a spokesman for the Pennsylvania was obliged to announce that eighty-five per cent of the freight traffic east of Pittsburgh was moving on a top priority.

"The Railroads' War Board," said William G. McAdoo, who was as expert a witness as any man, "had no actual authority. It was merely an advisory body [depending] wholly on the good-will of its constituent members." Those constituent members were as fixed in their ways as so many automatons. As a matter of course the railroad operators fought for higher profits, and in the time they could spare from these efforts they fought to discourage the government from taking control of the railroads as, indeed, the governments of Great Britain, France, Germany, and Italy had already done. With such awful precedents staring them in the face, the operators of American railroads were scared stiff, no doubt about it; yet

139

they refused to take the steps that would have averted federal control. The pressures mounted implacably.

On November 1, 1917, the country was short one hundred and fifty-eight thousand freight cars, while nearly two hundred thousand cars stood idle on the tracks of the eastern roads. The Railroads' War Board singled out, as the cause of the crisis, the lack of skilled labor. At the time, some railroad workers were paid only ten cents an hour, and half of those employed by the railroads got less than seventy-five dollars a month. Meanwhile, in the fast-growing war industries, even unskilled laborers got up to five dollars a day.

Late in November, all the northeastern states were threatened with a coal famine. The Atlantic ports were crowded with ships that could not steam to Europe for lack of coal. Around the ports the tracks were too crowded to carry what was needed.

On December 1, the Interstate Commerce Commission sadly reported to the Congress that the Railroads' War Board had failed. Unification of the national railway system was "indispensable," but unification was just what the Board could not supply.

President Woodrow Wilson waited until all but the most intransigent troglodytes had acknowledged the vital requirements of the public interest. At noon on December 26, by proclamation, he took possession of the railroads on behalf of the United States. McAdoo, the Secretary of the Treasury, was appointed Director General of Railroads, with absolute power over the rate, over wages and working conditions, over all the facilities of the network of railways throughout the country.

Government control of the railroads lasted for twenty-six months—from January 1, 1918, to March 1, 1920—and no period in the industry's history has provoked such wild disagreement among the participants as to what happened. According to a chief spokesman for the industry, federal control was an unmitigated disaster which cost the taxpayers $2,280,000 a day; on the other hand, according to the director general of the

Railroad Administration, federal control was "a godsend to the railroads and their owners."

It is easy to see why the participants could not agree at every point. Suddenly and radically the most powerful industry in the land had been appropriated by the government in a transaction of staggering complexity that involved the transfer of five hundred and thirty-two railroad companies (with their 66,070 locomotives, 55,939 passenger cars, and 2,408,518 freight cars, their 366,197 miles of track, their terminals, bridges, stations, roundhouses, switching yards, and shops, their private-car lines, their two canals, their twenty-five steamship lines, their docks and wharves and harbor equipment, their grain elevators, their three waterworks companies, and their three hundred million dollars in cash), some of which were exceedingly wealthy and some of which were in receivership, and all of which, taken together, had a book value of some eighteen billion dollars.

Moreover, the transfer of this enormous property, the biggest in the history of the world, had been accomplished without evaluation of any item of the assets by the companies that owned them or the government that appropriated them. Was a given mile of track in good shape or bad? Was a given freight car brand new or falling apart? Did such a freight car even exist? Nobody knew; or, at least, if he knew, he had not proven the value or the existence of it to the party who had taken possession of it and who, it was assumed but not yet contractually agreed, would one day, nobody knew when, be obliged to return it in a condition and on terms that had not yet been settled.

In short, the entire transaction, save for its cause and its justification, was quite mad, and no prudent businessman could possibly have approved any part of it.

So much for the objective facts. The subjective considerations were even less likely to usher in an era of sweetness and light. A few simple-minded folk supposed that the long struggle between the greed for private profit and the obligation to serve the public interest had at last been resolved, if only temporarily, and, at least so long as the nation was at war, that the railroads would be run in sensible and harmonious fashion. It did not work out exactly that way.

One trouble was that too many railroad magnates could not shake off their old autocratic habits. These lordly fellows had now to take orders about the operation of their own trains over their own roads, and often from men who had been their bitterest competitors or, even worse, from Democratic politicians. Their mood grew ugly. Not only did they stand exposed as incompetent to manage their own business properly in a time of national emergency, but they found themselves barred from sharing in the juicy war profits that were enriching all the industrialists and financiers with whom they commonly consorted.

Moreover, McAdoo's Railroad Administration might do such a conspicuously good job that, after the war, there would be an overwhelming popular pressure to nationalize the railroads forever. Here was a very real and present danger; more than a few railroad presidents began to appreciate the gravity of the situation and to worry about the chances of government success.

At first the Railroad Administration had its hands full simply in freeing the railroads from the snarl in which their owners had entangled them. There were the angry shippers all over the country to be propitiated; there was the coal famine in New England to be averted; there were the thousands of empty cars to be sped west, not only to relieve the congestion in the east, and especially on the tracks of the Pennsylvania and the Baltimore & Ohio, but also to fetch freight essential to the war effort and long overdue. (A stretch of wicked winter weather, officially described as "the most severe ever recorded" in the Eastern Region, made the work of clearing the congested tracks more difficult.)

Another legacy from the good old days of private management was the wage scale, which was at or near the starvation level. McAdoo characterized the wages paid to railroad employees when he became the director general as "a long-stand-

142

ing national disgrace," and, curiously, he could find no railroad president to disagree with him, especially now that *he* was obliged to pay those wages. His old friend A. H. Smith, the president of the New York Central, assured him that he must at once raise wages, and across the board. "You have the power to do it," Smith reminded him. To insure a decent living wage for two million men and women, to bring the employees of the railroads somewhere close to parity with the employees of other American industries, McAdoo had to spend vast sums:

In 1917 railroad labor cost $1,739,000,000
In 1918 railroad labor cost $2,614,000,000

an increase of more than fifty per cent, and in the process McAdoo was able to guarantee that for the first time women would get equal pay for equal work and that for the first time Negro firemen, trainmen, and switchmen would be paid the same wage as white men in the same jobs. In short, a glorious victory for the progressives of Woodrow Wilson's New Freedom.

Yet here, looking wonderfully satisfied, even leading the applause, were the railroad presidents. It was odd. McAdoo, ordinarily a shrewd fellow, seems never to have been puzzled by their delight over the fact that their labor force was now to get eight hundred and seventy-five million dollars more a year.

But the railroad presidents had good reason to be cheerful: the wage raise would put a huge dent in the net earnings of the railroads while they were under government control, and the lower those earnings, the more powerful the argument against any future nationalization. For the railroad presidents the magic number was about nine hundred and forty million dollars. That sum was the average annual railway operating income for the three years from June 30, 1914, to June 30, 1917, and it had been fixed by the Congress as the sum the government had to pay the railroad companies for the use of their rails and equipment. (This generous arrangement guaranteed bondholders their interest and stockholders an annual dividend of eight and one half per cent.) If the Railroad Administration could earn more than nine hundred and forty million dollars a year, it would make the private owners look sick. But the big boost in wages made such an eventuality all but impossible.*

Meanwhile, earnings had been suffering for another reason. When the Railroad Administration was formed, McAdoo simply appointed the various railroad companies as his agents, to operate their properties in obedience to his orders and under the supervision of three regional directors. This naïve procedure inevitably led to confusion. The officers of the railroad companies were put in the impossible position of having to protect the interests of those companies against the government while at the same time having to protect the interests of the government against the companies. It took McAdoo five months to wise up. In those five months, "instances were brought to my attention," McAdoo wrote later, "where [the railroad men] were doing as much as they could to thwart the policies of the Railroad Administration." Earnings, he declared, dropped sharply:

Earnings, first five months of 1917: $346,439,522
Earnings, first five months of 1918: $215,278,241
Decrease in earnings: $131,161,281

a loss of thirty-eight per cent; most unusual; not to be sneezed at, even if conditions had been uniformly horrendous. But conditions, apart from the bitter January weather, had been excellent: the railroads had been running at full capacity, the wage raise had yet to be taken into account. The one suspicious factor in the equation was management, the men whom McAdoo had trustfully left in charge. Some of these men were guilty of "a kind of sabotage," McAdoo concluded, "carried

*When McAdoo raised wages, on May 25, 1918, he simultaneously raised the freight rates (about twenty-eight per cent) and the passenger fares (about eighteen per cent) to meet the added costs; but the wage raise was retroactive to January 1, and there was no way to make the higher rates and fares retroactive. This cost the Railroad Administration an estimated four hundred and twelve million dollars.

144

on by some high in authority, for the purpose of discrediting government operation of the roads." McAdoo accused Julius Kruttschnitt, the chairman of the board of directors of the Southern Pacific, of "consciously and deliberately [setting] out to cause all the trouble he could, with the purpose of bringing discredit on the Railroad Administration."*

So after five months McAdoo dismissed the railroad companies as his agents, instead appointing one responsible officer of each company as a federal manager to report to the regional director. Earnings at once began to rise.

Another difficulty arose because of the officers of the Pennsylvania, who have traditionally enjoyed an exaggerated sense of their own importance. When a railroad man was to be appointed eastern regional director, the officers of the Pennsylvania took it for granted that he would be one of their number, probably their president, Samuel Rea. (Their vice-president in charge of operations, W. W. Atterbury, had already been appointed the director-general of traffic for the American Expeditionary Forces; in later years he would prefer to be addressed as "General Atterbury.") But McAdoo chose Smith, of the New York Central, to be the eastern regional director. The officers of the Pennsylvania did not trouble to conceal their dismay. Smith would divert their traffic, they cried, and would disorganize their operations.

As he listened to these wails, McAdoo smiled grimly, for he had found the Pennsylvania to be disgracefully shoddy—"in a worse condition than any other railroad in the United States" —and he was already digging deep into the taxpayers' purse to put the road in a decent condition. The Railroad Administration, he wrote later, had to spend "far more money on the Pennsylvania than on any other railroad system in the country."

*This quotation and the others attributed to McAdoo in this section are taken from *Crowded Years: The Reminiscences of William G. McAdoo*, Houghton, Mifflin, 1931. I have also drawn on *War History of American Railroads*, by Walker D. Hines, Yale University Press, 1928. Hines was assistant director general of railroads in 1918 and director general in 1919 and 1920. Prior to his government service Hines had been chairman of the board of directors of the Santa Fe.

Freight in the eastern region, as elsewhere, continued to move over the most direct route; complaints about diversion of traffic were ignored.*

From first to last—despite the surly and fractious management, despite the inexperienced labor force, despite the rundown plant and the outworn equipment, despite the maddening frustrations of wartime—the Railroad Administration got the job done, and at a profit. The needs of war were met. Troops were moved (passenger-miles went up thirty per cent above the record period under private management) and their munitions and supplies were moved (more freight was hauled in 1918 than ever before in railroad history). The job could have been done only under federal control, only by means of the sensible procedures of unification that were introduced by the Railroad Administration.

Meanwhile, the temper of the executives of the railroad corporations inevitably grew more sullen. For more than two years they were thrust to one side, excluded from any decision over the management of an enterprise to which they had devoted their energies, even their entire careers. In these circumstances, no rational decision of the Railroad Administration could meet with their approval, yet every blunder was greeted by their applause and magnified to outrageous extremities. They were angered by the government's recognition of labor unions; they were resentful of the government's success in operating a nationally unified railway system; they were fearful that the government was slyly reaching out to control their railways forever.

In truth, there were more than a few senators and congressmen who had been solidly impressed by the achievements of the Railroad Administration. Two or three of the Interstate Commerce Commissioners were likewise reluctant to let the

*"In one instance that came to my attention," McAdoo recalled, "it had been the custom to haul coal cars one hundred and seventy miles to a destination which was only thirteen miles from the point where the shipment originated. That miracle of inefficiency served its purpose of getting the revenue for one road even if that road did haul the coal at a loss. We stopped all that."

146

railroads slip back into the grasp of a few financiers, stock-market speculators, and men hungry for power. But Morgan was dead, and Harriman was dead; it was always possible that their heirs, genetical or spiritual, would prove less anthropophagous than their sires; and so, after prolonged debate, the Congress turned the railroads back to their owners as the stroke of midnight proclaimed March 1, 1920.

At once a rude clamor went up from the executives of the railroad corporations, all of it directed against the Railroad Administration. Item: federal control had robbed the tax-payers of a fortune. Item: federal control had, by mollycoddling labor, crippled the railroad companies and jeopardized their future solvency. Item: federal control had wrecked the railroads physically; the roads were broken, worn, and irreparably ruined. Before long it came clear that this chorus of wails and woe was a carefully organized campaign of propaganda designed to sanctify a piratical raid upon the United States treasury, an assault that put to shame even the spoliation of the public lands that had marked the industry's earlier history.

The railroad companies put forward claims against the government for alleged damages to their properties in the staggering amount of $1,013,389,502.12. An inspection of the claims of some of the individual railroad companies is instructive:

The New York Central claimed damages totaling nearly eleven million dollars. They ended by paying the government twenty-three million for improvements made while the road was under federal control. A Central subsidiary, the Big Four (the Cleveland, Cincinnati, Chicago & St. Louis) claimed damages of three million dollars but was obliged to pay the government five million.

The B&O demanded thirty-four million but eventually had to pay the government nine million.

The Erie demanded sixteen million but glumly paid the government three and one quarter million.

The Reading demanded twenty-three million but settled

147

by paying the government eight million.

The officers of the Pennsylvania were too realistic to claim any damages. As they well knew, the Railroad Administration had spent $218,824,202.60 of public funds in improving the road and equipping it with new rolling stock. But when the government presented a bill against the Pennsylvania for $187,117,000, the howl of anguish could be heard all across the country, skillfully amplified through the massed flügelhorns of Professor Ivy Ledbetter Lee, the most eminent of the idealists retained to adorn and perfume the public image of private corporations. The Pennsylvania, it seemed, had been sorely afflicted by the Railroad Administration but, in an extraordinary access of patriotism, the company was nevertheless ready to pay the government $53,814,000 without a whimper. At length, after many bargaining sessions, the Pennsylvania reluctantly disgorged ninety million dollars, or less than half of what the government (i.e., the taxpayers) had spent to mend and meliorate the company's plant and equipment.

The Chicago, Milwaukee & St. Paul tried to get away with twenty-six million but ended by paying the government more than six million.

The Rock Island claimed twenty million but ended by paying the government two and one half million.

The Santa Fe demanded nearly ninety-eight million; the claim was shaved to twenty-one and one half million.

The Pullman Company alleged damages of $24,424,000, including $571,059 for sheets lost or stolen, $417,893 for towels, $256,233 for pillowcases, and $133,750 for headrest linen covers—sums that seemed more like a generous evaluation of a complete inventory than a claim for damages. The government shelled out $7,250,000 in recompense.

Of the more than one billion dollars the railroads tried to get from the treasury, the government disbursed, net, $48,574,901.74, or less than five per cent. On this ignoble note, the curtain came down on the period of federal control of the railroads.

# 10

*Turn of a new leaf: the Transportation Act of 1920. A grand plan for the consolidation of the railroads according to the public interest. The plan is rejected and destroyed by the railroad companies. Scramble for conquest and imperial domination. The Van Sweringens. The big bull market and the crash of 1929.*

WHEN THE CONGRESS returned the railroads to their owners on March 1, 1920, an effort was made to turn a new leaf, to start from scratch; all the old sins forgiven, all the old sinners shriven. The public, by way of its elected representatives, undertook to forget the past behavior of the railroad men and asked of them only that they mend their ways and commence to act like sensible and civilized capitalists.

To coax them into the strait jacket of proper capitalistic behavior, the Congress offered the railroad men a fair return on the value of their property and instructed the Interstate Commerce Commission to raise the freight rates and the passenger fares so that their fair return would be guaranteed. Such an approach to the vexing problems of the railroads spawned several other uncomfortable questions, among which were:

What was the real value of railway property, so often and so villainously overcapitalized with issues of worthless securities?

What was a fair return on such property and how could it be estimated?

149

How could the railroad executives and, more especially, their financiers be effictively restrained from inundating the public with still greater floods of worthless securities?

How could the Commission, by setting a rate that would guarantee a fair return for a weak and poorly organized railroad, avoid pressing an exorbitant profit on a strong and prosperous carrier? Conversely, if the Commission pegged the rates at a level designed to yield the powerful railroads a fair return, might not the weak roads be further impoverished?

How might the chances for a fair return be affected by the wages paid to railroad labor, higher in 1920 than ever before but still well below the level in other industries?

The Congress sought to answer all these questions at once with the Transportation Act of 1920. The great value of the act was that it treated the railroads not as so many corporate devices for the making of private fortunes but as a national transportation system; its great weakness lay in the assumption by its advocates that the men who ran the railroads would agree with this emollient approach and would help to make it work. The Congress had every reason to hope for and to expect co-operation from the railroad companies. Earlier federal legislation had either policed the industry or punished it, but this act was designed to establish a rational railroad economy and to protect railroad investors. This act reversed a public policy of long standing and intense partisanship by encouraging and even instructing the combination and consolidation of railroads "into a limited number of systems." It did not seem within reason that the men who ran the railroads would spurn such a splendid opportunity.

The argument that railroad rates should be based upon an equitable valuation of railroad property had originated with Senator Robert M. La Follette away back in 1906, in a lengthy speech almost totally ignored by the Senate.* La Follette had

* When La Follette, then a very junior senator from Wisconsin, violated senatorial tradition by launching into his well-informed demand for rate regulation, the chamber was all but emptied. Only one other senator of

patiently reintroduced his bill for railway valuation in one session after another until it was finally enacted on March 1, 1913. Ever since, experts of the Interstate Commerce Commission had been toiling to establish an accurate valuation of the railroads, despite the bitterest resistance of the railroad operators and their bankers. Nevertheless, in 1920 most people imagined the job would soon be finished. In any event, since a beginning had to be made, an arbitrary valuation had to be set. The railroad men, pointing to their books, proclaimed a value of $20,040,572,611. The Commission's experts, using what data they had already gathered (and perhaps picking about in the entrails of some sacred poultry), divined the value to be $18,900,000,000.

The Congress decided that a fair return (that is, a fair annual net railway operating income) lay somewhere between five and one half and six per cent of the valuation. To assure the carriers such a net income, the Commission thereupon hiked the freight rates up twenty-five per cent in the south, thirty-five per cent in the west, and forty per cent in the east— the biggest boost in history. In this way the Transportation Act brought about regulation of railroad income. Since other sections of the act stipulated regulation of railroad securities by the Commission and regulation of wages by a Railroad Labor Board, the octopus of monopoly seemed to have been tanked at last, and fairly comfortably.

There remained, however, one problem. What of the railroad company able to earn far more than six per cent, thanks to the new high rates? Here again Congress had an answer: any carrier earning more than six per cent on the valuation

the ninety remained, as a watchful guard against some parliamentary emergency. La Follette at once capitalized on the rudeness of his fellows. "I cannot," he said, "be wholly indifferent to the fact that Senators, by their absence at this time, indicate their want of interest in what I may have to say upon this subject. The public is interested. Unless this important question is rightly settled, seats now temporarily vacant may be permanently vacated." There was applause in the galleries. Six years later La Follette noted with satisfaction that twenty-four of his standpat Republican opponents had been ousted from the Senate.

151

of its railroad property would be required to pay half the
excess to the government, to be administered by the Commission "in furtherance of the public interest in railway transportation"—say, for example, to pay for the cleaning of the
public washrooms in passenger cars—or used for loans to less
fortunate carriers. The other half of the excess was to go to a
reserve fund, against the day when the carrier might earn less
than the magic six per cent.

Now it may be taken as axiomatic that no railroad president
who can report to his stockholders a net income of, say, ten
per cent, will cheerfully fork over one fifth of that gaudy profit
to the government. Even the Congress of 1920 could appreciate so much. These so-called "recapture" provisions were,
then, regarded as only temporary expedients. The Congress
imagined that its truly novel provisions—those that governed
the consolidation and combination of railroads into "a limited
number of systems"—would make for a uniformity in which
rich roads would be joined with poor roads in sound systems,
each system able to compete on equal terms with the others,
each prudently financed, each stable, and each earning—to
quote the act—"substantially the same rate of return upon the
value of [its] railway properties."

The task of regrouping the railroads into "a limited number
of systems" was dumped on the Commission along with all its
other tasks, such as evaluating the railroads, fixing their freight
rates and passenger fares, supervising their safety, regulating
their securities, and making sure that they kept themselves
clean, including the backs of their necks and behind their ears.
This new consolidation policy required of the Commission
public planning of immense importance and enormous complexity, yet, in issuing its instructions, the Congress neglected
even to suggest how many systems of railroads might be
evolved from the more than five hundred railway companies
then in existence. Should there be four systems? twenty? fifty?
one hundred? The Congress dropped no hint. Moreover, while
the Congress bade the Commission to "prepare and adopt a
plan for the consolidation of railway properties," the whole

procedure of consolidation was voluntary. The Commission could not require consolidation; it could only refuse to approve a merger that was not "in harmony with" its over-all plan.

In other words, if the Transportation Act of 1920 were to succeed, the men who ran the railroads would have to suppress their competitive ambitions, co-operate intelligently, and proceed according to the highest standards of the public welfare. In short, pigs would have to learn to whistle. Twenty years later, a report of a Senate committee appointed to investigate these matters phrased the difficulty with utmost delicacy:

> It is, perhaps, fair to say [the committee reported], that the consolidation provisions of the Transportation Act presupposed a higher sense of public responsibility on the part of the railroads and railroad investors than was warranted by experience.*

The Transportation Act of 1920 was made to fail. The opposition was sometimes artful, sometimes brutal, but it never let up; at no point was there any concession by the men who ran the railroads either to the spirit or to the letter of the law. Appropriately enough, the opposition was led by the biggest railroad company in the country, the Pennsylvania Railroad Company. The Pennsylvania led the artful attack against the consolidation clauses of the act; the Pennsylvania led the brutal attack against railroad labor.

When W. W. Atterbury, vice-president of the Pennsylvania in charge of operations, came home from the war, he was scandalized to find that in his absence the American Federation of Labor had been encouraged by the federal government to organize more than thirty thousand workmen in the Pennsylvania's shops, and that their average annual wage was up from $944 in 1916 to $1,883 in 1920. Atterbury rallied the other railroads under the slogan, "No contracts with labor unions," and plunged into the work of crushing them utterly. The Rail-

*Report of the Committee on Interstate Commerce, 74th Congress, Part II, p. 524. This was the so-called Wheeler Committee, which investigated the connections between railroads, their holding companies, and their investment bankers.

153

road Labor Board had declared that the national wage agreements made during the time of federal control should remain in effect until July, 1921. Atterbury ignored the Board and signed separate wage pacts with company unions of his own contrivance. When the Board investigated and declared his "elections" illegal, he found a judge who would enjoin the Board from making any such charges. He restored piecework; he abolished collective bargaining; his company spies were busy in every shop and yard.

The hard times of 1921 led the Board to order a general reduction of wages. When the depression persisted, Atterbury and the other railroad operators pressed for still further reductions. The Board was cautious about cutting the wages of the powerful brotherhoods (the engineers, firemen, conductors, trainmen, and switchmen), but the fourteen A.F. of L. shop-craft unions were weaker, more vulnerable. The Board ordered their wages to be cut again, this time by twelve and one half per cent. On July 1, 1922, four hundred thousand shopmen across the country struck.

To alarm the public about the dangers of the strike, many passenger trains were unnecessarily withdrawn from service. (But the freight trains, which represented about eighty per cent of railroad revenues, ran as usual.) Violence was reported, sabotage was alleged. President Harding issued a proclamation. The strikers persevered through July and into August. They were not winning, since they lacked the support of the brotherhoods, but neither were they losing; and so there was room to negotiate a settlement. A dozen railroad presidents heeded the counsel of Daniel Willard, the president of the Baltimore & Ohio, and sat down with the union leaders to bargain. Atterbury fumed. But he had still one recourse.

An agreement was all but signed when, on a motion by Harding's complaisant Attorney General, Harry Daugherty, a federal judge issued an injunction that paralyzed the unions, an injunction bitterly characterized by their counsel, Donald Richberg, as designed "to prevent the settlement of a strike." Atterbury promptly announced that the Pennsylvania had

154

reached an arrangement with its company unions. The strike had been broken.

Atterbury had succeeded to the presidency of the Pennsylvania when, on January 14, 1926, he appeared before the Senate Interstate Commerce Committee to testify in favor of the railway labor bill. The chief provisions of the bill guaranteed railroad workmen the right to bargain collectively and to choose their own representatives without coercion. Yet Atterbury pleasurably purred his approval of the bill. Had the old rascal hit the sawdust trail? Not at all: the bill, as slyly amended, included a proviso under which the Pennsylvania's company unions (and those of any other railroad) might be sanctioned by the courts. A vice-president of the Pennsylvania, Elisha Lee, had personally assisted in drafting the clause.

Atterbury, bland as ever, was still in defiance of the will of the Congress, still in defiance of the public interest.*

The effort opposed to the consolidation clauses of the Transportation Act was more subtle and more complex. It called for stealth, sharp practice, financial cunning, skill in exploiting the hopes of the investing public, and, of course, an utter disregard for the law. The main arena of the conflict against the public interest was once again the so-called Official Region— that is, the northeastern quarter of the country, the section dominated by the trunk-line railroads that reached from the Atlantic seaports to Chicago and St. Louis. What happened in the Official Region was bound to affect what happened to the railroads elsewhere in the country, for two reasons. First, the rate structure for the nation as a whole was designed by the Trunk Line Association. The Interstate Commerce Commission could raise the rates or lower them; the Commission could intervene to raise or lower a tariff within a given region; but the Trunk Line Association, through its classification com-

*Not until the Railway Labor Act was amended in 1934 were company unions effectively outlawed. One by one the most intransigent antiunion citadels—the Lackawanna, the Nickel Plate, the Missouri Pacific, the Northern Pacific, the Union Pacific—were toppled. The Pennsylvania was the last to cave in.

155

mittee and its freight committee, still fixed the rates in the first instance and, from New York, influenced the decisions of similar committees meeting in Chicago and Atlanta. Second, the investment banking houses of Wall Street were best fitted to manipulate, meddle, and scramble for profit in the Official Region, where the competitive ambitions were fiercest. A word about these eastern trunk lines is in order, since the balance of power among them had somewhat shifted since last we examined them.

The Pennsylvania was the biggest railroad company and one of the biggest companies of any kind in the country. Its officers rejoiced in gross assets worth more than two billion dollars and a well-developed system of more than eleven thousand miles of track. While all its holdings of stock in the Baltimore & Ohio and the Chesapeake & Ohio had been sold, it still maintained tight control of the Norfolk & Western.

The New York Central operated more miles of line than the Pennsylvania, but in 1920 neither its assets nor its revenues were quite so large. One change in the system was significant: the threat of proceedings by the government under the anti-trust laws had led in 1916 to the sale of the Nickel Plate, the road between Buffalo and Chicago that W. H. Vanderbilt had grumpily purchased back in 1882. The new owners were O. P. and M. J. Van Sweringen, a pair of Cleveland real estate operators who had little capital, no railroad experience, but a superb wizardry in the juggling of credit. They had bought the Nickel Plate with borrowed money; they liked this way of doing business and planned more of it.

The B&O was, by comparison, poorly developed. In the east, the system depended on the Reading for trackage to New York's harbor; west of Ohio it was little more than two string lines reaching to Chicago and St. Louis. Its assets were less than half those of the Pennsylvania.

The Erie was a sickly thing, not much more than a backbone from New York to Chicago, lacking the ribs and arms to reach out to other industrial cities or interior ports. Its assets were less than one fourth those of the Pennsylvania.

156

Quite evidently, if these four systems were to be made competitive and were to earn "substantially the same rate of return upon the value of their railroad properties," the B&O and the Erie would have to be beefed up considerably. Just as evidently, if the Pennsylvania were to maintain its hegemony in the Official Region, its officers would have to dig in their heels and resist any and all consolidations; in short, they would have to scuttle the Transportation Act.

The recapture provisions of the act, which required a carrier earning more than six per cent on the valuation of its railroad property to pay half the excess to the government, proved useless as a means of hustling consolidation along. Valuation was a quicksand. What were the criteria? How to account for costs? Lawyers for even the weakest roads eagerly assisted in the work of sabotaging the machinery of valuation. It was easily done. Consider:

In 1912, spokesmen for the railroads had argued that valuation should be based on the original cost of building a railroad and had insisted that the valuation of all roads should be fixed at approximately fourteen billion dollars.

In 1920, the railroad spokesmen claimed a valuation of some twenty billion dollars and even prayed the Congress for legislation to fix it at that level.

In 1923, less than five billion dollars having been added to their property by investment, the railroad spokesmen would claim a valuation of some thirty-five billion and would argue that values should be based upon the cost of reproducing the railroads at current prices.

To fix the freight rates so that the railroads might earn up to six per cent on a valuation of thirty-five billion dollars would have cost somebody (guess who?) an additional one billion dollars a year. Here, then, were the propositions for an interminable debate. Only some supernatural force could have obliged the railroad operators to submit to an accurate valuation of their properties and a consequent transfer of their excess profits to the government.*

*About eleven million dollars were paid to the government, first and

157

But valuation or no, the Commission had been charged with the preparation of a plan for the consolidation of the nation's railroads. To advise them, the commissioners retained William Z. Ripley, a professor of economics at Harvard who had won a considerable reputation as an expert on transportation, had written several books about the railroads, and had as a result been elected a director of the Rock Island.

Professor Ripley's appointment was of course noted by investment bankers and railroad executives across the country. They were encouraged to invent and begin to play a delightful new parlor game, called Let's Consolidate the Railroads. Each of them, it seemed, was blessed with the wisdom to devise the perfect scheme; those who did not importune Professor Ripley directly filled the magazines and newspapers of 1920 with their quack panaceas. Some were content with fourteen systems for the country and four for the Official Region; others insisted on thirty systems for the country and found six work-

---

last, under the recapture clauses, and even this trifling sum was paid under fiery protest and sequestered until the courts could agree on its eventual disposition. In 1926 the Interstate Commerce Commission found a case on which it was ready to stand: the St. Louis & O'Fallon Railroad, an exceedingly profitable coal carrier that extended nine miles into southern Illinois, had in 1921, 1922, and 1923, according to the Commission, amassed a profit of $452,000 in excess of six per cent of its official valuation and therefore owed the government $226,000. The railroad's lawyers, flanked by a battalion of lawyers representing the richest systems in the country, hotly denounced the Commission's findings.

The official valuation had been determined after a compromise. When the Commission was "unable to ascertain" original costs from the accountants of one railroad after another, the commissioners decided to value each railroad by a formula that comprised: the cost of its reproduction in 1914, the actual cost of any betterments and additions since then, and the current value of the land on which stood its tracks, terminals, and other structures.

In May, 1929, the Supreme Court found, five to three (Justices Brandeis, Holmes, and Stone dissenting), that the Commission had not given "due consideration" to the reproduction costs since 1914. The decision was worth hundreds of millions of dollars to the railroads.

The recapture clauses of the Transportation Act were repealed by the Congress in 1933, at the pit of the Great Depression, by which time they were, in any event, academic.

able trunk lines in the Official Region. Professor Ripley wavered but he was inclined to compromise: twenty-two systems for the country, five of them in the east. (The professor's fifth trunk-line system was to be based on the Nickel Plate, the Lackawanna, and some smaller roads.)

The policy of the Pennsylvania was made quite explicit in a letter to Professor Ripley from A. J. County, the vice-president of the Pennsylvania in charge of corporate matters. County questioned the value of any plan for consolidation whatsoever; if, however, despite all the legal, financial, and technical difficulties, a plan were to be devised, it should call for forty or fifty systems. In short, the Pennsylvania refused to contemplate the possibility that any system, anywhere in the country, might threaten its primacy.

The Commission's tentative plan, announced in August, 1921, generally resembled Ripley's; the differences from it would seem to have been suggested to stimulate a discussion of the alternative possibilities. Five trunk lines were projected, and nearly forty eastern railroads, rich and poor, were to be divided up and parceled out to one or other of these five systems. The details of the division are of no particular importance, since both the plan itself and the hearings held by the Commission to debate its merits, if any, were greeted by the railroad operators with snorts of derision. In a memorandum to President Rea of the Pennsylvania, Vice-President County wrote that "the whole idea may be safely relegated to the wastepaper basket. . . ."

The hearings maundered along, hazily and purposelessly, from April, 1922, until January, 1924, toward inevitable stalemate. Meanwhile, in the real world, a railroad empire was a-building right under the Commission's nose, an empire that would pulverize the Commission's plan even as the hearings on it were droning on.

The candidates for imperial rank were the brothers Van Sweringen, who, with borrowed money and unseemly haste, purchased five railroads—the Lake Erie & Western, the Clover Leaf (more formally known as the Toledo, St. Louis & West-

159

ern), the Chesapeake & Ohio (which in turn controlled the Hocking Valley), the Erie, and the Pere Marquette—a spectacular expansion from one 525-mile string line to a well-articulated trunk-line system more than nine thousand miles long, with assets worth more than one and one quarter billion dollars, a system substantially bigger than that of the B&O and more profitable, at least in 1924, than even that of the Pennsylvania.

It is a sad duty to report that most, if not all, of this empire was assembled in ways that were naughty, dishonest, and often downright illegal. It is equally grievous to report that the Van Sweringens were advised and assisted in their dubious career by the officers of the New York Central system; the partners of J. P. Morgan & Company; George F. Baker, the president of the First National Bank of New York; and sundry other respectable, conservative bankers, lawyers, and railroad executives of Cleveland, New York, and other cities, all of whom should have known and probably did know better.

The Van Sweringens bought roads with money borrowed from banks. They formed holding companies, the stock of which they sold to the public. The money raised in this way they used to reduce the amount of the sums they had borrowed. The bankers profited, as bankers always do when someone uses their money. The Van Sweringens profited, not only in cash and credit but also in control of a vast and lucrative railroad system. The profits came, as always, from the public, the hard-working, thrifty public, ignorant of what the insiders were up to, hopeful of a sound investment, greedy for unearned money, and dumb.

Only one voice was consistently raised against these financial shenanigans. Joseph B. Eastman, a Yankee commissioner who fought almost alone for the public interest throughout the 1920s, had no stomach for the way in which the Commission vacated its responsibilities, nor for the resurgence of railroad autocracy.

The Commission authorized the Van Sweringens to merge their first two acquisitions—the Lake Erie & Western and the

Clover Leaf—into the Nickel Plate, despite serious procedural irregularities. The law stipulated that such a consolidation could be approved only after the Commission had (1) valuated the properties of the companies involved and (2) published its final consolidation plan. Neither of these steps had been taken, but the consolidation was nevertheless permitted, over Eastman's vigorous dissent. The decision, Eastman argued, "will gravely impair, if it does not destroy, our power to administer successfully" the consolidation provisions of the Transportation Act. He was right, but he was ignored.

The Van Sweringens took control of the C&O without reference to the Commission, for the authors of the Transportation Act had not foreseen the sly uses to which a holding company might be put; but the brothers did need the Commission's approval to become directors of the C&O. Once again the Commission obliged them; once again Eastman dissented, but in vain.

The brothers added the Erie to their system so that they might have access to the port of New York. They would have preferred to buy control of the far more profitable Lehigh Valley, a road that also linked Buffalo and New York, but their friendly bankers controlled the decision, and their friendly bankers (who were also the bankers for both the Erie and the Lehigh Valley) chose to hold on to the fat dividends of the Lehigh Valley and to dump the hapless Erie. With the moral support, whatever that might be worth, of J. P. Morgan & Company, the Van Sweringens formed a syndicate with George F. Baker of the First National Bank and bought both the Erie and the Pere Marquette, the strongest road in Michigan.

In less than three years the Van Sweringens, by borrowing and shrewdly spending less than forty million dollars, had become the owners of a powerful fourth trunk-line system. They were a force to be reckoned with, a force that had exploded the Commission's tentative plan for consolidation of the eastern railroads and, what was more, had crippled the Commission's power to curb the railroads' management.

161

In the Congress these developments were eyed with mistrust and disgust. Senator Albert Cummins, the Iowa Republican who had helped to draft the Transportation Act, began to talk of the need for compulsory consolidation; so did the Secretary of Commerce, Herbert C. Hoover.

Still the Commission lagged. Most of the commissioners wanted no part of the responsibility for planning consolidation. One of them, Mark Potter, sent the president of the Pennsylvania a querulous memorandum: "I am out of tune with present provisions . . . regarding consolidations. . . . The complete plan should be abandoned." Potter wanted "representatives of the railways" to confer "in a practical businesslike way," after which he expected that "everybody, carriers, shippers, and security holders" would be happy. In Potter's view, "everybody" did not include the labor unions, the passengers, or the public generally.

And so, when Daniel Willard of the B&O and the Van Sweringens proposed to the Commission that a plan for consolidation be formulated by the railroad executives themselves, the idea was endorsed by the Commission with alacrity.

The pattern for the 1920s had now been set. The men who ran the railroads, and their bankers, would struggle aggressively for dominion just as they had for fifty years; the Commission would vacate its responsibility for planning a rational transportation system; the public interest would be forgotten.

The presidents of the four trunk-line systems held conferences off and on from 1924 to 1932, seeking agreement on the division of empire. They got nowhere. They were like four unruly little boys playing Monopoly, with one or another of them losing his temper, upsetting the board, and swinging his fists whenever a throw of the dice went against him.

Behind the presidents, as they squabbled over empire, were the shadowy figures of their bankers, always ready to lend money at suitable rates, already ready with advice, strategical or tactical; but when the infighting around the conference table got particularly nasty, the bankers must have had to think fast to remember exactly whom and what they were

162

advising. J. P. Morgan & Company had to protect the interests of the New York Central and the Van Sweringens; they had also to bear in mind what might be best for the Lehigh Valley, the Reading, and the Lackawanna. Kuhn, Loeb & Company had to be even quicker on their feet, for they represented both the Pennsylvania and the B&O, whose interests were usually at loggerheads; they were also concerned for the Wabash and the Delaware & Hudson, small fry that might at any moment be swallowed by bigger fish. To cite one example of the result of these divided loyalties: the presidents of the trunk lines disputed who should own the Lackawanna for more than five months before W. H. Truesdale, who was only the president of the railroad concerned, heard the first word about it. (And then he heard about it not from his bankers but from the president of the Pennsylvania.)

The advice of the bankers was, indeed, indispensable when it came to the major railroad strategy of the 1920s. For whenever their fruitless four-party conferences were in recess (and often while they were in clamorous session), the carriers greedily sought to accomplish unifications of railroads by operating in a stock market already made feverish, as Commissioner Eastman had pointed out, precisely by their operations. From January, 1927, to the end of 1929 the four big eastern systems spent *almost a half billion dollars* to buy the stock, and consequently the control, of various smaller railroads. This enormous expenditure, every penny of it speculative, was advised and directed by the bankers and brokers of Wall Street.

Often the purchases of railroad stock were in violation of the Clayton Act, were recognized as such, but were made anyway. Usually the purchases were, as the Wheeler Committee would later say of the Pennsylvania's acquisition of stock of the Norfolk & Western, "bold and almost defiant in their relation to the question of Government regulation." Always the purchases were stupid, since the money should have been conserved for the purposes of rational transportation rather than poured into dubious, imperialistic schemes.

As the big bull market soared onward and upward, the purchases got to be insanely extravagant and could be undertaken only because railroad profits had exceeded one billion dollars a year, from 1925 onward, and in 1929 would reach a record one and one quarter billion. When the B&O, which owned twenty-five per cent of the stock of the Reading, began in 1928 to add to its holdings, the price paid was $100 a share; by September, 1929, the price was $145 a share and that wise old Nestor of finance, Bernard Baruch, a director of the B&O, sent a message to Dan Willard, the president: "Suggest following competitive buying aggressively if necessary to prevent absorption of possible control by others."

Apart from its graceless phrasing, this message made no sense, for no others were trying to "absorb" control. The B&O nevertheless kept on buying stock of the Reading until November 11, just as though the worst financial crash in history had never taken place; in all, the B&O bought two hundred and fifty thousand more shares, at a cost of some twenty-six million dollars.

The B&O was by no means the only carrier to persist in buying railroad stocks right through the disastrous crash of October, 1929, and long after it. The Pennsylvania spent, from October, 1929, to May, 1931, about twenty-five million dollars for stock of the New Haven, a road that soon afterward bubbled into bankruptcy. From July, 1929, until January, 1932, the New York Central spent seventeen millions to buy stock of the Lackawanna at an average price of $110 a share; four months later, the same shares could have been picked up for $12 apiece. The Van Sweringens, who realized profits of more than thirty million dollars from the sale, during the summer of 1929, of nearly six hundred thousand shares of their Alleghany Corporation, spent all that vast sum and more on stock of the Missouri Pacific; the road went into bankruptcy in 1933 and was followed, a year later, by Alleghany itself.

Since such purchases can never be justified, how to account for them? Otto Kahn, a partner in Kuhn, Loeb & Company, made a brave try in 1933, before the Senate Banking and

Currency Committee. The railroads had to "scramble," said Kahn, "to put themselves in a position where possession was nine points of the law." When Kahn used the word "scramble," he was characterizing the carefully considered policies of the four big trunk-line systems in dealing with the problems posed by consolidation. What he meant was that each of them would recklessly spend its substance, regardless of the future, to seize an empire and, if possible, expand it.

Meanwhile, here came the Commission, limping along the dusty right of way, having prayed the Congress for five consecutive years for relief of all responsibility as to consolidation but still required by law to do *something*. At last, in December, 1929, having ineffectually sweated and strained for an unconscionable time, the Commission produced its so-called final plan. It laid a bomb. It was predicated on five trunk-line systems, but the masters of the four trunk-line systems that dominated the Official Region had long since decided there was no room for a fifth. The Commission's suggestion for a fifth trunk line involved consolidating the Wabash (a road between Kansas City and Detroit, with trackage rights through Canada to Buffalo) with the Lehigh Valley, the Norfolk & Western, and the Seaboard Air Line. Control of the first three of these roads was vested in the Pennsylvania, which would not have yielded any one of them without protracted, bitter, expensive litigation.*

*Atterbury of the Pennsylvania had bought, for $62,500,000, forty per cent of the stock of the Lehigh Valley and a like amount of the stock of the Wabash from Leonor F. Loree, an ambitious fellow who, as president of the Delaware & Hudson, had essayed in 1927 to construct a fifth trunk-line system. Atterbury continued to buy shares of both the Lehigh Valley and the Wabash until he had spent, from the Pennsylvania's treasury, $106,592,757.75. (It may be pertinent to note that, in 1935, these stocks were worth about $6,600,000.)

Was control by the Pennsylvania of these two roads not in blatant violation of the Clayton Act? The Commission thought so, but a federal circuit court of appeals in 1933 magisterially reversed the Commission's decision on the grounds that the Pennsylvania had bought the stock "solely for investment." In 1934 the Supreme Court sustained the lower court, four to four.

Meanwhile, in 1931, the Wabash had gone into receivership.

165

The Commission managed to produce another "final" plan in 1932, but nobody paid much attention to it. It was not, indeed, a plan at all: it was only a rubber stamp to ratify a sly, greedy, aggressive, and often illegal compact made by the four most powerful operators in the east. The planlessness of the plan was emphasized by the fact that the Commission (with Commissioner Eastman as usual in lonely dissent), by obsequiously approving the four-party compact, had demolished its own project for consolidating the railroads elsewhere in the country.

Nothing was done about it. No carrier was punished. Nobody cared. Who in 1932 had time or energy to address himself to the excesses of the railroads or to bring charges against those responsible for them? In 1932 every other consideration was dwarfed by one single awful fact—the Great Depression.

In its time the railroad industry had faced and weathered some tolerably severe panics and depressions—those of 1873, 1893, and 1907 stand out—but this one was different. Always before the railroad industry had been able to recover quickly because the resilient strength of American production had flooded the railroads with commerce. Always before the railroads had been the only carriers available to do the job, and so they had prospered. This time it was different. This time there was competition—tough, resourceful, imaginative, hard-working, ready to get the job done quicker and cheaper.

The masters of the railroads could not complain that this competition had taken them unaware. They had known that trucks were being manufactured and highways built to accommodate them, but they had smiled with condescension, dismissed the threat of trucks and highways as inconsiderable, and gone about the profitable business of their comfortable monopoly. In 1921 a journalist suggested to a railway executive that he might need "good transportation salesmanship" to keep his road profitable. " 'Good transportation salesmanship,' " the railroad man repeated, his tone amused and mocking; "what funny words!" After all, why should a railroad freight agent worry about salesmanship? In 1921 a truck that could haul

166

one ton of freight was an exceptional monster, and the average railroad freight car carried a load of more than thirty-seven tons. Yet in 1921 the Commission had just granted the railroads a whopping increase in rates, and it was natural for a shipper with narrow margins of profit to pluck at his lip, and consider the truck, and wonder.

In 1921 there were less than four hundred thousand trucks competing for the carriage of freight.

During the 1920s the federal government spent seven hundred and fifty million dollars to build highways, and the various states spent many more millions. During the first half of the 1930s federal aid to highways was beefed up by the Public Works Administration; it amounted to more than one billion dollars.

In 1933 there were more than three million trucks hauling freight over those new highways, and the trucking industry was being run by hard-bitten, hungry men who had nothing but contempt for the freight agents who sat in railroad depots and waited for business to come to them.

In the time they could spare from their gross and futile speculations on the stock market, the masters of the railroads had kept a shortsighted eye on the activities of the truckers. Busy with their schemes to obstruct the Transportation Act, they had nevertheless found time in 1924 to delegate representatives to a National Transportation Conference in Washington and to push through a resolution "that there is need for truck transportation in co-operation with, not in competition against, railroads."

Something, perhaps, like the Railway Express Agency, a trucking firm that was wholly owned by the railroads.

Most of the railroad companies formed subsidiary trucking companies, during the 1920s, to haul freight between factories and rail terminals. The shippers seemed to want the extra service.

There was even a moment, early in the 1930s, when the railroad companies were in a position to seize the infant trucking industry and control it utterly.

167

If the masters of the railroads had been shrewd enough . . .
If they had not been so preoccupied with their schemes of conquest . . .

But then the moment was gone, and the Great Depression closed in, and masters of the railroads no longer commanded enough cash, or even enough confidence, to try to take over a competitor which, they nervously assured each other, would never amount to much.

# 11

---

*The railroads prostrate. The government to the rescue.*
*Another plan for nationalization. The Transportation Act of*
*1940. War restores the health of the industry.*

---

THE PLIGHT of the railroads in the 1930s must wring from even
the most stonyhearted—well, perhaps not a sob, but at least a
pang of compassion. The mighty were fallen so low! And laid
out so flat! To be sure, they had nobody to blame for their
plight save themselves (though they industriously sought to
shift the blame to fate, or to the Commission, or, after 1935,
to That Man in the White House), but there is still something
affecting about a menace overnight transformed into a mendi-
cant.

The railroads were, no doubt about it, sick unto death.
Throughout the 1930s they were like a drunk nursing a horrible
hangover, an epic Katzenjammer that even time could not heal.
And the worst part of the affliction has been that two generations of Americans have been born and one of them has grown
to maturity during a time when the railroads have been
stripped of their sometime glory and have looked like nothing
but a bunch of dreary old bums.

Let us examine first the pathology, the morbid details of the
disease. They stink, as do all festering wounds; but our interest
is clinical, so on with the surgical masks and up with the lights.

The net profits of the major railroads plunged, with terrifying speed, down from their uttermost peak of prosperity:

169

|      |                |
|------|----------------|
| 1929 | $1,251,698,000 |
| 1930 |   868,879,000  |
| 1931 |   525,628,000  |
| 1932 |   326,298,000  |

and those profits for 1932 would have all but vanished if the twenty-one unions representing railway labor had not, on January 20, 1932, signed a contract that authorized a wage cut of more than two hundred and ten million dollars.

In 1932, railroad companies operating seventy-two per cent of the nation's tracks did not earn enough money to meet their fixed charges.

By 1938 those railroads had lopped six hundred and sixty thousand men off their payrolls, thereby condemning them to service in the vast army of the unemployed and reducing the payrolls by one billion dollars.

Of one hundred and forty-seven Class I railroads, thirty-eight were in bankruptcy or receivership. These thirty-eight roads operated thirty-one per cent of the country's railroad mileage and represented twenty-four per cent of the industry's capital investment. The total of bankrupt roads would have been catastrophically higher if it had not been for the Reconstruction Finance Corporation and the Public Works Administration, which together loaned the railroads seven hundred and thirty-eight million dollars.

In 1937 more than three billion dollars' worth of railroad bonds were in default of interest. This meant that investors were not being paid one hundred and fifteen million dollars of annual interest. One half of all railroad bonds were owned by national banks, mutual savings banks, and insurance companies, and in turn this meant that every investor, down to the humblest, had had his income shaved.

So much for the statistics, which quiver and bleed only when they are translated into the human tragedies, the misery and despair, the blighted neighborhoods, even the slow strangulation of entire cities like Altoona, Pennsylvania, a company town which has never recovered from the mortal slash of *fifty-*

170

*six per cent* made in the payroll of the Pennsylvania from 1929 to 1933.*

During the 1930s all sorts of physicians prescribed all sorts of nostrums for the disease that ailed the railroads. The net effect was futility with a tonic dash of farce.

Calvin Coolidge, Bernard Baruch, and Alfred E. Smith harmonized in a denunciation of competition and a proclamation that only compulsory consolidation into "a single national system" would save the railroads. Not so, said Frederick H. Prince, a Boston financier who specialized in railroad securities; consolidation should proceed voluntarily into seven systems—two eastern, two southern, three western—and would result in savings of seven hundred and forty-three million dollars. Not so, said Joseph B. Eastman, who had been named Federal Coordinator of Transportation by President Roosevelt; the savings would be less than two hundred and twenty millions, and the disappearance of competition would prove calamitous; much waste could, however, surely be avoided if the railroads would agree to use joint terminals and to pool their equipment. Not so, chorused management and labor, the one jealous of

---

*General Atterbury also suffered in order that the Pennsylvania might maintain its proud record of payment of dividends: his annual salary dropped from $106,000 to $60,000. But the men in the Pennsylvania's shops, members of company unions which had signed sweetheart contracts with the company, never forgave or forgot the sixty-seven thousand men and women fired outright by 1933, or the many months when those who had survived were granted only two or three days of work, or the way in which skilled molders and machinists were paid only a common laborer's wage, or the technique by which skilled artisans were made to bid against each other for the privilege of being employed to do piecework.

The Pennsylvania was, during the Great Depression, easily the most hated railroad and General Atterbury the most hated railroad executive. When Atterbury died in 1935, the men of the Pennsylvania shared a black and bitter joke:

His coffin, they said, was being carried down the aisle of the Episcopal cathedral when suddenly the lid snapped up, the eyes of the corpse glared at the eight pallbearers, its mouth snarled, "Lay off four of these men," and the lid slammed down again.

It was not until 1947 that the American Federation of Labor began to get a toehold in the shops of the Pennsylvania Railroad.

171

competitive advantages, the other fearing loss of even more jobs. Well, then, said Eastman, if the railroads won't voluntarily undertake economies, the government should form a United States Railway Corporation which, by flexing the federal muscle of eminent domain and issuing debenture bonds guaranteed by the federal treasury, would take the railroads over and acquire them, once, finally, and for all time. Yes, cried Senator Burton K. Wheeler, and he introduced a bill authorizing a federal corporation to acquire "any common or contract carrier of property or passengers for hire by any means of transportation." Hey! This meant not only railroads but also trucks, omnibuses, pipelines, barges, steamships—great heavens, what not? The entire transportation industry shuddered and gathered its strength for a collective onslaught upon the Seventy-Fourth Congress to defeat the Wheeler bill.

Instead, the Congress passed the Motor Carrier Act, which brought part of the trucking industry under the same sort of regulation that governed the railroads but left an even bigger part of it unregulated. (Here was doleful evidence of the low estate to which the railroads had fallen: their lobbyists, who once had swept all before them, were now less effective than the aggressive lobbyists for the truckers.) But regulation of the trucks made little difference to the plight of the railroads. The railroads were stuck with an archaic rate structure which, as the Commission pointed out, continued to develop "with no thought to the competitive agencies of transportation which now exist." Rather than seeking to increase their freight traffic by cutting their rates, the railroad operators asked the Commission for a general rate increase—a policy that directly encouraged the expansion of highway transport.

This odd behavior intrigued the editors of Fortune—it was, they suggested, like a lady standing on her head at a dinner party—and in April, 1938, they examined the men responsible for it. The average age of the presidents of the fourteen biggest railroads, they found, was sixty-two years. None of these executives had spent less than thirty-six years in the railroad business; their average experience of the business was forty-two

172

years; one man had spent fifty-one years in it. Most of them had attended either a second-rate college or none at all. Their average annual salary was fifty-seven thousand dollars. None of them owned stock in his own road. The composite profile suggested an aging fathead with a parochial point of view, a man who would have been startled to death by a fresh idea.

There was, however, one newcomer among the railroad bigwigs who could never have been accused of hostility to a new idea. Robert R. Young was a cheeky little gambler from Texas; he was not, to be sure, a president, but at forty-one he was scrambling fast to become the chairman of the board of a most profitable railroad, the Chesapeake & Ohio, and so he was an impudent refutation of the railroad maxim, "A man can't get to be a vice-president before he's got arthritis." Young's rise was instructive, showing that all a man needs to take over a railroad empire is a gallon of gall and one well-heeled friend.

At thirty-two, Young had got suddenly rich by being shrewd enough to go short on the market in October, 1929. Still in funds in 1933, he bought twenty thousand shares of the Alleghany Corporation, the principal holding company of the Van Sweringen railroads, and hung on to them, watchful. He watched with interest when Alleghany went into bankruptcy despite fifty-five million dollars loaned by the Reconstruction Finance Corporation, and when J. P. Morgan & Company took Alleghany over in default of loans made to the Van Sweringens Young was even more interested. On September 30, 1935, at a carefully arranged auction, J. P. Morgan & Company sold Alleghany (which controlled twenty-three thousand miles of railroad tracks) to George P. Ball, the glass-jar manufacturer of Muncie, Indiana, who was a friend of the Van Sweringens. The price was $2,803,000. Young was a most interested bystander. He wanted Alleghany, because whoever controlled Alleghany controlled the lucrative C&O.

Before long, Young learned that some Wall Street bankers and some executives of the General Motors Corporation were forming a syndicate to buy Alleghany. He hankered for a modest participation in this syndicate, but no sooner had he wedged his way in than he found he was being elbowed out. He made a hurried trip to Washington and, sure enough, all at once Senator Wheeler began to threaten an investigation of any deal by which General Motors might try to get into the railroad business. The syndicate obligingly collapsed, and Young promptly bobbed up with a friend, Allen P. Kirby, whose inherited bankroll was plump with profits from F. W. Woolworth's five-and-ten-cent stores. In 1937, Young and Kirby bought Alleghany from Ball for $6,375,000, only to find that, owing to the tangled complexities resulting from the collapse of the Van Sweringen empire, control of the company could under certain circumstances be exercised by the Guaranty Trust Company, a New York bank.*

Young was furious. He began to refer to "dambankers" as a southerner refers to "damyankees." He suspected that Ball had rigged the price of Alleghany's securities before selling, so that the dambankers might hold a continuing authority over the C&O. His control of the railroad might not yet be complete, but he could still operate it. In 1938 he did an unprecedented thing: he called for competitive bids from the dambankers on an issue of thirty million dollars' worth of C&O bonds. He was delighted to be able to award management of the issue to a Cleveland bank. For the first time a major railroad financing had been arranged by other than eastern bankers. (Six years later the Commission would tardily rule that all railroads must invite sealed competitive bids for their bond issues.) Young next turned his attention to George Ball and sued him for eight million dollars, alleging collusion with the dambankers on the price of Alleghany's stock. Ball eventually settled out of

*Nearly three fourths of Alleghany's common stock was held in trust as security for the company's long-term obligations—eighty-five million dollars' worth of bonds that would variously mature in 1944, 1949, and 1950. When Young and Kirby bought Alleghany, they also bought these obligations. The Guaranty Trust stood as trustee for the bondholders: so long as the debts were paid, the bankers were content; if, however, Alleghany's common stock fell below a certain point on the exchange, the bankers could vote the stock and control the company and the C&O as well.

174

court for four million dollars, including enough Alleghany stock to give Young and Kirby uncontested control of the C&O. Young was promptly elected chairman of the C&O's board and began to look around for new railroads to conquer.

At the very least, the appearance of this maverick promised that some of the fusty notions of the old-time railroad shell-backs would get a good shakeout. But in 1938 the condition of the industry was still pitiable: net railway operating income had been lower only in 1932; the hard-nosed truckers were grabbing business of all kinds, in all parts of the country; once again the railroads were on the verge of collapse. And once again the politicians groped toward a solution by compromise: in the spring of 1938 President Roosevelt appointed a Committee of Three (all members of the Interstate Commerce Commission) to study the situation, and they naturally urged that the Commission be authorized "to require a unification" of railroads; in the fall he appointed a Committee of Six (three railroad executives and three officers of railway labor unions) and they naturally recommended that "all initiative in the matter [be left] to the railroads themselves." By that time, with the railroads hauling only about three fifths of the nation's freight and their share of the total steadily dwindling, their future looked bleak indeed. But suddenly a Committee of One (Adolf Hitler) came to a terrible decision, and at once matters improved for the railroads.

As the war in Europe spread over the world, the struggle to kill more human beings more efficiently was reflected in a rising net railway operating income and in a gratifying increase in the rate of return on investment:

|  | Net Railway Operating Income | Rate of Return on Investment |
|---|---|---|
| 1938 | $ 372,874,000 | 1.62 per cent |
| 1939 | 588,829,000 | 2.56 |
| 1940 | 682,133,000 | 2.95 |
| 1941 | 998,256,000 | 4.30 |
| 1942 | 1,484,519,000 | 6.36 |

The railroads were even able to chalk up a gain in their share of the market: by 1943 they would be hauling more than seventy per cent of the freight and more than seventy-five per cent of the passengers. Happy days were here again; who could ask for anything more? To enhance their bliss, the railroad operators were never, during this war time, confronted with any nonsense about the nationalization of their companies.* They were, to be sure, marshaled, drilled, bureaucratized, overregulated, exhorted by beardless experts in political economy, prevented (unlike their lucky counterparts in other industries) from gouging excessive profits out of the public and the public treasury, and ordered to heel-and-toe by an Office of Defense Transportation which was directed by their ancient critic and censurer, Joseph B. Eastman; but at least they were healthy, they were breathing, they stood a chance of justifying their exuberant salaries to their stockholders.

Meanwhile, in the Transportation Act of 1940, the Congress had got around to declaring and defining a national transportation policy, no less. It was

> to provide for fair and impartial regulation of all modes of transportation . . . , so administered as to recognize and preserve the inherent advantages of each; to promote safe, adequate, economical, and efficient service and foster sound economic conditions in transportation . . . , to encourage the establishment and maintenance of reasonable charges for transportation services, without unjust discrimination, undue preferences or advantages, or unfair or destructive competitive practices . . . ; and to encourage fair wages and equitable working conditions— all to the end of developing, coordinating, and preserving a national transportation system by water, highway, and rail. . . .

In theory, the Act empowered the Commission to regulate and control barges, steamships, tankers, and other vessels in do-

*In December, 1943, President Roosevelt actually issued an executive order that brought all railroad companies under federal control. But the order was canceled when the companies were able to settle their squabbles with the labor unions.

mestic commerce just as it regulated and controlled railroads, pipelines, trucks, and buses. In fact, however, lobbyists for various industries had taken aim on the Act and shot it full of so many gaping holes (called "exemptions") that not more than ten per cent of water carriage was effectively regulated. In theory, the Act instructed the Commission to make rates for all carriers with an even hand, considering the effect of those rates only on "the carrier or carriers for which the rates are prescribed," and here the intent of the Congress was clear: the railroads, which for a century had victimized the public, now actually needed protection from the more ingenious or more efficient modes of transportation that had been developed. All modes would be regulated but, as the Senate Committee on Interstate Commerce had warned, in urgent italics: *If one or more forms of transportation cannot survive under equality of regulations, they are not entitled to survive.*" But in fact the trucking industry and the water carriers persevered, as why should they not have done, in every conceivable competitive practice, persistently undermining the railroads' right of way.

So long as the war lasted, the railroad managers could not have cared less. Before them, they liked to imagine, there stretched a limitless future in which their net operating income would soar effortlessly beyond the billion-dollar mark, perhaps beyond the two-billion-dollar mark; in their euphoria they totted up the movement of troops (more than ninety-seven per cent of them by train), the movement of army equipment and supplies (more than ninety per cent of it by train), and the movement of naval equipment and supplies (nearly ninety per cent of it by train). They were proud of themselves.

But after the war—thud.

# 12

---

*Revenues decline after the war. Robert R. Young bobs up:*
*will he save the passenger service? The railroads fight the*
*truckers. Revenues continue to shrink. The Pennsylvania and*
*the New York Central announce plans to merge. Help from*
*the Congress: the Transportation Act of 1958.*

---

THE GLUM FACT of the matter is that the railroad industry
began to display morbid symptoms even before the end of the
war. The railroads' share of the freight business, which was
more than seventy per cent in 1943, thereafter declined steadily, each and every year for the next twenty years, until it
amounted to less than forty-three per cent. Their share of the
paid passenger business slumped far more swiftly, from better
than seventy-five per cent in 1944 to well below twenty per
cent today; and it shows no signs of leveling off but, on the
contrary, seems to be headed straight toward absolute zero. (If
the traffic of passengers by private automobile were included
in the figures having to do with intercity travel, the railroads'
share would shrink to less than two per cent.)

Statistics like these are puzzling, especially during a time of
national growth and a time—interrupted, to be sure, by occasional recessions—of general prosperity. Are the railroads
merely struggling to contend with the problems that any erst-
while monopoly must contend with, when suddenly confronted by resourceful competitors? Are they governed by incompetent executives, men who in any other industry would
be ruthlessly shoved aside to make room for their betters, men

hagridden by tradition and rutted in outworn ways of doing business? Have the railroads gradually subsided into a morass of inefficiency, neglect, and slovenry, to be preserved from extinction only by the enforced subventions of the mutinous taxpayers, now and forever, world without end, Amen? Some shrewd observers insist that the railroads as now constituted are a cyclical industry, capable of producing substantial profits only in time of martial emergency, such as during the war in Korea or the war in Vietnam. As noted earlier, the railroad operators themselves prefer to blame the government, snarling that all would be well if the Commission would quit regulating them or if the Congress would quit subsidizing their rivals. But the questions still nag, and to answer them we must delve behind those dismal statistics that show how pitifully diminished is the share of the transportation business enjoyed by the railroads.

To begin with, a glance at the passenger traffic, but only a glance, since we shall examine the matter in some detail in a later chapter. For the moment, it will suffice to say that all the evidence shows that the most influential railroad pooh-bahs, the chairmen of the boards of directors, the presidents, and the vice-presidents in charge of operations and finance, had decided to dump this traffic many years before. Passenger service, to most railroad men, is a nuisance, an irritation, a running sore. It interferes with the potentially lucrative business of hauling freight. Freight is infinitely superior to passengers. Freight, since it is usually inanimate and invariably inarticulate, cannot complain about delays, stupidities, inconveniences, impudences of petty officials, discomforts and shabbinesses of railroad cars, filth, squalor of public facilities, breakdowns, derailments, wrecks—in short, the ordinary, day-to-day routine of the railroads. Freight makes money, passengers make headaches: there could be only one conclusion. It was a wrong conclusion, of course; but to dull-witted men it seemed right. Beginning as early as 1920, the presidents of the biggest railroads in the Official Region began to prune passenger trains from their schedules by the dozens and by the hundreds,

179

"and," as a contemporary journalist friendly to the railroads pointed out, "the running-times of many others have been so lengthened as to make riding upon them a dreary business indeed." At least as early as January, 1928, and very likely long before then, the presidents of the biggest eastern railroads discussed in detail how best they might get out of the passenger business. Downgrade it, they concluded; abandon lines and stations throughout the Eastern Region; if here came the automobiles and the motorbuses, retreat in good marching order; let there be no bloody, competitive combat; yield the field. Off to the left there, does some overzealous passenger agent sound his trumpet in the charge? Quell him forthwith. No panic; fight for every bridgehead suitable for freight traffic, every wharf and pier, every terminal, every foot of track over which there may be air rights to be exploited by some fly-by-night promoter of real estate; but show the white flag to any who may contend for the passenger business, for we don't want it, we despise it, we wish to expunge it from our books forever.

So throughout the 1930s, especially in the Official Region; so again after the War of 1939–1945, while a chorus of yelps and yips proceeded fortissimo from most railroad spokesmen about the so-called deficits accruing from the so-called passenger service.

South of the Potomac and west of the Mississippi there were perhaps a dozen railroad companies that persisted in promoting their passenger trains, but in the east only one important railroad executive dissented from the prevailing policy of defeatism. Vigorously and with some wit, Robert R. Young of the Chesapeake & Ohio lambasted all the old inherited notions about the passenger business. He placed full-page advertisements in the newspapers to taunt us all on the inconveniences of travel in our proud republic ("A Hog Can Cross the Country Without Changing Trains—But You Can't"), and his campaign actually forced a few companies to experiment, briefly and at least two generations too late, with uninterrupted service between New York and Houston, even between New York and San Francisco or Los Angeles. Young was derisive about the

180

antiquated rolling stock the railroads used to discourage their potential passengers. Pullman sleeping cars were, in his pungent phrase, "rolling tenements." He maintained the railroads could double the passenger revenues they had rung up in their palmiest days if they would only put on modern equipment of decent design, keep it clean, move it quickly, and merchandise it with some imagination. He was *for* giving school children free excursions on the railroads, *against* having to wait for seats in the dining car, *for* new passenger cars every seven years, *against* the practice of locking toilets while a train stood in the station, *for* lavish expenditures on advertising, *for* the sale of tickets aboard trains, *for* carrying passengers' automobiles on flatcars hitched to passenger trains. In short, Young approached the problems of passengers like a prospective passenger, and he whooped up a vast enthusiasm on the part of the public and a vast and acid indigestion on the part of the paleologues of the Association of American Railroads.

In the fall of 1946 Young pulled the C&O out of that august Association, denouncing it for having "lobbied for three years to exempt [the railroad industry] from the antitrust laws when its money and energies might better have gone to improve equipment and service. . . ." He was already testing his heretical ideas with a new streamlined train between Detroit and Grand Rapids, which had dramatically reversed the downward plunge of passenger revenues by carrying seventy-six per cent *more* passengers than its tacky predecessor of 1945. He had, moreover, doubled his bets by spending thirty-three million dollars to replace the whole fleet of C&O passenger cars. There was a glint in his pale blue eyes. He was going to revitalize the entire industry. Already he was planning his giant next step—to take over the New York Central.

For twenty-four years the Central's revenues and profits had been slipping steadily downgrade; in the late 1940s almost any of Young's arguments would have stirred the Central's stockholders and provoked them into a rebellious mood. To influential journalists, Young issued sardonic comments on the Central's slowpoke management. Why should the Central's

181

passenger service have eaten up fifty-five per cent of the system's train-miles, yet returned only twenty-five per cent of the system's revenues? Why shouldn't the Central pony up a trifling one hundred million dollars to replace its two thousand grimy, decrepit passenger cars and so offer a service that would attract new customers in the millions?

Just at that time Governor Thomas E. Dewey was wooing the voters with promises of a broad new turnpike between New York City and Buffalo. Might this possibly put a crimp in the Central's passenger business? Young was undaunted. He persisted in taunting the Central's management. How much of what he said was for real and how much was only a grandstand play is impossible to estimate. At any rate, after a sharp squabble over proxy votes, and no doubt assisted by the votes of those shareholders who yearned for an improved passenger service, Young grasped control of the New York Central in January, 1954.

Almost at once a remarkable thing happened: Young discovered the bogus passenger deficit and began to whimper about what it was doing to the Central's revenues.* Before long, Young was demanding that the Interstate Commerce Commission permit him to hike the Central's first-class fares up forty-five per cent and to rocket the Central's rates for commuters up a stratospherical three hundred and ninety per cent. To perdition with the passengers, and long live the freight traffic!

In this way, all hope for a decent passenger service in the Official Region was stomped to death. The only influential voice raised from within the industry on behalf of the passengers had changed its tune. Since early in 1954 no chief executive of an eastern railroad has uttered a peep to encourage either the commuter or the traveler from one city to another. On the contrary, the earnest effort has been to convince every commuter and every intercity passenger that he should drive his car, or take a bus, or fly. But, in any event, get lost, and the sooner the better.

*The so-called passenger deficit is examined in detail below, at pp. 246–249.

182

The sooner the passengers vanished entirely, the sooner the railroad men could concentrate all their attention on their freight traffic, an item that required that their intellectual powers be turned up to maximum amperage. On the one hand, the railroads were caught in a squeeze between rising costs and the often inconsistent, always frustrating regulations of the Interstate Commerce Commission; on the other hand, their share of the freight business steadily shriveled as the resourceful truckers moved in, and so their revenues were beginning to suffer from a chronic anemia.

What to do? To the canniest railroad strategists, the answer seemed clear: they must fight savagely, no holds barred, no quarter given, for a heftier share of the traffic; and meanwhile they must strive to shove the freight rates higher. Such a course appealed to most railroad executives. It was what they had always done and so, since what is traditional is always best, it must be right. The strategy meant that there would be two fields of battle: one out in the open, where the struggle would be conducted under the procedural rules of the Interstate Commerce Commission; the other clandestine, as if in a dark alley, a dirty fight in which the railroad men would jump the truckers from behind and slug them impartially with brass knucks, bung starters, and sap sticks.

According to the evidence (later presented in the U. S. District Court for the eastern district of Pennsylvania) the fight against the truckers was first discussed in May, 1949, by the chief executives of the Pennsylvania Railroad. Their scheme was to gather together the owners of automobiles and other groups of private citizens in organizations, innocent of aspect, which would holler for so heavy a burden of federal and state taxes on the truckers as to take all the profit out of the trucking business. (It is worth noting that Pennsylvania was then the only state that levied no tax on the real estate owned by railroads.) These proposed organizations would also whoop it up for other legislation inimical to the truckers, such as laws limiting the weight of the load a truck might haul. Needless to say, these organizations would be inspired by a natural and spontaneous loathing of the truckers on the part of the public; the railroads would have had nothing whatsoever to do with their creation.

This scheme the gentlemen of the Pennsylvania Railroad took to a conclave known as the Eastern Railroad Presidents Conference, where it was greeted with glad cries. Before long the scheme had been turned over to Carl Byoir & Associates, a firm skilled in the manufacture and the manipulation of public opinion. The Byoir outfit undertook to make the scheme work for a fee of $75,000 a year and expenses estimated at more than $350,000 a year. Four years later the Byoir expense account was much bigger, for the fight against the truckers had been joined by associations of western and southern railroad executives; the fight had spread across the nation, and it had grown ever dirtier and more dishonest.

The Byoir outfit created phony Associations of Automobile Owners and phony Citizens' Tax Leagues. It rigged "independent" surveys of public opinion. It recruited college professors whose prestige could be used to conceal all deceits and distortions. It subsidized "independent" journalists to write syndicated columns of political "news" which were in fact artful attacks on the trucking industry. It retained "independent" consultants in public administration and finance to analyze the use of highways and to show that revenues from highway users were insufficient for maintenance. Having carefully doctored the so-called research, the Byoir outfit spiced it with ersatz statistics about the truckers and peddled it to newspaper editors, to conferences of mayors, to associations of chiefs of police, to county supervisors, to organizations of farmers, of rural letter carriers, of all sorts of citizens.

The response was gratifying. In one state after another legislation was passed raising the truckers' fees for licenses, lowering the weight of the maximum permissible truck load, and stipulating mileage taxes on trucks.

All proceeded smoothly. Byoir agents were able to insinuate themselves into the Interregional Council on Highway Transportation, a group of public officials from fourteen states which, with the help of the federal Bureau of Public Roads, was conducting a technical study of a stretch of highway by deliberately subjecting it to extraordinary stresses. If the tests proved anything, they proved that a properly constructed concrete pavement would support indefinitely, without structural failure, trucks hauling more than seventy thousand pounds; but the Byoir agents skillfully distorted the technical findings and narrowed them down to one highly publicized and arrantly dishonest conclusion, to wit: that big trucks and only big trucks inevitably destroy highways.

The Byoir outfit—and of course its clients, the presidents of the eastern railroads—now had some boffo material which, thanks to Byoir's sly tactics, could be palmed off as if it had been guaranteed to be accurate by a respected federal bureau. How best to use it? In Ohio, a Byoir representative was palsy-walsy with the director of the Department of Highways and with the chief of the Department's Bureau of Public Relations; this intimacy won him easy access to the office of the governor, at that time the Hon. Frank J. Lausche. Before long Byoir's man had made such adroit use of his fake facts that the truckers were required to pay thirty per cent more for their fees. Copies of Governor Lausche's replies to those truckers who protested were in the Byoir office even before they reached the United States mails, and, to quote the smug comment of the Byoir agent, Lausche's replies "contained our poison." The agent was also able to persuade the Hon. Mr. Lausche that he should base his campaign for re-election in 1952 on a vigorous advocacy of a ton-mile tax on the truckers. In consequence, the hon. gentleman plugged the ton-mile tax in all but one of his campaign speeches, and always he based his so-called arguments on the gaudy nonsense supplied him by Byoir's agent. "Lausche's astonishing victory," a writer for The Cleveland Plain Dealer noted, "against the political tide, can be construed as an indorsement of his highway program." The Byoir agent had done his job so deftly that the truckers were obliged to jettison their charges that the Hon. Mr. Lausche's "bills were railroad inspired"—which of course they were.

Meanwhile in Pennsylvania Byoir's tainted facts had been used even more triumphantly. The commonwealth of Pennsylvania, squashed firmly under the thumb of the Pennsylvania Railroad, allowed on its highways no trucks with a gross weight of more than fifty thousand pounds. (In the states surrounding Pennsylvania, a gross weight of seventy-three thousand pounds was permitted; the lower limit in Pennsylvania forced long-haul truckers to haul their freight on expensive, roundabout routes and reserved to the Pennsylvania Railroad a lucrative traffic in shipments of steel from the mills around Pittsburgh.) Attempts by the truckers to persuade the legislature in Harrisburg to relax these limitations had failed in 1945 and again in 1947. In 1949 the Hon. James A. Duff, then governor, instructed the chairman of the legislative committee on highways to send to his desk no bill authorizing an increase in the permissible weight of truck loads. But by 1951 the truckers had decided the time had come to fight back, and truckers are likely to fare rather better in a brawl than, say, dry goods clerks or interior decorators. Later it would be alleged that the truckers began by bugging the room in the Biltmore Hotel, in New York City, where the Eastern Railroad Presidents Conference customarily held its meetings; however that may be, the truckers began to use techniques that remarkably paralleled those of the railroad gentry.* Nor, in Pennsylvania, did the truckers neglect their homework: they raised a vast sum to help elect the Hon. John S. Fine as governor, generous sums to help elect various key members of the legislature, and other substantial sums to buy time on radio and television stations and to buy space in all the most influential newspapers; they undertook some intensive lobbying in

*In the lengthy opinion he delivered after trying the suit that was later brought by the truckers against the eastern railroads and Carl Byoir & Associates, Judge Thomas J. Clary remarked: "There is no doubt that [the Pennsylvania truckers association] was at all times, through its officers, committees, and public relations director, fully aware of the continuing railroad campaign, particularly in Pennsylvania, to convince the public that the heavy truckers did not pay their proportionate share for road building and road maintenance."

Harrisburg. All this pressure was mounted to win passage of just one bill, nicknamed the Big Trucks Bill, which would permit the maximum gross weight of truck and load to be raised from fifty to sixty thousand pounds. The Byoir agents worked shrewdly and effectively and, on at least one occasion, in violation of the Federal Communications Act, to thwart the truckers, but the bill was nevertheless passed by big majorities of both houses of the legislature and sent to Governor Fine for his signature. The Hon. Mr. Fine temporized. The State Highway Department, he had been informed, was against the bill. Why? Its officials had been fed a stiff dose of the phony Byoir statistics, including those which had apparently been authorized by the Bureau of Public Roads. A few minutes before the bill would have automatically become law, the Hon. Mr. Fine vetoed it. "Veto of this bill," the Byoir account executive noted, smacking his lips, "meant that some $5,000,000 worth of freight was retained on the Pennsylvania Railroad, because the trucking limit was not raised." Who cared about a few hundred thousand dollars spent to buy the honor of a few public officials, the reputation of two or three college professors, and the conscience of one or two dozen press agents? The Pennsylvania Railroad had retained (and would retain until 1955) millions of dollars' worth of freight.

Governor Fine's veto was, for the truckers, the ultimate outrage. They brought suit against the Eastern Railroad Presidents Conference, two dozen eastern railroads, and Carl Byoir & Associates, alleging a conspiracy in violation of the Sherman and Clayton Antitrust Acts and seeking injunctive relief and compensation for damages sustained. Judge Thomas J. Clary of the U. S. District Court found for the plaintiffs. Judge Clary said, and the italics are his: "*It was the purpose and intent* of [the railroad men and the Byoir outfit] *to hurt the truckers in every way possible even though they secured no legislation; it was their purpose to restrict the activities of the truckers* in the long-haul industry *to the greatest extent possible,* and finally, if possible, *to drive them out of that segment of the entire transportation industry.*"

The Court of Appeals for the Third Circuit, one judge dissenting in part, sustained the judgment of the District Court.

The Supreme Court, while agreeing with the courts below that the campaign against the truckers was "vicious" and "reprehensible," nevertheless held that the campaign had not violated the Sherman Act. The judgment was therefore reversed.

What is more important, the suit and the trial of it ended the covert brawl between the railroad men and the truckers. Instead of slugging away at each other in a dark alley, they subsided into a sullen, suspicious truce, both parties tacitly agreeing that they must conduct their quarrels in public, with the Interstate Commerce Commission acting as referee, and even sulkily conceding that they might possibly be able to co-exist.

The hope of the railroads pooh-bahs—that they might throttle their competition and so conjure up the dulcet days when they had enjoyed a monopoly—had vanished, and they were still stuck with a whole complex of problems that must have seemed to them to have been deliberately designed to put a crimp in their net operating income. Their fixed charges (chiefly the interest on funded debt) were high, costs of labor and of materials were steadily rising, taxes took from revenues a billion-dollar bite every year, and the volume of their business steadily diminished.

So far it had not occurred to most railroad men that, if they improved their service, the shippers of freight and the passengers might once again throng their terminals and depots. To be sure, there were a few gestures toward better service: in 1952 Diesel locomotives for the first time outnumbered steam locomotives; and in 1954 the hauling of truck trailers on railroad flatcars was for the first time authorized by the Commission despite the doleful howls of the truckers, who protested that this piggyback service was a kind of carriage by motor vehicle which was illegal if undertaken by the railroads. But most railroad men were still mired in the old way of doing things and eyed anything new with suspicion.*

Another classic shortcut to a greater volume of business, of course, is to lower prices. The railroad men raised their prices. From 1945 to 1958 the railroad industry prayed the Interstate Commerce Commission to grant higher freight rates on no less than fifteen different occasions, and the compliant Commission duly approved increases that raised the cost of shipping freight by rail by more than seventy per cent.

And down went the railroads' share of the freight traffic, down from sixty-seven per cent in 1945 to forty-six per cent in 1958, down, steadily down.

Now this policy of raising their rates, which seems so wilfully, even suicidally, stupid, was at least to some extent forced on the railroad managers by the infuriating inconsistencies of the Commission's decisions on competitive rate making. (The commissioners, for their part, could retort that they were merely administering a statute, and that all complaints should properly be addressed to the Congress.) To most railroad managers even the concept of competitive rate making was strange, new, and therefore somehow dismaying. In the good old golden days of monopoly, the railroad rate had been compounded by a kind of magic. Most of the ingredients were costs, simple enough to compute—the cost of capital investment in equipment and of maintenance of equipment, the cost of handling and switching freight at a terminal, the cost of hauling it from one terminal to another, the cost of returning empty freight cars (always charged to a one-way haul), the liability for loss or damage, and so on—but the most important ingredient was not a cost at all but a mystique disguised as a theory. In brief, the theory required that each

*Judge Clary had noted that "the greater flexibility of the truck and the speedier delivery of goods were elements in the competitive market which the railroads might themselves have attempted to meet by the use of trucks or otherwise. . . . However, the record in this case is barren of any attempt on the part of the railroads to adjust their thinking and their actions to meet this definite threat to a segment of business theretofore enjoyed by them."

189

commodity be charged as much as it could pay, so that all commodities might circulate as freely as possible. In other words: charge whatever the traffic would bear. (Railroad executives prefer to describe this mystique as "the value of the commodity" or, even better, "the value of the service.") The greater the value of the commodity, the higher its rate, and the more artificial the rate structure. How artificial that structure came to be can be gauged from a refinement in the way it was described. Around the turn of the century, Professor William Z. Ripley of Harvard termed it "a house of cards"; by 1936 a writer for the magazine Fortune called it "a patched and gum-stuck house of cards in which the railroads dare not breathe except in careful unison." It took very little huffing and puffing for competition to blow this crazy house down: the truckers simply walked off with the more valuable commodities (chiefly manufactured products) by quoting the shippers a realistic rate based on the cost of the transportation, after which the railroad managers were obliged to ponder the perplexing question of competitive rate making. Costs would play a determining part in their new rates; the Commission had made it clear that any new minimum rate would have to be compensatory—that is, it would have to equal or exceed "out-of-pocket costs" and "fully distributed costs."*

Nobody who is hot after a fat profit wishes his pursuit to be

*The terms are those used by the Commission. In an attempt to clarify meaning, the Commission has stated: "Fully distributed costs based on the out-of-pocket costs plus a revenue-ton and revenue ton-mile distribution of the constant costs, including deficits, indicate the revenue necessary to a fair return on the traffic, disregarding ability to pay." (New Automobiles in Interstate Commerce, 259 I.C.C. 475, at p. 513.) All clear now?

The whole business of cost analysis has been elaborated into what seems, to an innocent bystander, the densest opacity. See, for example, "The Role of Cost in the Minimum Pricing of Railroad Services," by Burton N. Behling and nine other distinguished economists, in The Journal of Business of the University of Chicago, Vol. XXXV, No. 4, October, 1962. This brief monograph alludes to no less than twenty-five different kinds of costs, including (hold on, now) incremental costs, fixed costs, common costs, joint costs, variable costs, traceable and non-traceable costs, economic costs, social costs, allocable and unallocable

190

regulated. The general hell of competitive rate making was that the Congress, by way of the Commission, required the railroads, most of the truckers, some of the carriers on inland waterways, the owners of pipelines, and the freight forwarders to run an ungainly kind of obstacle race in which the rules for each runner differed. For the railroads, the particular hell of competitive rate making was that the Commission, in arbitrary and capricious fashion, too often decided that a low railroad tariff, while fully compensatory, would take too much business away from the truckers or the water carriers and so ordered the railroads to maintain a higher and noncompetitive rate. Throughout the 1940s and well into the 1950s the Commission behaved like a kind of benevolent czar, graciously willing to confer upon each mode of transportation a fair and equal share of the traffic but conspicuously unable to define what was a fair share. (One congressman, who presumably knew his way around a race track, referred to the Commission as "a giant handicapper.") Despite the obvious inherent advantages of economy and efficiency they could offer, the railroads were discouraged by the Commission from asserting those advantages and on occasion were even forbidden to assert them.

The situation was not improved by the fact that the railroads were (and are) far more straitly regulated than their competitors. The tariff on everything hauled by a railroad was (and is) subject to challenge or protest but, thanks to gaping loopholes in the Interstate Commerce Act, the truckers could haul many kinds of agricultural produce without let or hindrance and, by the same dispensation, the water carriers could as freely haul the so-called bulk commodities—grain, coal, ore, sand, gravel, stone, petroleum, chemicals, and such. By the most conservative estimate, these exemptions accounted

---

costs, short-run and long-run costs, forward-looking costs, constant costs, unit costs, and "so-called 'full costs.'" Incremental joint costs, we are told, are not traceable; common costs which are incremental are traceable in principle, although maybe not in practice.

No wonder the old-time railroad executive was bewildered.

191

for *more than half* of the freight of the nation.

And so, faced with a dwindling share of traffic in an expanding market, thwarted by the Commission from competing for a larger share, blind to the possibilities of offering their shippers and passengers a better service, most of the railroad executives yielded to the luxury of self-pity. They could think of only one way to cover their rising costs. In 1957 they asked for and were granted the next to last of fifteen general rate increases.

Meanwhile, and with considerable vigor, their lobbyists in Washington had been fighting for legislation that would enable them to compete with their rivals, if not with an even hand, at least on a more reasonable basis. These men smoothly pleaded the urgency of the railroads' plight, arguing that it amounted to a crisis in transportation. They claimed that the railroads were in a financial pickle that grew steadily more sour. Look, they said, at the balance sheet of the industry: here was the proof: the rate of return on investment was less than four per cent in 1956, and by 1958 it would be less than three per cent. At this rate, where were the railroads to find new capital? At this rate, what would become of the railroads? The bleating of the railroad executives came to be as piteous as it had been back in the worst years of the Great Depression. Betimes their skillful publicists flourished the banner of free enterprise, warning the more impressionable congressmen of such deadfalls as government ownership, nationalization, socialism, and disaster for the national defense.

Was the matter really so grave? The truckers scoffed at the idea. After inspecting the railroad industry's consolidated balance sheet, they pointed to other entries—the gross revenues and the net income—which indicated that during the 1950s the railroads were clearing a profit of better than seven cents on the dollar. This may not have been a spectacular showing (back in 1929 the profit had been almost twenty cents on the dollar), but it was almost as good a showing as General Motors or United States Steel could boast for the same period. Moreover, the truckers argued that the low rate of return on railroad investment meant, in fact, that the railroads were stuck with a huge investment in an unprofitable plant; and with this argument even the most pigheaded railroad executive was bound to agree.

The truth is that, while most railroads were doing fairly well, a few were not earning even enough to cover their fixed charges; and these sickly few included the two most influential railway companies in the country, the Pennsylvania and the New York Central. When these two began to howl, they could make it seem that the whole industry was gurgling its death rattle.*

The Pennsylvania and the Central had both begun to taste the bile in 1954, a year of business recession:

|  | Net Railway Operating Income | Fixed Charges and Other Deductions |
|---|---|---|
| Pennsylvania | $48,061,181 | $49,438,340 |
| New York Central | 33,034,962 | 47,325,402 |

but they had alike been spared the indignity of a deficit by their income from other than railway operations—chiefly the rents from real estate given them, decades before, by right of eminent domain. In that year, 1954, Robert R. Young had taken control of the Central, proffering himself as the vigorous Napoleon whose financial wizardry would revive the senile railroad business. Sure enough, in 1955 the Central's net railway operating income was most handsome; indeed, there was none better in the industry. But thereafter Young proved conspicuously unable to keep the Central from a steep downgrade:

|  | Net Railway Operating Income | Earnings per Share |
|---|---|---|
| 1955 | $73,897,427 | $8.03 |
| 1956 | 58,320,739 | 6.02 |
| 1957 | 29,532,256 | 1.02 |

In 1956 the Central's slim dividends were supplemented by a

*The other big railroads that failed at least twice, during the 1950s and the early 1960s, to earn enough to meet their fixed charges were: the New York, New Haven & Hartford (which went into bankruptcy in distribution of the shares of a subsidiary, the United States Freight Company. (Concerning this interesting transaction, there will be more in a moment.) In 1957 the Central's dividends amounted to one dollar per share in cash, to which were later added some shares of the Reading, taken from the Central's capacious treasury.

In August, 1957, for the first time since Young had taken control, the Central lapsed into the red.

The Pennsylvania was in almost as distressing shape, and that fall its president, James M. Symes, made it his business to talk to Young. On November 1, spokesmen for the two companies announced that studies were under way, "looking toward a possible merger into a consolidated system."

There could have been no more dramatic confirmation of the low estate to which the railroad industry had fallen. The Pennsylvania and the Central had always been among the top three or four on any list of the richest and most powerful railroad companies in the country; for a century they had been the bitterest of rivals; each knew the other only as a mortal enemy; and now they spoke sweetly of marriage? The shotgun was their sudden impoverishment.

On Monday, January 20, 1958, the directors of the Central, meeting in Young's palatial shebang in Palm Beach, Florida, voted to skip the dividend due in March because of "the currently depressed national economy, which, together with long-standing industry problems, has led to a virtual crisis for the railroads."

On Saturday, January 25, Young shot and killed himself. A spokesman for the Central denied that there was any connection between the suicide and the Central's financial woes, and almost certainly he was right; but for those who recalled Young's illusory ambitions the coincidence seemed overwhelm-

1961); the Chicago & North Western; the Erie and the Delaware, Lackawanna & Western (which were consolidated in 1960); the Baltimore & Ohio; the Chicago, Milwaukee, St. Paul & Pacific; and the Northern Pacific.
Note that this list includes all four of the big eastern trunk lines.

ing evidence of cause and effect.

The affairs of the Pennsylvania and the Central continued to deteriorate with an astonishing rapidity. For 1958:

|  | Net Railway Operating Income | Non-Railway Net Income | Net Income After Fixed Charges and Taxes |
| --- | --- | --- | --- |
| Pennsylvania | $11,738,011 | $37,229,364 | $3,544,073 |
| New York Central | $11,824,179 | $37,469,980 | $4,050,995 |

Never had two great corporations lost so much business so fast. Already the Pennsylvania was in the process of firing twenty per cent of its employees, and the Central's layoffs cut almost as deep; less money was being spent on capital improvements; even executive salaries were being shaved by ten per cent. Was all this the result, or the cause, of still another business recession? At all events, the chairmen of the two congressional committees charged with supervision of the country's commerce found it necessary to schedule hearings on the plight of the railroads. The Senate's committee later reported that "not only were the railroads being adversely affected by the business recession which was then appearing, but . . . the sickness of the railroads was contributing greatly to the deepening recession. . . ."

After taking testimony for several weeks, the committee concluded that the reasons for the cramps and clonic spasms afflicting the railroad industry were four:

1. The "development of newer methods of transportation that offer intense competition to the railroads." The committee had in mind not only the other common carriers, like the truckers; they were also thinking of the hundreds of shippers who had decided, in the face of rising railroad rates, to buy and operate their own fleets of trucks, free of state and federal regulation. "The enormous growth of commercial private carriage of property by motor vehicle in recent years, resulting as it has in a continuing erosion of huge volumes of traffic that would otherwise be available for transportation by public

195

carriers, is a serious problem for the railroads and other common carriers."

2. "Government assistance offered to the railroads' competitors." Here the committee could point to the vast annual expenditures—from the public purse—for highways, for airfields, for direct subsidy of small airlines, for maintenance of inland waterways, and so on.

3. "Over-regulation." Here of course the accusing finger stabbed at the Interstate Commerce Commission and at the various state regulatory agencies. These bodies, said the committee, "dictate to the railroads, usually under laws and procedures that are ancient and outmoded."

4. The wretched incompetence of railway management. "There has been a failure," the committee scolded, "to recognize changing conditions, times, and tastes. A failure to compete aggressively for business by use of modernized equipment, by adjustments in plant and financial structures, as well as failure to adjust rates to compete effectively for traffic."

To this last point, the House committee added a hearty amen, noting that the railroad industry afforded "a picture of obsolete equipment, nineteenth century economics, and antiquated thinking—all detrimental to the economy and dangerous to the defense of the country."

What the Congress could most effectively do about the plight of the railroads, it did. A paragraph was added to the rule of rate making, encouraging the railroads to publish competitive rates and instructing the Commission to consistently permit each carrier to assert its inherent advantages, whether of service or cost.*

*The amending paragraph, section 15a (3) of part I of the Interstate Commerce Act, provides:

In a proceeding involving competition between carriers of different modes of transportation subject to this Act, the Commission, in determining whether a rate is lower than a reasonable minimum rate, shall consider the facts and circumstances attending the movement of the traffic by the carrier or carriers to which the rate is applicable. Rates of a carrier shall not be held up to a particular level to protect the traffic of any other mode of transportation, giving

But still, from 1958 through 1961, every railroad indicator pointed down. Gross revenues: down. Ton-miles of freight: down. Share of freight traffic: down. Passenger-miles: down. Share of passenger traffic: down. Net railway operating income: down. Rate of return on net property investment: down, down below two per cent in 1961. Net income: down.

What was to be done to keep the railroads from plunging into oblivion? The Senate Committee on Interstate Commerce called for another study of national transportation policies.

---

due consideration to the objectives of the national transportation policy declared in this Act.

This prose is a fair example of what lawyers have to write, who are aware that powerful interests will soon be tugging at every word and phrase in an effort to prove that the paragraph means what they want it to mean. Did the paragraph mean that the railroads might make lower, competitive rates? Yes, said the railroads. No, said the truckers and the coastwise water carriers. Yes, said the Supreme Court on April 22, 1963, four years, eight months, and ten days after the paragraph had been enacted into law. Did that end the matter? Of course not. It will never end, so long as there are new cases to test, new "facts and circumstances" to adduce, and fresh legal talents to be hired by greedy litigants.

# 13

An improved freight service. Piggyback, auto-rack cars, Big John hoppers, unit trains. More mergers. Plot and counter-plot. Commissioner Tucker and the much-neglected public interest.

EVEN AS THE SENATE'S study group was toiling away at its report (which would eventually fill seven hundred and thirty-two printed pages and then be filed away and forgotten), the railroad industry was being startled by timid hints of change. Such a phenomenon seemed a contradiction in terms. What! *Change* in the *railroad* industry? It was so staggering an idea that the industry's press agents doubted the public would credit it; to cushion the shock, they began to talk of a "new breed" of railroad managers, as though an eccentric biological explosion had spontaneously produced a group of mutants wholly unrelated to the past.

In truth, there *was* something new: a realization that the railroads simply had to supply better service.

Traditionally, service had meant leaving a forty-foot boxcar on a siding and letting the shipper figure out how to pack it with his freight. Or maybe the shipper wanted a flatcar, or a hopper car. In any case, as like as not what he got would be obsolete or unsuitable, and almost certainly it would be dirty and in need of repairs. In 1958 the chances were three in four that a freight car, any freight car, would be at least ten years old, two in five that it would be at least twenty years old, and one in five that it would be a decrepit antique at least thirty

198

years old. Every shipper was discouraged, if not actually estopped, from any converse with the manufacturers of freight equipment, for who knew what wildly expensive notions might not be hatched? And what railroad company was so foolish as to spend capital funds on custom-built equipment? In the event, most shippers developed their own private carriage or harkened to the seductive sales pitch of the truckers, who were full of bright ideas about new equipment.

But around 1958 the industry began to sense a tremulous ferment, an exquisite itch. It derived, no doubt, from the revised rule of rate making, which encouraged the masters of the railroads to lower their rates and so to dream of an expanding traffic. Here and there a railroad executive could be found wondering whether his company's service might not somehow be improved. More often the executive found himself being shoved toward this bizarre decision by an impatient shipper. Of all the shippers, the most impatient and the most imaginative was the late Morris Forgash, a soft-spoken, stocky little man who was the president of the United States Freight Company.

Forgash was a freight forwarder—that is, a man who gathers up the small consignments of various shippers and consolidates them into carload lots, finding his profit in the difference between what he pays the carrier for a full carload and what he charges the shippers for fractions of it. To the railroad pooh-bahs a freight forwarder had traditionally been a kind of peddler; a huckster who saved them the nuisance of picking up, hauling, and unloading small shipments; a humble creature who tagged along after them, hippety-hop, like a sparrow after a horse's droppings, ever anxious to please, never daring to displease. So until the 1930s; but with the advent of the truckers the freight forwarder was able to expand, using the trucks for his short hauls and the rails for his long, and so in effect coordinating the two modes of transportation. In 1942 the Congress, impressed by the growth of freight forwarding, had required its regulation by the Interstate Commerce Commission. At that time the United States Freight Company, a

199

holding company, owned a dozen subsidiaries which, taken together, comprised the biggest freight-forwarding outfit in the world. But U. S. Freight in turn was in thrall to the New York Central, which controlled its stock through still another holding company; as a consequence, Forgash was stuck with the job of filling the Central's boxcars and his annual net income was stuck at less than two million dollars.

In 1956, Robert R. Young of the New York Central, desiring to keep his shareholders happy, found it expedient to distribute 295,000 shares of the stock of U. S. Freight as a dividend. Forgash at once got U. S. Freight to buy from the Central the rest of its stock—150,000 shares—and so won its independence.

Forgash was then free to show the railroad men how they might expand their business. He had been pondering the concept of freight by piggyback—that is, the hauling of truck trailers or similar containers on flatcars. In 1957 this service, still primitive, took two forms:

*Plan I.* The railroad moved trailers owned by truckers, carrying freight solicited by truckers and billed by truckers at truckers' rates. In effect, the railroad acted as a substitute for the highway.

*Plan II.* The railroad moved its own trailers or containers on its own flatcars, carrying freight for which the various complex railroad rates were charged. In effect, the railroad substituted a trailer for a boxcar.

By the end of 1957, fifty-seven railroads offered the service, but equipment was sketchy and impromptu; since each road had its own half-baked idea as to how the trailers should be loaded and held fast, interchange of traffic between roads led to lengthy, costly snarls. The one effort to bring order from this chaos was by the Trailer Train Company, a co-operative venture spawned by the Pennsylvania and boasting, as its owner-members, an inconsequential nine railroad companies.

Piggybacking was, clearly, an inauspicious business. Yet Forgash had a scheme to transform this business so that it would revive the railroads and make of them once again a growth industry, a scheme so simple, so elegant, that it was

200

well beyond the powerful minds of the railroad magnificoes. Swiftly raising some cash by an issue of new stock, Forgash bought hundreds of forty-foot trailers and the tractors to pull them; simultaneously he leased more than two hundred specially designed flatcars that would each accommodate two of his trailers. Thus primed, he entered into negotiations with the railroads.

The railroad experts on traffic and rate making had their heads crammed with all the ancient and arcane intricacies— the value of the freight, its bulk, its weight, its classification; the liability of the carrier for loss or pilferage; the cost of returning empty cars; the cost of handling freight at the terminals and so on—but Forgash brushed aside this baroque edifice of nineteenth-century mythology. He wanted to know only one thing: how much would he be charged to ship two of his trailers on a flatcar? He was given two rates: fifty cents a mile if he owned only the trailers, forty-two cents a mile if he supplied his own flatcar as well. The tariffs were hedged about with cautious conditions: if the loaded trailers weighed more than so much, the rates went up; and the freight could not be limited to one commodity, lest the railroads be priced out of their precious bulk loads. These provisos were, however, so much spinach. The fact was that, for the first time since away back of beyond, the railroads were selling transportation, pure and simple. The cost of transportation, for carrier and shipper alike, had been stripped to its essentials. Two new forms of piggybacking had suddenly been born:

*Plan III.* On flatcars furnished by the railroads, any shipper could have any freight hauled in his own trailers at unprecedentedly low rates and could take his freight to and from the railhead on his own trucks.

*Plan IV.* On his own flatcar, any shipper could have any freight hauled in his own trailers at still lower rates and, with his own trucks, move his cargo door to door.

Here was a new, bold, simple, elegant system of pricing transportation, based only on the cost of line haul—that is, the cost of moving so many cubic feet of loaded space so many miles from here to there. The impact on the industry of these two new plans was immediate and stunning. Companies that had been planning to engage in private carriage began instead to piggyback their goods according to Plan III. Other companies switched from long-haul truckers back to the railroads.* The short-haul truckers—those who operated within, say, five hundred miles of a railroad terminal—rejoiced, for they perceived that piggyback would bring them a great volume of business; but the long-haul truckers howled bloody murder and began to fight Forgash's rates before the Commission, in the courts, and on Capitol Hill. Forgash smiled and tended to his knitting.

In 1957 the speediest cross-country freight service took seven days, but in July, 1958, Forgash's U. S. Freight Company dispatched the first piggyback train from New York to Los Angeles in six, and by 1959 he had shaved the time to five days and his companies were the railroads' most important customers.

Some of the railroad men who had watched this bravura performance, eyes apop, saw something sinister in it. Forgash, they said, had undermined the whole rate structure, and they feared malign, perhaps bolshevik, consequences. A few of the shrewder brethren, however, glimpsed in Plan III a splendid opportunity for hanky-panky. Reaching far back into the storehouse of their memories, they brought forth that ancient device, the rebate, and offered it to favored shippers, in violation of the Elkins Act of 1903. (Under Plan III, the shipper properly receives only ramp-to-ramp rail transportation. The criminal procedure was the loading or unloading of trailers either at no cost to the shipper or at a negotiated price.) In Decem-

*As an example of the first type, the Interstate Commerce Commission has cited the Monsanto Chemical Company; of the second, the Eastman Kodak Company. These companies were, the Commission stated, "typical of many others." The Commission further reported: "There can be little doubt that piggybacking has been a decisive factor in returning to the railroads a substantial volume of traffic that previously had been moving by other modes of transportation, private and for-hire." (See 322 I.C.C. 307–308.)

ber, 1961, the B&O and the Erie-Lackawanna each pleaded *nolo contendere* to criminal informations alleging such wrongful behavior; each company was fined one thousand dollars. The Pennsylvania, the Burlington, and the Santa Fe were similarly charged, but the charges were dismissed at the request of the United States attorney, under circumstances that left the Commission puzzled as to how far a railroad might go in making private arrangements with a shipper for such incidental services.

One thing was certain: piggyback, thanks chiefly to Plan III, was prospering. The member-owners of the Trailer Train Company would soon comprise forty Class I railroads (operating more than nine tenths of the country's line-haul track) and one freight forwarder (the U. S. Freight Company); already in sight was the time when two million trailers a year would be hauled on flatcars; and two examiners, assigned by the Commission to study regulation of piggyback, could report: "The bounds of this service and its total effect on transportation are as wide and as long as the imagination of the men who are providing this service to the nation."

If the examiners had Morris Forgash in mind, what they meant was that the bounds of piggyback were limitless.

Other improvements in railroad freight service were belatedly introduced during the early 1960s. Of these, perhaps the most conspicuous were the auto-rack car, the so-called Big John hopper car, and the so-called unit train. To the truckers, the bargemen, and the operators of pipelines, these very tardy and very modest betterments were hideous instruments contrived by the Prince of Darkness, and they set up against them a fearful outcry which has not yet entirely abated and probably never will.

The auto-rack car inflamed especially the truckers. Once, long ago, the railroads had hauled nearly all the new automobiles, three or four to the boxcar, and they had soaked General Motors more than ninety dollars apiece to ship them from Detroit to New York. Then the truckers developed trailers that could haul automobiles faster and cheaper and

203

door to door. The railroads' press agents keened about the danger to the public of these big rigs on the highways, and probably they *were* dangerous, but they were also profitable, and so they kept on rolling, with some of James R. Hoffa's pals collaring a good piece of the business. By 1959 the truckers had cut their rates so efficiently that they were hauling eighty-eight per cent of automobile production.

After many long years of this legalized highway robbery, some railroad executive, less dimwitted than his fellows, finally thought of mounting the automobile trailers on flatcars and so showed Detroit that the railroads could haul them even cheaper and faster. Meanwhile, agents of the Santa Fe and the St. Louis-San Francisco had happened to notice that the European railroads (despised by all one-hundred-per-cent Americans because they are nationalized) had developed an apparatus of racks that made it possible to haul twelve automobiles on one flatcar. When the American railroads adapted the device and published competitive tariffs, the truckers at once began to howl that the competition was destructive and therefore un-American. The Congress was flooded with mail from truck drivers pleading certain unemployment and from trucking bosses warning of their imminent bankruptcy. James Hoffa, the *fons et origo* of this deluge, flatly predicted the extinction of an entire industry. Nothing so dire has happened, but the railroads, which in 1959 had hauled less than eight per cent of the new automobiles, had by 1966 recaptured nearly half the traffic—all thanks to their sixteen thousand new double-deck and triple-deck rack cars.*

The Big John, a monstrous covered hopper car made of aluminum and designed to carry more than one hundred tons of grain, went into service on the Southern Railway System in 1961 and promptly shot off as many sparks as a Catherine

---

*The most spectacular instance of this railroad resurgence is afforded by the New York Central. Once the world's largest auto carrier, by 1960 the Central had lost almost all such traffic. But in 1966 the Central was back on top with a remarkable record of having hauled *more than two million* new automobiles in the year.

wheel. Some of those sparks highlighted the dubious practices of the unregulated, long-haul, gypsy truckers; some dully reflected the delinquencies of the more conservative railroad operators; some glared down on the incredibly frustrating behavior of the Interstate Commerce Commission; and what few were left bedazzled the reputation of the president of the Southern Railway, Dennis W. "Bill" Brosnan, a hard-working, hardhanded, tough-minded Georgian who is considered a traitor by those railroad men whose minds are still mired in the Mesozoic ooze.

Brosnan is a very representative example of the so-called "new breed." He is said to be "unrailroadlike," to insist upon the hiring of assistants who will not "think railroad," to shun whatever is traditional in railroading; and so he is duly adored by the industry's Young Turks. All this blather to one side, what has chiefly lifted Brosnan from the ruck is his remarkable zeal for snatching freight traffic from any and all competitors in the southeastern states crisscrossed by the Southern's 10,400 miles of track.

Beginning around 1955, officials of the Southern noticed a heavy movement of grain from the midwest into the southeast, transported by unregulated long-haul truckers. Investigation showed that these truckers typically hauled exempt commodities—fruit and vegetables—into the midwest and then, to provide themselves with what is called a backhaul, i.e., a remunerative return trip, fetched back grain at very low rates, sometimes no more than the cost of their gasoline. By 1960 this gypsy traffic amounted to some six million tons, and the Southern was hurting. "It was as bad," said Brosnan, "as losing your wallet and not even knowing you'd lost it." Much more grain was being cheaply moved on barges.

After a careful analysis of costs, the Southern spent thirteen million dollars to build five hundred enormous hopper cars, the Big Johns. In July, 1961, the Southern published tariffs for moving grain in multiple-car lots that cut the shipping costs by sixty per cent. The legal battle that followed involved the Southern Governors Conference; the Southeastern Association of Railroad and Utilities Commissioners; the common-wealths of Kentucky and Virginia and the states of Alabama, Georgia, Mississippi, North Carolina, and South Carolina; the Department of Agriculture; the Department of Justice; the Louisville & Nashville Railroad and a half-dozen other southern railroads; the Tennessee Valley Authority; the State Corpora-tion Commission of Kansas; the Southeastern Association of Local Grain Producers, Processors, Merchandisers, and Con-sumers; the Tennessee River and Tributaries Association; the Waterways Freight Bureau; the American Waterways Oper-ators, Inc.; dozens of millers, farm co-operatives, grain mer-chants, grain exchanges, trucking companies, and grain-elevator operators; seven hundred and forty southern cities and towns; four hundred and twenty chambers of commerce; the American Farm Bureau, the National Grange, and the National Farmers Union; the Interstate Commerce Commission; federal courts in four different districts; the United States Supreme Court (twice); and the United States of America. After four years and two months of hearings and legal wranglings, the Commission having twice reversed itself and thrice been scolded by sundry judges and justices, the Southern Railway was permitted to cut its rates for shipping grain by sixty per cent. Which is to say, everything was back where it had started.

Except for one thing: the Southern's movement of grain had jumped from seven hundred thousand tons a year to more than two million tons a year.

The lesson of this toothsome increase was not lost on the other railroad operators or on their bankers. Did they dare risk their money on such big, new, expensive rolling stock? At first most of them thought not, but a few of them cautiously ven-tured a little capital on bigger boxcars, sliding-roof hopper cars (a model first developed in Europe), longer flatcars, and much bigger tank cars (up from five thousand to fifty thousand gallons in capacity). Not many, though: in 1961 the railroads retired 54,051 of their cars as impossibly ramshackle, and to take their places they put in service only 25,633 new ones. In

206

1962 a survey by the American Railway Car Institute showed that the "badly depleted fleet" of freight cars had not been in worse shape since the years of the Great Depression, back in the 1930s. Frederic J. Schroeder, the chairman of the Institute, has since observed: "Freight cars were being scrapped [in 1961-1962] faster than new ones were being built; the fleet had shrunk . . . despite expansion of the nation's economy; and ten per cent of the [1,604,241] cars . . . were unfit for use."

This survey was obsolescent almost as soon as it was printed, as was still another study of the already scupulously scrutinized railroad industry, one handed to the Secretary of Commerce by a committee of the National Academy of Sciences and the National Research Council.* What made them antiquated was, quite simply, that in 1962 and 1963 the railroad business began at last to be profitable again. Once more in funds, the railroad managers began to spend with a free hand to improve motive power, rolling stock, and communications, to install data-processing equipment, to automate freight yards and terminals, to rationalize traffic control, to investigate marketing procedures; in short, to make competition, not merely attempt to meet it.

Specialized freight cars were the most visible improvement; first rolling out at the rate of thirty thousand a year, then suddenly at the rate of sixty thousand a year; one billion dollars' worth, most of them designed for specific shippers with specific needs: a boxcar to haul an entire tobacco crop of eighty acres, a flatcar with bulkheads to haul thirty-two cords of lumber, a ten-thousand-gallon tank car insulated with urethane foam to keep liquids at near-freezing temperature, a hopper car that hauls one hundred tons of coal and can be

*The latter report, which was sharply critical of railroad management for its "conservative and unperceptive attitudes" toward technology, marketing, systems analysis, and long-range programing, was for obscure reasons never given any publicity in the general press. Insofar as it deals with the railroads' freight operations it is by now out of date. Its strictures on passenger operations, however, are more pertinent today than ever, and they will be taken into account in the later chapters on commutation and intercity travel.

207

emptied in twenty-three seconds, a pressurized car that can whoosh out more than a hundred tons of cement or flour or lime in a matter of minutes, thermos bottles on wheels, twenty-thousand-gallon wine vats on wheels (but don't ask how the wine travels), high-cube boxcars for auto parts, outsize hoppers for ores and phosphates, cars with covers like clam shells, cars that can be swung upside down and emptied while their train keeps moving along, cars moving on roller bearings, on cushioned underframes, with air brakes—suddenly, belatedly, every conceivable kind of a car, built to delight the shipper of every conceivable kind of commodity.

And more than specialized freight cars: whole specialized freight trains.

The specialized freight train, the so-called unit train, is typical of recent railroading in that it was conceived to meet competition and has grown so swiftly that it has in five years become a distant target at which its competition sights in vain. The notion of the unit train was evolved in 1961 when officers of the eastern railroads learned, to their dismay, of plans to move coal slurry from West Virginia to New York through a pipeline.* Both technically and economically the project was feasible (already such a pipeline was operating from southern Ohio to Cleveland), and the thought of losing a traffic traditionally regarded as in fief to the railroads was a chilling one. Yet the big buyers of coal—the public utilities companies, which have traditionally burned coal to generate power—keep a sharp eye on costs, and slurried coal looked cheap to them. Most of the worried railroad executives argued that they should meet the threat in the good old traditional way, by lobbying in state capitols and convincing state legislators to refuse the right of eminent domain to the prospective pipeline operators. Jarvis Langdon, Jr., disagreed. Langdon, who was

*Slurry is defined as a thin, watery mixture. Coal can be sent through a pipeline for hundreds of miles in a slurry. Other commodities, such as grain, can be similarly slurried, although as yet they wait upon a more economical technology. If you imagine today that the bread from your local supermarket tastes like soggy blotting paper, just wait four or five years.

then the president of the Baltimore & Ohio (he is now chairman of the board of directors of the Rock Island), is another splendid specimen of the "new breed," as is demonstrated by his behavior in this emergency. Instead of contributing to a slush fund for starving state senators, Langdon flouted tradition by exploring the possibilities of lowering the cost of hauling coal by shuttling a hundred or more big, efficient, reconditioned hopper cars back and forth, between mouth of mine and siding of utility, swiftly and regularly, without holding them up for classification at intermediate freight yards or breaking them out of their original consist. The B&O experiment took more than a year, but in the spring of 1963 its officers reckoned they could slice their rate on coal shipments of nine thousand tons by a dollar a ton and still make a tidy profit. This, they figured, would enable them to compete successfully with any projected pipeline. In New York City, their chief customer, the Consolidated Edison Company, agreed.

The Norfolk & Western Railway admired the idea of the unit train. N&W hopper cars were soon shuttling back and forth between the mines of West Virginia and the N&W port facilities at Lambert's Point, Virginia; coal was headed north to New York City on N&W colliers; and the N&W had cut the rate a dollar and a quarter a ton. B&O executives growled and met the new rate.

The Pennsylvania Railroad admired the idea of the unit train. *Its* officers published a tariff that clipped the old rate by a dollar and a half a ton. Langdon, no doubt wondering if this was the price he had to pay for being of the new breed, sighed and followed suit. And still the B&O made money.

The New York Central admired the idea of the unit train but, for a wonder, its officers wasted no profit margins by competing along the seaboard. Instead, they posted new rates for hauling coal from West Virginia to Cleveland, Ohio, in competition with the one established coal-slurry pipeline in the country. Before long that one pipeline had been closed down.

By 1966 the Association of American Railroads was reporting, with some complacency, that one third of the nation's coal

209

traffic was moving by unit train; that, thanks to the economies of this transport, coal was competing successfully with nuclear energy in the generation of electricity; and that the annual saving to the utility companies (if not to the consumers) was more than one hundred million dollars. Moreover, the system of shuttling trains on tight schedules between a single origin and a single destination had spread across the country and had been applied to a variety of commodities. The Santa Fe was shuttling ore in one-hundred-ton gondola cars eleven hundred miles from a Kaiser mine in New Mexico to a Kaiser steel mill in California; the New York Central had converted the unit train into a segment of the Bethlehem Steel Company's assembly line by fetching hot steel slabs five hundred miles from a mill at the eastern end of Lake Erie to a mill on the southern shore of Lake Michigan; other unit trains were moving grain from Duluth to Buffalo.

And the squeals of the inland water carriers were rising to a frenzied crescendo. The Lake Carriers' Association, representing two dozen Great Lakes shipping lines, vowed it would "pursue every available remedy" in the battle against the "predatory and discriminatory rate practices" of the railroads. But the only proper remedy is to do what the railroads had finally and at long last done: to devise a means of more efficient competition, to provide a better service.

All these belated improvements of service, plus some selective rate cutting, enabled the railroads to recapture some part of their former freight traffic. At least temporarily the long steady decline in their fortunes had been halted—thanks in part to the growing demands of the war in Vietnam, in part to the general industrial prosperity. But what would happen when the war ended? What if the prosperity took a nose dive? The experience of the previous forty years had taught one unvarying lesson: that the railroads—and especially those in the Official Region—had, in one economic cycle after another, always climbed a shorter peak and then tumbled into a deeper depression, despite the strong and steady growth of the national freight and passenger traffic.

210

In short, the invigorating net incomes of the 1960s could prove short-lived and cruelly deceptive.

The difficulty was still with the low rate of return on the net property investment of the Class I railroads:

| | |
|---|---|
| 1961 | 1.97 per cent |
| 1962 | 2.74 per cent |
| 1963 | 3.12 per cent |
| 1964 | 3.14 per cent |
| 1965 | 3.69 per cent |

Although healthier, this rate was in every year grievously below that of nearly every other industry in the country. Unquestionably this rate discouraged new funds for capital investment in a competitive market.

The railroads own a huge plant, most of which stands idle most of the time. They have the capacity to increase their volume of traffic without proportionally increasing their costs; contrariwise, when their volume or traffic declines, they are stuck with the impoverishing burden of paying taxes on and maintaining a big, fixed, unused plant. The ebb and flow of traffic, then, affords the leverage beloved by all speculators in railroad securities: when the volume of traffic rises, profits soar sharply; when the volume declines, the fixed costs of the vast plant gobble up the reduced revenues. At either turn of the teeter-totter the speculators gather for their predictable feast.

In effect, the operators of the railroads today are paying for the excesses of the operators of the railroads yesterday. The operators today must pay the fixed interest on the bonded indebtedness contracted yesterday, and they must also pay the crushing obligations of thousands of miles of duplicative track greedily and unnecessarily laid down yesterday.*

The urgent need is to shrink the plant. To a limited extent,

---

*Perhaps the classic instance of a long-term bonded debt is that of the New York Central's West Shore 4s, created at the time (1886) when J. P. Morgan forced a settlement of a squabble between the Central and the Pennsylvania (see pages 90–92). These bonds, issued in the amount of $48,775,000, will mature, if we are all very good and drop no hydrogen bombs and provoke no revolutions, in the year 2361.

211

improved technology has been helpful: one electronically controlled freight yard can handle the load borne by a dozen or fifteen old-fashioned yards; another electronic system—centralized traffic control, which enables one operator seated at a console to guide trains so efficiently that two main-line tracks can smoothly handle a traffic that once required four tracks—makes it possible to rip up thousands of miles of costly, unnecessary rails. (A mile of track yields about five thousand dollars in salvage; after it has been torn up, the carrier typically saves an estimated three thousand dollars a year in maintenance costs and as much as two thousand dollars a year in taxes.) But to bring the railroads to optimum operating efficiency, what is most sorely needed is the wholesale consolidation of the railroad companies, especially in the northeast, where the tracks are thickest.

Ever since the Congress passed the Transportation Act of 1940, the railroads have had authority to develop and consummate mergers—always subject to approval by the Interstate Commerce Commission. The Act stipulated various criteria to be considered by the Commission in judging merger proposals; of these the most important was that any consolidation had to be shown to be consistent with—what else?—our old friend, "the public interest."*

But even after they had been invited to initiate their own mergers, the railroad executives seemed strangely reluctant to do so. To be sure, the extraordinary traffic generated by the War of 1939–1945 kept them unusually busy, but in the postwar decade, despite the urgent inducements, if not the actual obligation, to consolidate, they filed no significant merger application with the Commission. The reason was not hard to find. The carriers were sophisticated enough to realize that

*At about the same time the Supreme Court essayed to nail down the elusive concept of "the public interest" once and for all. In United States v. Lowden (308 U.S. 225) the court said that "public interest . . . is not a mere general reference to public welfare, but . . . has a direct relation to adequacy of transportation service, to its essential conditions of economy and efficiency, and to appropriate provision and best use of transportation facilities."

212

the Commission would reject as against the public interest any consolidation of rich roads that were likely to injure the traffic of weak roads, and no wealthy road cared to assume the obligations of a poor one. What got the merger movement out of the deep freeze was the impoverishment of even the wealthier roads.

In the overbuilt Official Region, the merger movement began when, as noted earlier, James Symes, the president of the Pennsylvania, invited discussions with Robert R. Young, looking to the consolidation of the Pennsylvania and the New York Central. When these two titans sat down together, the officers of every other eastern railroad experienced a natural thrill of alarm and dismay; there was an immediate scurry to explore other possible mergers. Since these consequent conferences were private, there was no need for pious invocations of the public interest. The other carriers simply reacted to the threat of a huge Penn-Central system in their midst. Their concern was commercial; their anxiety was for their gross revenues and their net profits, if any. Their posture was one of self-defense.

Young's sudden, shocking death seemed not to affect the complex negotiations between the Pennsylvania and the Central, but much of the impetus behind them was gone. Young's successor as the Central's chief executive officer, President Alfred E. Perlman, had never been happy about the prospective merger; he had considered it ill-timed. In his view the Central was a run-down carrier which he had only just begun to refurbish; until his program of modernization was well advanced, he believed the Central would suffer in any merger transaction.

Even as Perlman of the Central began to drag his feet, Symes of the Pennsylvania was stepping up the pressure. It was announced that the Virginian Railway and the Norfolk & Western were contemplating a merger. Superficially, such an arrangement would merely combine a pair of relatively prosperous but relatively small coal carriers in the Pocahontas region; in fact, however, the mighty Pennsylvania was reasserting its leadership in the railroad community and warning the Central

213

to get back in step. Translated, the Pennsylvania's warning ran: We know the Virginian has traditionally transferred to the Central a lucrative traffic in coal, but that traffic can be made to vanish, for we control the Norfolk & Western.*

If the warning accomplished anything, it provoked Perlman, who is a notably stubborn man, into greater intransigence than ever. In November, 1958, he called Symes to say that he was canceling all further Penn-Central negotiations. Later, when their separation was official, the two men issued statements to the press. "Before we marry the girl," Perlman said, "we want to make sure no other heiress is around that might fall into our lap." Symes was sadder and wiser. "It's going to cost us all a hundred million dollars a year," he said.

Meanwhile the officers of the Erie and of the Delaware, Lackawanna & Western had been deeply involved in discussions of a merger. Perlman gave them scarcely a glance: in 1958 the two roads had sustained a net loss of nearly eight million dollars, and their efforts would be still worse in 1959: here was no heiress to fall into his lap.

Meanwhile the officers of the Baltimore & Ohio and the Chesapeake & Ohio had also been deeply involved in discussions of a merger. Perlman was most interested: in 1958 these two roads had cleared a net profit of nearly sixty-eight million dollars; surely the public interest would be well served by merging the Central with the C&O and the B&O. During 1959 and the first few months of 1960 the presidents of the three roads amicably studied the possibilities. They looked good.

*The officers of the Pennsylvania subsequently denied that they controlled the N&W either directly or indirectly. Their protestations may be charitably characterized as disingenuous, and one is permitted to wonder who the officers of the Pennsylvania imagined would believe them.

It could easily be shown that the Pennsylvania owned forty-three per cent of the N&W's stock; that the consent of the Pennsylvania was absolutely required for any N&W merger; that the chief officers of the N&W were elected only at the pleasure of the Pennsylvania; that the Pennsylvania maintained, for the convenience of its officers, rooms for the president of the N&W at its headquarters in Philadelphia; and that in these rooms were held some, if not all, of the meetings of the N&W's board of directors.

Savings might amount to as much as one hundred and fifty million dollars a year.

Meanwhile the officers of the Pennsylvania had not been idle. Their unacknowledged subsidiary, the Norfolk & Western, had assimilated the Virginian with no digestive difficulty and was now fatter than ever; perhaps it should now undertake to swallow the Nickel Plate (a road that successfully competed with the Central over much of its length) and also consider leasing the Wabash (a road almost entirely owned by the Pennsylvania). Stuart Saunders, the president of the N&W, promptly undertook to open negotiations with the Nickel Plate.

|  | Net Income in 1958 | Net Income in 1959 |
|---|---|---|
| N&W | $55,080,192 | $60,741,953 |
| Nickel Plate | 10,433,465 | 13,288,922 |
| Wabash | 4,124,035 | 3,781,487 |

It would make a sound system, enabling the N&W to reach away out to Chicago and St. Louis, even to Kansas City, and to double back to Detroit, Cleveland, and Buffalo.

Now, to the casual eye, there were two comprehensive railroad systems a-borning in the Official Region. The one comprised the Pennsylvania, the N&W, the Nickel Plate, the Wabash, and perhaps also the Lehigh Valley; the other comprised the New York Central, the Chesapeake & Ohio, and the Baltimore & Ohio.

Was everybody happy? No; of course not. A dozen smaller railroads in the Official Region had not been taken into consideration and all of them—the Erie-Lackawanna (now merged), the Delaware & Hudson, the Reading, the Central of New Jersey, the Boston & Maine, and the New York, New Haven & Hartford were the biggest, but there were several others—wailed like babes lost in the wood.

The officers of the Pennsylvania bided their time, cautious and alert. They were playing a risky game, and timing was exceedingly important. Early in 1960 they did not believe there would be only two comprehensive railroad systems in the

Official Region: they were hazarding the future of the Pennysl-
vania that there would be three such systems, but much depended on how the executives of other companies would size
up a situation that seemed quite clear to the executives of the
Pennsylvania. Specifically, would the directors of the C&O
undertake to merge with two roads at once? In May, 1960, the
C&O announced its plan to acquire control of the B&O and
eventually to seek the Commission's approval of a merger.
The decision had the effect of isolating the New York Central,
just as the officers of the Pennsylvania had hoped would
happen.

Perlman first fought the C&O for control of the B&O by
trying to buy a majority of its voting stock. The expensive
and unseemly scramble that followed was reminiscent of the
gaudy financial excesses of the late 1920's. Perlman lost.

When the Commission held hearings on the C&O's application to control the B&O, Perlman fought to have the New
York Central included in any unification. He lost.

When the Pennsylvania gently applied pressure by seeking
the Commission's approval of a plan to control the Lehigh
Valley, Perlman fought it bitterly. He lost.

When the N&W filed its application to consolidate with the
Nickel Plate and to lease the Wabash, Perlman insisted that
the Central be included. His demand was rejected.

Where was the Central to find a consort? There was only one
possibility. The directors of the Central were obliged to conclude that misery loves company:

|      | Pennsylvania's Net | New York Central's Net |
|------|--------------------|------------------------|
| 1960 | $7,819,112 (deficit) | $ 1,038,253 (profit) |
| 1961 | 3,515,586 (profit) | 12,549,048 (deficit) |
| 1962 | 3,209,885 (deficit) | 3,835,538 (deficit) |

Late in 1961 Perlman of the New York Central and Symes
of the Pennsylvania spoke to each other by telephone. In
November the directors of both companies met together, and
the next day the two presidents announced that the two rail-

roads would be merged (the Commission and the Supreme Court willing) as soon as possible. Barring any hitches, something called the Pennsylvania New York Central Transportation Company, with invested capital of three billion three hundred million dollars and assets of more than six billion dollars, would in the fullness of time be born. It would be the fruit of the biggest merger in capitalist history. Two senescent giants would have tottered into a grim embrace.

The merger movement in the Official Region, with its attendant conspiracies, betrayals, feuds, raids, and heartbreaks, had so far lasted four years and had caught up in its toils every carrier with any perceptible prospect of profitability. To be sure, the sicklier roads were still making reproachful outcries, but the shape of the restructured railroad industry seemed to have emerged by 1962, and all that was wanted was for the Commission to give its official blessing to three systems—the C&O-B&O, the N&W-Nickel Plate-Wabash, and the Penn-Central—which would operate more than eighty per cent of the trackage and haul more than ninety per cent of the rail freight in the northeastern quarter of the nation. The applications for these various unifications could be dealt with piecemeal or they could be joined into one proceeding in order that the Commission might judge, from the standpoint of the public interest, how this sweeping realignment of railroad properties would serve travelers and shippers of freight during the next generation.

Wisdom dictated that the Commission consider all three applications together, if only so that a master plan might at last be conceived and implemented for a rational railroad system in the crowded northeast. Various states, cities, port authorities, federal agencies, and railroad companies urged the Commission to follow such a course. A majority of the commissioners, however, heeded the arguments of the C&O, the B&O, and the Pennsylvania and agreed to review each application separately. On this basis it is possible to tell what happened very simply:

In 1962 the Commission authorized the C&O to acquire control of the B&O through ownership of capital stock.

In 1964 the Commission approved the consolidation of the N&W, the Nickel Plate, and the Wabash, on the condition that the Pennsylvania divest itself of its holdings of stock in the N&W and the Wabash.

In 1966 the Commission approved the merger of the Pennsylvania and the New York Central.

Set down thus baldly, the Commission's decisions appear to have been forthright, reasonably prompt, and commendably sagacious. Alas, it is not so: and the disagreeable facts once again demonstrate how the railroad pooh-bahs can (a) manhandle the public interest and (b) win the Commission's sanction of their schemes while (c) managing to make the Commission seem an intolerably slowpoke and bumbling paradigm of bureaucracy.

The process began with the application by the C&O for control of the B&O. A chief issue was whether the application should be delayed so that all the eastern unifications could be considered together. The C&O urged that speed was of the essence, that any delay would be calamitous to the B&O and hence to the public weal. Look, said the C&O, at the B&O's wretched financial condition: a net deficit of more than thirty-one million dollars in 1961; help should not be postponed for even a day; only the C&O can revive the moribund B&O; therefore, approve our application forthwith.

Most of the commissioners were persuaded by these panic-stricken pleas. Not so, however, Commissioner William H. Tucker. It seems to be a tradition of the Commission that its dissenting conscience shall be from New England, and Tucker, who is from Boston, may turn out to be a worthy successor to such stalwarts as Charles Prouty and Joseph B. Eastman. At all events, Tucker filed a scathing dissent from the majority opinion favoring the C&O's application. He characterized that application as "overstated . . . misleading . . . exaggerated . . . contradictory . . . suspect . . . dubious . . . circuitous . . . false." His analysis of the B&O's so-called plight was an instructive lecture on how railroad accountants can rig their books and juggle their balance sheets: the net deficit for 1961 had been adroitly established by suddenly reducing the book value of certain securities, by writing off claims for bills, taxes, uncollected interest, and other disputed charges, some of which went back as far as 1933, and by making other adjustments not related to the carrier's operations in 1961. These items amounted to more than sixty-seven million dollars. A case could have been made that the B&O had actually earned a handsome profit in 1961, and the road's officers themselves proudly predicted there would be a profit in 1962, i.e., prior to any rescue mission by the C&O. All this the Commission's majority ignored.

Tucker then turned his guns on the Commission itself and raked it with warnings and censures:

> Because of the extensive consolidation proposals now before us, our decisions, irrespective of their nature, predetermine to a great degree the future of the American railroad system. . . . Certainly the implications of the instant applications and the two other principal eastern proposals are without precedent in the history of this Commission. Never before has the Commission been placed where the exercise of its guardianship of the public interest has been so imperative. . . . What kind of railroad system should the present generation leave to the generations that follow? . . . The answer [of the Commission's majority] seems to be that whatever the carriers prove to be good for themselves is good for the country. . . .
>
> [T]he Commission's role in this proceeding has been passive from the beginning to end. . . . Our status as a quasi-judicial body does not compel this Commission to make decisions based solely on the narrow interests of the private parties as exemplified by their testimony before this Commission. . . . The public interest is not going to evolve automatically by simply balancing interests of those actively concerned with a particular proceeding. This may be the popular or least controversial course for independent commissions to steer but the rewards of passivity and judicialitis, over the long haul, will be made at the expense of the public interest. . . . I can foresee the probability of substantial injury to the public. . . .

The decision to isolate this case from the others is going to haunt this Commission for many days to come. . . .

But only two other commissioners agreed with Tucker. Eighteen months later, the Commission approved the unification of the N&W, the Nickel Plate, and the Wabash, with Tucker this time in solitary dissent. It seemed quite clear that the railroads of the Official Region were to be based on three systems. As a reward for his skill in designing and consummating the merger, Stuart Saunders, the president of the N&W, was invited to become the chairman of the board and the chief executive officer of the Pennsylvania, a very considerable promotion.

And then, in greatest secrecy, a small group of railroad executives and Wall Street financiers began to concoct a scheme that would simultaneously torpedo the three-system structure of eastern railroads and make the Commission look more foolishly ineffectual than ever. The scheme was conceived in the lively intelligence of John P. Fishwick, the senior vice-president of the N&W. It was "ingenious," said Herman Pevler, the new president of the N&W; it was "most constructive," agreed Walter Tuohy, the chief executive officer of the C&O. It was, in brief, a scheme by which the N&W and the C&O would merge and, in the process, undertake to acquire five other eastern roads—the Erie-Lackawanna, the Delaware & Hudson, the Boston & Maine, the Reading, and the Central of New Jersey. If all hands agreed, the scheme would create a system that would operate 26,460 miles of road, earn gross revenues of nearly two billion dollars a year, and boast assets of nearly six billion dollars.* For ten months the small group of railroad executives elaborated their secret scheme and at length, late on the last day of August, 1965, Pevler and Tuohy

*The proposed Penn-Central would operate 23,271 miles of road, earn gross revenues of nearly two billion dollars a year, and boast assets of more than six billion dollars. By these criteria, then, the two proposed systems would be substantially comparable. Because of their lucrative coal traffic, the N&W-C&O system would, however, seem better able to convert gross revenues into net profits.

detonated their torpedo before a group of reporters hastily gathered in the Waldorf-Astoria Hotel.

Reactions were predictable.

Cyrus S. Eaton, the chairman of the board of the C&O, said: "The proposed N&W-C&O system . . . will greatly enhance the benefits to the shippers and receivers of the eastern United States. The public interest is paramount in this regard."

Stuart Saunders, the chairman of the board of the Pennsylvania, was speechless for some little time. Eventually he said: "It would not be in the public interest. It would create a system that we can't live with competitively."

The moral is: When the chairmen of the boards of railroad companies start talking about the public interest, it is time to count the spoons.

The time had now come for the Commission to make its decision on the merger of the Pennsylvania and the New York Central. Approval was necessarily unanimous; even Commissioner Tucker concurred. But, for the most pardonable of reasons, he could not resist the joys of I-told-you-so. He reminded his brethren that they had been continually advised "that the three-system idea would rationalize the eastern rail merger situation," yet they were now presented with a two-system idea. "In my view," said Commissioner Tucker, "it is evident that the resolution of the eastern railroad merger movement really has not been adequately attuned to the needs of the public in the east, or to the public interest in general." The merger movement, he said, had been only a "gigantic game of dominoes."

The merger movement in fact has proved to be an unconscionable mess. No sooner had the Commission announced that its approval of the Penn-Central merger was conditional on inclusion of the freight and passenger operations of the New York, New Haven & Hartford than Perlman of the Central and Saunders of the Pennsylvania were complaining that they would have no part of the New Haven's passenger service. Likewise, when the Erie-Lackawanna and the Central of New Jersey demanded immediate absorption into the N&W, Pevler of the N&W insisted that he would have no part of *their* passenger service. Translated, these outcries meant simply that the railroad corporations in question were leveling their artillery at the governors and legislators of the several states most concerned and were demanding that these politicians fork over millions of dollars every year from the several state treasuries, or else. Pay up, in order that the railroad corporations might continue to pay out fat dividends to their stockholders. Pay up, or else.

In terms of economics, how is such a procedure to be defined? Is this good old American venture capitalism? Is it state socialism? Is it creeping socialism? Is it some kind of under-the-table nationalization? Or is it, quite simply, blackmail?

Whatever it is, one thing is clear: the railroads haven't changed much in the last one hundred and some years. When first they were built, their entrepreneurs had their greedy fingers deep in the public purse for their own private profit and lo! it is still the same today.

# 14

*A study of the deteriorating passenger service. Did the passengers jump off the trains, or were they pushed? The so-called passenger-service deficit examined. The Post Office and the passenger service.*

> *A passenger train is like the male teat—neither useful nor ornamental.*—James J. Hill, president of the Great Northern

OUR INCOMPARABLE AMERICAN INGENUITY has developed a system for moving us back and forth, and around and about, which is at only one remove from insanity. Whether the system will collapse completely before a rational alternative can be agreed upon and put into effect is still moot, but already it has begun to crumble at the edges. Consider just a few aspects of our remarkable achievement:

We own more than eighty-six million automobiles, most of which were designed to travel twice as fast as the law permits but few of which can move along city streets faster than could the horse and buggy, seventy years ago.

To accommodate this huge fleet of lethal instruments, we have carved nearly four million miles of roadway from our land and have paved nearly three million miles of it. In the conglomerate, this is as though we had given half the state of Wisconsin over to the automobile. We have additionally paved God knows how many square miles of parking lots, but probably enough to obliterate the state of Connecticut.

This expanse of asphalt and concrete, vast as it is and fast as it proliferates, does not avail. The traffic jams simply get bigger. Not only in the cities: on July 31, 1965, congestion on

223

a forty-five-mile stretch of highway in New Jersey lasted seven hours and reached out to tangle more than one million automobiles—and, of course, a good many buses as well.

We have evolved a ludicrously complex and costly technology—including radar, computers, closed television circuits, and surveillance by helicopters—to channel this traffic and assist it to trickle along the expressways leading to and from our big cities.

We rejoice in a splendid webwork of airlines, each boasting jet-propelled airplanes that can cruise at just less than the speed of sound; but we spend as much time to go to and from the airport as to make a three-hundred-mile flight.

Over most of our busy airports, on fine clear days or nights, it is not uncommon for airplanes to be stacked up in holding patterns, some of them having to circle in space for more than an hour beyond the time of their scheduled arrival before they are permitted to land.

This doleful state of affairs is sufficiently familiar, as is the fact that things are getting worse every day. No sooner are bridges and tunnels built than they are obsolete. More highways mean only greater congestion on city streets and parkways. The so-called expressways and freeways, intended to ease the impact of superhighways on the cities, are likewise engulfed even before they are completed: the Congress Street Expressway and the Dan Ryan Expressway in Chicago are daily choked with more automobiles than they were designed to carry, as are the Los Angeles—Hollywood Freeway, the John C. Lodge Freeway in Detroit, and a half-dozen parkways and expressways around New York City. At Chicago, the O'Hare Airport had already reached the saturation point by 1966, and so had the National Airport outside Washington; the three airports in the New York metropolitan area—Kennedy International, LaGuardia, and Newark—were strained to their uttermost by late in 1967, and the same was true of the airports at Los Angeles, Philadelphia, Boston, and elsewhere.

Our population increases steadily. More of us come to live in the crowded urban areas. More and more of us want to use the glutted highways and airspaces. The statistics of the problem are terrifying—or would be, if they were not so obviously lunatic. Here they are: our travel between cities already exceeds nine hundred billion passenger-miles each year, and those who are expert at projecting trends predict that this figure will have doubled in twenty years. The experts notwithstanding, this will not happen, since it cannot happen; but the fact that such a traffic has been soberly forecast is a measure of our dilemma.

How to extricate ourselves? Should we build more highways? The countryside where highways are most needed is already hideously scarred by blacktop, and the angry citizens of suburbs and exurbs are alike in revolt against any further wounds. Moreover, the cost of limited-access highways is already exorbitant, if the cost of expressway connections with bypassed cities be included; and the howls of protest from the cities against still more expressways are enough to give even the most hardened politicians pause. In San Francisco the board of supervisors spurned two freeways even though it meant kissing good-by to a quarter of a billion dollars of federal funds; successive Democratic and Republican administrations in New York City have blocked plans for an expressway designed to soar across lower Manhattan.

Perhaps we should built more airports? But they would have to be even farther away from the cities they would serve than the existing ones, and so the greatest presumptive advantage of travel by air would be negated.

Various strange and wonderful devices have been proposed, some so novel that new words have had to be coined to describe them, others denoted by arcane acronyms. There are helicopters and other aircraft that take off and land vertically (VTOLs and VSTOLs); hovercraft have been designed to ride a cushion of air between concrete guideways; other cushioncraft have been conceived to be jet-propelled through tubeways buried underground and so to shoot us lickety-split, like so many panic-stricken moles, from coast to coast in a couple of hours. For one reason or another, none of these devices promises

225

much during what is left of this century. Some are too noisy, some would intolerably pollute our air, some are technically dubious, some would be psychologically traumatic for human beings as presently constituted, and all are prohibitively expensive.*

And so, in the face of the stubborn contrariety of the railroad managers, the notion has begun to take hold that the most sensible way of traveling between cities a few hundred miles apart, the most efficient way, the cheapest, the most convenient, the surest, the safest, potentially the most comfortable, the easiest, and the best way, is the way that has been available for a hundred years or more; in short, the railway.

Proponents of this notion are not, of course, plumping for railroad passenger service as we know it today—the slow, dirty, noisy, unpunctual, inconvenient jouncing about that is contemptuously provided in dilapidated equipment. They have in mind a smooth, comfortable ride at speeds up to one hundred and fifty miles an hour, regularly available in pleasant, modein coaches and parlor cars—no more than could and should have been provided since 1946 or thereabouts, if the officers of the railroad companies had been alert to the public interest and aggressive in competing for the public custom; no more than what has in fact been provided in Canada, in Japan, and in Europe, which is to say, by railroads that have been nationalized.

Until quite recently, such a notion has been poison to the directors of American railroads, and most of them still regard it as a threat to all they hold dear. For at least a generation all of them have, for sundry reasons, persistently sought to scuttle most of their passenger service, and some of them have contrived to slaughter their passenger business entirely. There has been nothing sly or underhanded about this policy; on the

*The fact that a mode of transport is outrageously costly does not, of course, necessarily discourage our peerless leaders. The Congress has already appropriated five hundred million dollars of our money to develop the ultimate folly, a supersonic airplane. Those who question any aspect of the SST are made to feel, as The Wall Street Journal has pointed out, that they are "somehow unpatriotic."

contrary, it has been diligently plugged by the presidents of the biggest and most influential railroad companies. As long ago as July, 1956, Donald J. Russell, then the president of the Southern Pacific, in an interview with a reporter of The San Francisco Chronicle, cheerfully predicted the demise of the Pullman car and the virtual extinction of long-distance travel on rails; he acknowledged that most railroads would like to get out of the passenger business completely. A month later James M. Symes, then the president of the Pennsylvania, told a reporter of The New York Times: "I've just about given up hope as to the future of long-haul passenger travel." These gentlemen were not so much advocating as describing a process that had been in full swing since 1929 and would proceed even more swiftly after they had spoken:

| | Miles of Road in Passenger Service, Class I Railroads | Passenger-carrying Cars in Service, Class I Railroads |
|---|---|---|
| 1929 | 226,703 | 47,797 |
| 1939 | 172,031 | 30,353 |
| 1949 | 156,821 | 27,903 |
| 1959 | 99,989 | 17,695 |
| 1966 | 72,796 | 10,687 |

Precise figures as to intercity passenger trains (as distinct from commuter trains) are harder to come by, but in 1929 there were at least twenty thousand of them. In September, 1965, Wayne Hoffman, the executive vice-president of the New York Central, estimated that their number had dwindled from eleven thousand in 1946 to thirteen hundred in 1964. As of August, 1967, there were less than nine hundred. At least two states and several sizable cities had no railroad passenger service whatsoever. There was no through service between Washington and Cleveland, Cleveland and Detroit, Cleveland and Pittsburgh, Detroit and Indianapolis, St. Louis and Louisville, Atlanta and Jacksonville, or Dallas and San Antonio. Efforts to discontinue service between New York and Boston and to reduce and downgrade service between San Francisco and Los Angeles had been mounted but, at least for a time, rejected.

To the directors of most railroad companies, this was a very satisfactory state of affairs. They were content. One could almost hear them purr as, through the 1960s, the Dow-Jones average of railroad stocks maintained a jagged ascent. These men had only to close their eyes and count to ten; when they opened their eyes again—presto! chango!—the passenger business would have vanished; or so they hoped. But instead they began to hear talk of a rejuvenated passenger service. Their exasperation may be imagined.

The talk was started by a few dreamy, meddlesome scholars —professors of urban planning or of transportation who should have known better. They were ignored; after all, their voices could not carry very far.

But then an imaginative politician spoke up, one who, by an awful mischance, actually preferred the railroad for travel back and forth between Washington and his constituency and so was vividly aware of all the railroad's shortcomings and all its wasted potentials. Claiborne Pell, the junior senator from Rhode Island, after pondering these shortcomings, went so far as to draft a set of specific, simple proposals for the resuscitation of railroad passenger service, at least in the northeastern states. Pell was new to the Senate (he was first elected in 1960) but he was no stranger to men of considerable influence. He took his plan to an old friend, Arthur Krock, the Washington columnist of The New York Times, who, he rather hoped, might deem his piece worth recommending for publication in The New York Times Magazine. Krock at once appreciated the right of the matter: the Pell plan was reported on the front page of the newspaper in May, 1962.

In the executive offices of several railroad companies, that Monday morning in May was a bleak one. All along the Atlantic seaboard railroad directors were recalling the words of the poet Burns about the best-laid plans of mice and men. The president of one great eastern railroad system picked up his telephone and spoke forcefully to Pell for a half hour, from

228

long distance, seeking to dissuade him from his fool notion of an improved rail passenger service. Too late. Within ten days the editors of ten big newspapers published in the northeastern states had jumped, with glad cries, aboard the Pell band wagon; and before long the editors of a half-dozen railway labor weeklies were whooping their approval.

A public debate on intercity railroad passenger service had been assured.

For years before it was moved into the arena of public policy, the debate had been conducted in the pages of such trade magazines as Trains, Railway Age, and Modern Railroads; and it had boiled over, too, at nearly every public hearing called (by the Interstate Commerce Commission or by one of the state regulatory agencies) to judge whether specific passenger trains might be discontinued. A salient aspect of the debate was the attempt to fix responsibility for the calamitous decline of the service, in the face of a growing population and an expanding travel market.

The relevant figures on the intercity travel of revenue passengers by Class I railroads are these:

|  | Total of Passengers (Excluding Commuters) | Railroad Share of Public Carriage | Share of All Travel (Including Automobiles) |
| --- | --- | --- | --- |
| 1929 | 321,449,000 | 77% | 17.1% |
| 1939 | 219,896,800 | 65 | 8.45 |
| 1944 | 595,299,438 | 74.2 | 34.13 |
| 1949 | 245,994,418 | 47.5 | 7.27 |
| 1959 | 129,824,369 | 28.6 | 2.89 |
| 1966 | 105,286,419 | 15.2 | 1.6 |

The lonely eminence of 1944, projecting above an otherwise mournfully steady slope toward the vanishing point, resulted from the extraordinary demands made upon the railroads during wartime, when gasoline for private automobiles was curtailed and travel by airplane was governed by a system of priorities.

229

The number of people who prefer to travel between cities by rail, it is worth noting, is still a substantial one. What imaginative businessman would not drool over a market firmly founded upon one hundred million customers? Only a railroad director would depreciate it.

The lords of the railroads have had no difficulty in identifying those responsible for the loss of their passengers, and they seem honestly bewildered that anyone else can hesitate to do so. They point, in summary fashion, to the automobile and the airplane and to the distressful manner in which those competitors have been pampered and cosseted by politicians at every level from the county courthouse to 1600 Pennsylvania Avenue, all to the ruinous detriment of the railroads. Moreover, evidence abounds to back up their lamentations. In the 1950s the federal, state, and local governments spent hundreds of millions of dollars each year to build highways and airports and in other ways to promote and subsidize travel by airplane or automobile. In the 1960s more than one billion dollars a year have gone to beef up air transport and more than ten billions a year to build still more highways. Some part of these monstrous sums—perhaps as much as two thirds of them—has been recovered by excise taxes on gasoline, tires, and the like, or by tolls and other imposts levied on those who choose to use the highways or the airways; but the vast remainder has been extracted from the general taxpayer, including, of course, the railroad company.

The worst of this inequity has been that the railroad company, being privately owned, has had to pay property taxes on its stations and tracks and other real estate; but the automobile and the bus have rolled over public highways, and the commercial airplane has used untaxed municipal airports. Indeed, as the managers of railroads have grown painfully aware, there was often a suspiciously proximate relationship between the property tax paid, say, on a railroad station and the sum needed to defray the expenses of the airport serving the same city. (In 1956 the New York Central paid a tax of $59,904 on its passenger station in Albany, New York; the operating

230

deficit of Albany's municipal airport that same year was $57,784.) Of all the states, New Jersey seemed to the railroad industry to have the most outrageous tax policies: in 1956 New Jersey exacted tribute at the rate of $10,244 per mile of road, a tax bite more than five times as deep as the national average. The New Jersey tax officials, moreover, assessed railroad property at its full value, while permitting other industrial and commercial taxpayers a more sympathetic valuation.

But in every state, while the government fed their competitors lavishly with one hand, with the other it snatched from the railroads. And fewer passengers climbed on board the trains.

To the railroad operators it seemed quite clear that their passengers were quitting them for the swifter airplane and the more convenient private automobile, and that the Interstate Commerce Commission and the various state regulatory agencies were nevertheless forcing them to maintain an unpopular, archaic, and hideously expensive service. That the costs of the service were climbing dizzily there could be no question. In the early postwar years, the cost of labor rose even though the number of employees was reduced:

| | No. of Employees in Passenger Service | Total Compensation | Average Straight Time Hourly Pay |
|---|---|---|---|
| 1947 | 42,850 | $194,902,365 | $2.36 |
| 1957 | 29,504 | 237,776,436 | 4.65 |
| 1966 | 16,767 | 179,450,000 | 6.03 |

This pay is based upon work rules that have been in force since 1919. For engine crews, the rule reads: "One hundred miles or less (straight-away or turn-around) . . . shall constitute a day's work; miles in excess of one hundred will be paid for at the mileage rate provided. . . ." For conductors and trainmen a day's work is one hundred and fifty miles or less (straight-away or turn-around). Engine crew and train crew alike are paid overtime "on a speed basis of twenty miles per

231

hour computed continuously from the time required to report for duty until released at the end of the last run." Since 1919 the average speed of passenger trains has somewhat increased, so that the day's work has diminished from about five hours to about three hours and twenty minutes.

Translated into operational examples, this means that the New York Central must employ eight engine crews, whose members divide about nine and one half basic days' pay, to move its Twentieth Century nine hundred and sixty miles between New York and Chicago, or that the Burlington must employ eight engine crews, whose members divide ten and one third basic days' pay, to move its Denver Zephyr a little more than one thousand miles to and from Chicago.

The cost of equipment rose even more sharply:

|      | Average Cost of Coaches | Average Cost of Sleeping Cars | Average Cost of Dining Cars |
|------|-------------------------|-------------------------------|-----------------------------|
| 1947 | $ 79,019                | $ 85,265                      | $101,903                    |
| 1957 | 189,483                 | 265,044                       | 358,341                     |

Not many passenger cars have been built since then.

And each year fewer passengers have stepped on board the trains.

The Interstate Commerce Commission, using a statistical formula of its own contrivance, concluded in 1957 that the passenger service had for the previous seven years saddled the railroads with an annual deficit of more than five hundred million dollars. Since many of the biggest railroad companies were, at the time, suffused with red ink, their officers indicted the traffic in passengers as an intolerable burden. On cue, spokesmen for the shippers likewise began to yowl that the passenger-train deficits were crippling the railroads and preventing them from the efficient discharge of their divine duty, to wit, the carriage of freight.

Responsive to these protests, the Commission undertook to investigate the passenger-train deficit. The hearings ambled along like an accommodation local, from June 18, 1957, to June 23, 1958 (while the deficit itself, by the Commission's intricate formula of accounting, mounted in 1957 to an all-time record seven hundred and twenty-four million dollars); and they served to convince at least the hearings examiner, Howard Hosmer, that the passenger service was deteriorating so swiftly that, as he predicted, "the parlor and sleeping-car service will have disappeared by 1965 and the coach service by 1970."

That was precisely what most (but by no means all) the lords of the railroads had hoped would be predicted. They had already besought the Congress for relief, and in August, 1958, they had got it. An amendment (Section 13a) to the Interstate Commerce Act put a gratifying zip into the process by which passenger trains, whether interstate or intrastate, could be forever curtailed, canceled, and discontinued. The extermination picked up speed and proceeded merrily apace—until all at once Senator Pell's consarned plan burst into the public prints.

The extermination has proceeded, but cautiously, more slowly, with much greater difficulty, for now the other side of the debate has been given a hearing and a respectful attention.

The opposition holds that the lords of the railroads are solely responsible for the deterioration of the passenger service, just as they have always been responsible for the incivil and contemptuous treatment that has been the passenger's traditional lot on most railroads. This argument has never been articulated or documented with so much skill as has the railroads' argument, for while full-time railroad presidents abound who can summon adroit attorneys, even research institutes, to plead their cause, no man is a full-time railroad passenger, devoting himself professionally to the protection of other passengers from the annoyances and delinquencies that commonly afflict them. Everyone else in this industry has an organization to fend for him—there are associations of security owners, of railway labor executives, of traffic agents, of rate experts, of car builders, of state commissioners, and of shippers; there are brotherhoods of railway workers and conferences of railway presidents—but nobody speaks for the passenger.

The lack has never been too consequential: the plight of

the passenger has always spoken eloquently for itself.

At no time in the history of American railroads have passengers failed to remark the singular reluctance of railroad presidents to afford comfortable, even minimally decent accommodations. Whatever provides ease or convenience may subtract from financial profit, and, as has occasionally been hinted in this essay, the railroad president has ever been spurred by his quite natural greed for profit. To select at random an early example, here is an extract from a letter written by Charles Elliott Perkins, the president of the Chicago, Burlington & Quincy, to John Murray Forbes, the chairman of his board of directors, on March 24, 1879:

> In planning a sleeping car . . . *if you improve on your neighbors* [in the matter of luxury] they will overtake you. That kind of competition has cut very largely into profits from passenger transportation. The public has been educated to expect too much. . . . I have had the sleeping car conundrum on my mind. . . . I have rather concluded that [the solution to the conundrum] is not to be found in cheaper sleeping accommodations so much as in the abandonment of *through lines* of sleepers.

President Perkins was at least eighty years before his time. But the trains of 1879 were poor things, made of wood, perfectly designed to roast their passengers when, as occasionally happened, a stove in one of the coaches overturned and a coach was converted into a chamber of incineration.

Let us turn to happier times, to the first truly radical change in the manufacture of railroad cars, when wood was replaced by steel. This revolution began in 1894, with freight cars. Fourteen years later, in 1908, the Pullman-Standard Car Manufacturing Company began production of all-steel passenger cars. The company was obliged to make this extraordinary decision because of the very real hazard that steam locomotives, puffing up clouds of glowing sparks, might set afire the old wooden coaches they would be made to haul through the tunnel the Pennsylvania was then building (to be opened in

234

1910) under the Hudson River from New Jersey to New York City.

The all-steel sleeping car came later, making a modest appearance in 1910 and no considerable splash until the mid-1920s, when passenger revenues from Pullman cars were at their zenith. This was the car now considered high camp, the car that evokes memories of the romantic Nights of the Green Curtains. Only those of us who are in our forties or older can recall those sleepers, characterized so aptly by Robert R. Young as "rolling tenements." They were ugly, uncomfortable dormitories, as lacking in privacy as a jailhouse. Each passenger swayed longitudinally in a berth cloaked only by a swaying curtain of a heavy dark-green fabric that might better have been used as an upholstery for the furniture in the lobbies of commercial hotels. At one end of each sleeper was the men's room—one toilet, a pseudo-leathern couch, and a meager triad of communal washbasins, inadequately equipped with mirrors, in front of which a gaggle of salesmen customarily postured and prattled, exchanging jokes of an unexampled vulgarity; at the other end was the women's room—similarly fitted, but littered with someone else's face powder and someone else's hair combings rather than someone else's cigar ends.

Spurred by a concern for the comfort of their passengers, the railroad executives required that three fundamental improvements be made in these hideous sleeping cars:

In 1924 receptacles for used razor blades were installed in the men's rooms.

In 1926 containers of fresh facial tissues were placed in some, but not all, of the women's rooms.

In 1929 the water coolers were adjusted so that they would no longer overflow on the strip of carpeting in the corridors.

There was also the matter of air conditioning. One would have thought the lords of the railroads would have snatched at air conditioning when first it became practical; would, even more likely, have themselves been first to conceive of it; for surely there are few surroundings in which the human being can more gratefully welcome a constant supply of cooled, clean air than a railroad coach drawn by a steam locomotive on a hot day. With windows closed, the passengers baked; with windows opened (presuming, of course, that someone had the Herculean strength required to open a coach window), the passengers were at once aspersed with soot and grime and coal dust, and their lungs filled with a noxious stench.

Yet long after the feasibility of air-conditioned passenger trains had been demonstrated, the railroad operators hung back. In concert, they declined to install the necessary devices; all their available funds were bespoken by their investment bankers, who were advising them in their calamitous ventures in the stock market. Not until their passenger revenues fell off sharply, after 1929, did they turn to air conditioning, and then they could ill afford it; not until late into the 1930s were most trains routinely equipped with air-conditioned passenger cars; and a few of the smaller roads waited until 1950 to grant their dwindling custom this minimal comfort.

The conclusion is inescapable that the general public, badly used by the railroads from the first day a flanged wheel rolled along an iron rail, could not wait for the opportunity to use another mode of travel. They had been fighting bitterly for nearly a century; now they wanted only to switch.

Belatedly a few railroads, especially those west of the Mississippi, engaged to recapture their passengers. In 1934 the Union Pacific put on a lightweight train that cut the time between Chicago and Los Angeles from sixty to less than forty hours; the Burlington began operating its swift, handsome Zephyrs; and in 1935 the Santa Fe was obliged to schedule lightweight trains of its own. Industrial designers were retained who made the first changes in the design of sleeping cars and lounge cars since the time, back in the 1870s, when those elegant creatures had first been built. For the New York Central Henry Dreyfuss redesigned the Twentieth Century, Raymond Loewy did the same for the Pennsylvania's Broadway Limited, and curious crowds gathered in the big New York depots of both roads to examine sleeping cars which, for a wonder, afforded privacy: drawing rooms, sections, bedrooms, compartments: each traveler enjoying a washbasin and a toilet of his own, each traveler withdrawn behind a door that he could lock: was it possible?

It was possible, but it had come too late. Of the rich and fastidious, fewer would patronize these expensive cars each year; and the masters of the railroads had ignored, in their calculations, the scores of millions of other Americans. In the summer of 1939 Joseph B. Eastman took a retrospective look at the railroads' passenger traffic. He deplored the rigidly negative attitude of most railroad directors toward new equipment for passenger trains and the new technology for its construction. "The promotion of lightweight, cheap, comfortable gas or gas-electric units, capable of combination into multiple-unit trains and furnishing flexible and convenient service," Eastman said, "has been so neglected that it is probably too late now, for the bus has occupied this field."

The bus, the noisome bus. It was typical of the footling way the railroads had operated their passenger service that an inelegant carrier like the bus should have emerged as a rival able to cut deep into the revenues of the noble railroad; able, indeed, to ring up half as many passenger-miles as the railroads by 1940.

Railroad executives had first taken irritable notice of the intercity bus back in the early 1920s, as on a picnic they might have noticed a wasp hovering over their jar of jam. They had at once begun to keen their familiar propaganda: the bus lines were "dangerous," they were "irresponsible," they were "unregulated," they "destroyed" public highways yet refused to pay taxes for highway maintenance. When these complaints got them nowhere, the railroad executives formed their own subsidiary bus companies and priced their fares so as to ruin the presumptuous competition. All this was routine business practice. But in 1925 one railroad president—Ralph Budd of the Great Northern—took the trouble to do some independent research into the passenger traffic at twenty-six railroad depots in Minnesota, and he came up with a remarkable fact: in eleven towns also served by Northland Greyhound, his railroad's traffic had gone off 63.7 per cent since 1920; but in fifteen towns *not* served by buses, the traffic had gone off 64.6 per cent. The conclusion was obvious: the automobile, not the bus, was stealing his passengers away. The moral was equally obvious: he should join forces with Northland Greyhound and so be free to kill off his unprofitable branch lines.

Once the complex arithmetic had been explained to them, other railroad presidents caught on quickly. For $330,000 the Pennsylvania bought stock in the parent Greyhound Corporation; in 1930 this stock was sold and the Pennsylvania took fifty per cent of Pennsylvania Greyhound. For $480,000 the Southern Pacific ended up with a one-third interest in Pacific Greyhound. The Burlington, the New York Central, the Union Pacific, the New Haven, the Chicago & North Western, and some smaller roads also had holdings in other Greyhound companies.

It was a most amicable arrangement. The railroads and Greyhound, the magazine Fortune reported, have "a mutual understanding that has kept a definite spread between rail and bus fares. Busses generally charged 10 per cent less than railroads; an actual rate agreement was made in New Orleans in 1934. There is none evident today [September, 1944], but probably none is necessary. Railroads have shown little inclination to indulge in all-out rate wars. . . ."*

With the connivance of the railroad men, their passengers left them for the bus. Even more they left for the automobile and, slowly at first, for the airplane. Yet most railroad executives persisted in proceeding as though the railroad still enjoyed a monopoly. If there has emerged a glaring contradiction, a lapse of logic, the explanation is that we are here dealing with the railroad industry.

A revolution was in full cycle, but the railroad managers,

*During the late 1940s and early 1950s the Greyhound Corporation acquired from the railroads most of their stock holdings. The last big purchase came in October, 1953, when the Southern Pacific and the Pennsylvania sold all but "certain amounts of preferred stock." Apparently the railroads were pulling out of every phase and aspect of the passenger business.

238

hidebound as ever, failed to measure its sweep. In retrospect, one can understand why they were so blinded, even while losing patience with them for their refusal to open their eyes to what was going on around them. The depression of the 1930s threatened to engulf almost every railroad company in ultimate disaster; the war of the early 1940s buried every railroad under an avalanche of traffic. During those fifteen years the managers of the railroads were so absorbed by their immediate concerns that they never paused to learn from the lessons of yesterday or to consider the possible exigencies of tomorrow.

Incredible as it may seem, when in 1946 the railroad managers began to struggle with the postwar problems of their passenger service, they knew almost nothing about their market. What was the flow and pattern of traffic? How many passengers traveled to or from a given city? Where were they going? Where did they come from? Were there more or less of them than a year before? than five years before? What did they like about the passenger service? What would they like to see changed? At which hours of the day or night did they prefer to travel? Might train schedules be better fitted to their convenience? What reason did each have for travel? To these and a hundred like questions, most railroad managers could answer only: We don't know, we have never troubled to find out. (Most of them cannot answer such questions even today.)

Into this dark backward and abysm of assumption and conjecture the railroad men bravely plunged. They were certain of only one fact: their passenger cars were old, shabby, and in dreadful disrepair; if they were to hold the custom of the scores of millions, in and out of uniform, who had been forced during wartime once again to ride the trains, they would have to buy new passenger cars, and quickly.

They spent with a free hand: more than five hundred million dollars in the five years 1946-1950 to buy more than four thousand new passenger-train cars, handsome, expensive, air-conditioned, and built according to the traditional heavyweight design to last for at least a generation. Yet in each year the number of their passengers dwindled. Discouraging. What could be amiss?

In the next five years they spent their money more cautiously. Less than two hundred and fifty million dollars went to purchase new equipment, and of that sum a larger share was paid to buy cars for the so-called head-end traffic—that is, cars built to haul mail and baggage and express freight. Yet in each year the number of their passengers diminished. Puzzling. Could it be that they had somehow overlooked some aspect of their passenger service?

During these same five years the Pennsylvania, the New York Central, and the B&O engaged Robert Heller Associates, consultants on problems of management, to inquire into the habits and preferences of passengers on every train east of the Mississippi and the Missouri, north from the Gulf of Mexico into the Maritime Provinces of Canada. Here was the most comprehensive and thoroughgoing study ever undertaken for any mode of transportation in the history of the republic. It cost about five million dollars. Motivation of travelers, operation of trains, costs and marketing of the passenger service—all this and much more was painstakingly investigated. The purpose of the study was to enable the directors of the three railroads to determine the feasibility of consolidating their passenger services. (Think what might have come to pass: a rational integration of terminals and depots, a saving of millions of dollars by elimination of unnecessary competition, a more frequent and more convenient schedule of trains, cheaper fares, swifter, more comfortable rides; in short, a paradise for those who prefer to travel by train in the overcrowded Eastern Region.) Nothing happened. The study itself, an invaluable research, was discarded, scattered, or destroyed; not maliciously, not with evil intent, but (as I have been told by one of those familiar with the research) only stupidly, only because the executives who had it in charge knew no better.

Much interest attached to a few of the cars built at this time, for these few, which cost less than ten million dollars, were genuine innovations in passenger equipment, proudly hailed as "the trains of the future"—streamlined, built of light-weight aluminum or stainless steel, and manufactured to run in fixed sets of six or eight or a dozen cars. They bore flamboyant names like Aerotrain and X-Plorer and RDC-Hot Rod. They were hurried into service early in 1956 and almost immediately proved to be a resounding flop. They trembled and shook at high speed; they were noisy; they broke down easily and often, but their consist could not be readily parted to detach an intermediate car for repair or maintenance; they could not be interchanged with cars of traditional design; they were too light to trip the devices that activated signal systems. By 1960 they had all been scrapped or relegated to service on suburban runs, and the whole episode had perfectly demonstrated what the venerables dodoes of the industry had known all along, to wit: "Never monkey around with damfool experiments." . . . "The old way is the best way." . . . "Whatever is old has been tested by time."

The old way is the best way, and if it doesn't work, cancel the service. Under this grim slogan the masters of the railroads now reformed their ranks in a sullen phalanx. What they had never properly understood they now condemned. Even before the new lightweight equipment had proved to be a costly mistake, the Eastern Railroad Presidents Conference was urged to seek a steep increase in passenger fares and especially in Pullman fares. This plan was proposed by the New York Central and heartily endorsed by the Pennsylvania. (The other eastern carriers at first declined to support it.) The plan was revealed on July 25, 1956, by a knowledgeable reporter of railroad affairs, Robert Bedingfield, in an article published on the front page of The New York Times. The headline put it neatly:

2 RAILWAYS PLAN FARE RISE
TO DETER PULLMAN TRAVEL

and just in case some reader might have missed the import of the headline, the president of a smaller railroad was quoted in unmistakable terms: "What they are trying to do is to dry up the Pullman service and switch the passengers over to the coach and the airplane." In fine, the big railroads hoped to use the fare—the rate for passengers—as an instrument of policy, a club with which to beat their ratepayers into doing as they wished.

This was by no means the first attempt to convert the fare into an instrument of policy; it has rarely risen or fallen, like other costs, in response to the pressures of the open market. Sixty years ago, in 1906 and 1907, when the state legislatures in Ohio, Indiana, Michigan, Illinois, and elsewhere compelled reductions of the fare from three to two cents a mile, the legislators were simply capitalizing on the obvious, which was that the railroads were universally despised for the long schedule of their crimes and delinquencies (detailed at pp. 126–130). In 1918 the Federal Railroad Administration fixed the fare across the nation at three cents a mile, and in 1920 the Interstate Commerce Commission bumped it up to 3.6 cents a mile. During all this time the lords of the railroads had held the passengers in their monopolistic grip, but early in the 1930s, when competition and the depression combined to push passenger revenues disastrously low, the operators began to wrangle and dispute among themselves about the fare. South and west the coach fare was cut to two cents and the first-class fare to three, and passengers returned to the railroads; but in the northeast, although Dan Willard of the B&O pressed for lower fares, Atterbury of the Pennsylvania balked. The Pennsylvania sold the most tickets; the Pennsylvania controlled the market; in the east the Pennsylvania set the fare. Not until 1936 did the Commission gather enough pluck to overrule the Pennsylvania, by a five-to-four vote, and once again fix the same basic fare over the entire country.

In 1942 the Commission, in an ex parte proceeding, approved a general ten-per-cent increase: 3.3 cents a mile for first-class fares, 2.2 cents a mile for coach seats.

In 1944 the magazine Fortune published a rollicking analysis and forecast of the postwar passenger service, a wondrous prediction of swift, smooth rides on streamliners crossing the continent in forty-eight hours at a fare of only *one cent* a mile.

242

The fare could be cut so low, Fortune's cheerful analyst estimated, because costs of a streamliner carrying one hundred and eighty passengers would be about sixty cents a mile, or one third of a cent for each passenger-seat-mile on a well-patronized train. Fortune's informants acknowledged that the lords of the railroads would have to move fast, if they were to snatch the traffic of the big postwar market, but they were, on the whole, most sanguine; they envisioned crowded trains and profits fatter even than those swollen to unprecedented heights by the war.

Happy dreams! Blissful dreamers! No railroad moved quickly to cut its fares; on the contrary, with the Pennsylvania, the New York Central, and the Southern Pacific leading the way, the basic fares were steadily raised all over the map. By May, 1956, this was the situation:

| | First-Class Fare per Mile | Increase from 1942 | Coach Fare per Mile | Increase from 1942 |
|---|---|---|---|---|
| Eastern Region | 4.725¢ | 43.2% | 3.544¢ | 61.13% |
| Southern Region | 4.0425¢ | 22.5% | 2.8875¢ | 31.25% |
| Western Region | 3.675¢ | 11.4% | 2.625¢ | 19.3% |

(Unlike the other western carriers, the Southern Pacific and the Missouri Pacific charged the same rates as did the southern carriers.)

In the summer of 1956, the New York Central and the Pennsylvania proposed to hike the first-class fares still another forty-five per cent. Their officers would have liked the proposal to have come from the entire industry, but the operators of the western and southern roads thought it too raw; they asked only another five per cent. The Commission approved the five per cent and, in a six-to-five decision, granted the Central and the Pennsylvania only a fifteen-per-cent boost of their first-class fares.

Manifestly, the railroads were not encouraging any return of their former passengers.*

*The fare has since been further inflated, especially in the Eastern Region. For several years the railroad operators complained bitterly about

There were other ways, in 1956, to enervate the passenger service. Advertising budgets, already minuscule, could be reduced still further. In 1946 the industry had submitted to a little self-criticism on this score from its creature, the Association of American Railroads. "Railroads," the A.A.R. said, in a report on passenger traffic, "spend insignificant sums for advertising in comparison with the amount of business done," and the reporters went on to point out that even in 1943, when travel by domestic airlines was constantly jeopardized by military priorities, the airlines had spent twenty-five times as much (in relation to revenues) as had the railroads, in trying to drum up their passenger business. But after 1950, instead of beefing up their advertising of passenger services, most railroad companies cut it to the bone and deeper, into the marrow.

This is not to say that the railroad executives were ignorant of the blessings of advertising. On the contrary, they had a lively awareness of such beguilements. And so, beginning about this time, they cluttered the spacious concourses of their noble depots with showy turntables on which were displayed —what else?—the latest glittering models of the automobile industry's most fetching products. The message was icy and unmistakable: Forsake the train! Go by automobile! More comfortable, more convenient!

Additionally, although travel agents are paid a commission by the airlines for any tickets they sell, the railroad companies either refused to make similar arrangements or paid a com-

---

a ten-per-cent excise tax on passenger fares, contending that here was another official government mischief, designed expressly to injure the railroads' efforts to make the passenger service viable; yet, when in 1962 the Congress repealed the excise tax, all the eastern carriers at once raised their fares by the same ten per cent, as did the Chicago & North Western, the Southern Pacific, the Missouri Pacific, the Western Pacific, the Frisco, and a few smaller lines.

As a consequence the Pennsylvania and the New York Central have ever since rejoiced in the highest basic fares in the country: 7.53 cents a mile for first class, 4.735 cents a mile for coach. These fares have been jacked up, respectively, one hundred and twenty-eight per cent and one hundred and fifteen per cent above the fares of 1942.

mission only after an elaborate set of conditions had been met.

When the Pullman Company showed, after an extensive study, that many travelers had never gone first class simply because they didn't know what was offered them, the suggestion was made that railroad ticket salesmen might sell more first-class tickets if they were offered an incentive. In 1955 a modest experiment was mounted: in nine sample markets, ticket salesmen were rewarded with merchandise, depending on how well they sold Pullman accommodations. At once sales went up thirty-one per cent, in proof that nearly fifty million dollars a year could be added to first-class revenues if the plan were adopted by the industry. The incentives, trivial as they were, nevertheless enormously improved the morale of the sales clerks, for not only did the first-class revenues increase but the coach sales were also up. If the plan were approved by all the railroads, some twenty-two thousand clerks in forty-four hundred ticket offices would be bucking to improve the industry's image in a market of scores of millions of travelers. Hays MacFarland, then the Pullman Company's advertising agent, all but drooled as he thought of the possibilities. "Any TV or auto maker would consider that kind of a distributor set-up almost priceless," he said.

The industry rejected the plan.

Every idea for attracting passengers back to the railroads or for making it easier to travel by rail was somehow flawed— it was too expensive, too impractical, too likely to be fought by the unions, too much trouble.

Whatever imagination and ingenuity the railroad industry possessed in the mid-1950s was never devoted to overcoming objections to improvements in the passenger service but rather was dedicated to the invention of schemes to downgrade the service. In 1959 only three railroad companies—the Pennsylvania, the New York Central, and the Southern Pacific —named a vice-president to operate their passenger service, and these three companies were apparently the ones most anxious and most determined to scuttle their passenger service. Certainly no other companies indulged in more bellyaching on the subject.

In the 1950s one figure glared from every railroad company's balance sheet: the alleged deficits accruing from the passenger service. These deficits were frightful. They were also exceedingly well publicized, for every railroad company had discovered that the sure-pop way to get its weaker trains discontinued was to agitate the public generally and the Congress particularly by pleading imminent bankruptcy unless these deficits were wiped out.

In the aggregate, these deficits for the years 1950–1957 amounted to more than five and one quarter billion dollars. Good grief! How could any industry survive under such a staggering burden? Obviously, none could. The passenger-service deficit, so-called, is and always has been a statistical mirage; a fraud, a phony; most useful, perhaps, as a means of singling out those railroad executives who will lie to the public (even, occasionally, to their own shareholders) and betray the public interest with the greatest effrontery.

Over the years their distortions have been designed to convince us all that the carriage of passengers by the railroads is ever and everywhere unprofitable and can be maintained only thanks to the profitable carriage of freight. Their flimflam has been and still is based on a venerable formula, prescribed by the Interstate Commerce Commission, by which the railroads are required to separate a set of imprecise costs that are imperfectly understood even by their own officers.

The formula is called "Rules Governing the Separation of Operating Expenses, Railway Taxes, Equipment Rents and Joint Facility Rents Between Freight Service and Passenger Service on Class I Line-Haul Railroads," and, as Stanley Berge has pointed out, even the title has a Victorian ring.*

*Berge, who is professor of transportation in the School of Business at Northwestern University, is the wittiest and most perceptive of the many critics of the so-called passenger-train deficit; I am much in his debt for my own discussion of it. Among his articles on the subject is one that was published in Journal of Marketing, Vol. 28, No. 1, January, 1964.

The formula was concocted by the Commission in 1887 when the public concern was chiefly to keep the freight rates and the passenger fares within reasonable bounds. Cost accounting was both unknown and unnecessary in that time of monopoly, and so the Commission required only that the railroads file a schedule separating expenses "chargeable to passenger traffic" from those "chargeable to freight traffic." Expenses chargeable to both services were to be divided in proportion to the train-miles of each service.

Almost at once the formula was assailed by the Association of American Railway Accounting Officers as "an arbitrary rule" that "will furnish misinformation if used . . . for any practical purpose." Soon afterward the formula was savaged by the state railway commissioners as "grossly erroneous, not to say preposterous." Taking the hint, the Commission itself retired the formula in 1894, but twenty years later it was revived and elaborated, and it still stands today, more bewildering than ever. In brief, the formula now requires that the railroad companies charge their passenger service with millions of dollars of maintenance and other overhead costs, all of which would still have to be paid even if every passenger train disappeared tomorrow.

This phantom deficit continued to bother a lot of people, in and out of the industry. In 1954 Richard F. Mitchell, then the chairman of the Commission, confessed publicly that he believed the Commission's estimate of the deficit (seven hundred million dollars in 1953) was "overstated" by as much as two hundred million dollars; six months later he was ready to slice another hundred million from the same figure. In January, 1955, the Association of American Railroads complained to a task force of the Hoover Commission that it cost the railroads three million dollars a year to report unnecessary statistics to the government; in particular the Association objected to "the separation of common expenses between freight and passenger services" because the task was "burdensome and produces information of questionable value." In 1956 the governors of the New York Stock Exchange, concerned lest

247

shareholders were being hornswoggled, asked the American Institute of Accountants to investigate "divergencies between accounting practices of railroads and generally accepted principles in other industries."

The spate of criticism led the Commission to hold hearings in 1957 on the separation rules that had created this bugaboo. More objections to the rules were at once voiced. The National Association of Railroad and Utilities Commissioners said:

> The Separation Rules [are useful only] in the development of purely statistical information [which] has resulted in much misuse and misunderstanding of the "Passenger Deficit." . . . The term "Passenger Deficit" . . . appears to the public and others not accquainted with the rules under which the expenses are assigned [to be] a total loss from operation of the passenger train service. Nothing could be so wrong because its true meaning is that of a statistical fantasia.

There were other protests: from the Post Office Department, from firms of public accountants, from the city of Philadelphia.

And then something most curious happened. The Association of American Railroads, in the person of the vice-president in charge of accounting, submitted a statement which in effect urged that the rules be left unchanged, since the Commission's formula produced substantially accurate and useful data for the purposes intended. It was a complete turnabout from the Association's position of two years before, when the formula had been derided for producing data "of questionable value." Complacently patting down its back hair, the Commission thereupon concluded that its separation rules were dandy and required no modification. The myth of the passenger deficit had once again prevailed.

How came this astonishing switch by the Association? Easily, quickly, once it had been determined by the lords of the railroads that the phantom deficit was a most useful hobgoblin with which to alarm impressionable congressmen. In 1957 and 1958 they were exerting pressure on the Congress to amend the Interstate Commerce Act so that unwanted passenger trains might be more easily lopped off; the bigger the deficit could be made to seem, the sooner the Congress would act.*

The amendment (Section 13a) was duly enacted. The butchery of the passenger service proceeded briskly. Between two and three hundred intercity trains vanished every year.

Now when a passenger train that moves back and forth between two cities is discontinued, in all likelihood the old-time way of hauling the mail between those two cities has been jeopardized. When several thousand such intercity trains are canceled, the disruption of the old-time mail service is almost complete. Back in 1935 the railroads had operated some ten thousand mail-carrying passenger trains, but by 1959 there were fewer than two thousand passenger trains available to carry the mails, and not all of these were running on schedules

---

*Once the amendment had been enacted, the deficit had served its immediate purpose; but, like other large lies and multiple untruths, it has been kept alive for other reasons. In evidence of its more recent vitality, one may cite:

1. The letter of Stuart T. Saunders, chairman of the board of directors of the Pennsylvania Railroad, dated February 23, 1966, which appeared in the annual report of that railroad company to its shareholders. At page three, Saunders wrote:

> Our freight business continued to subsidize our passenger service. Approximately 48 cents out of every dollar of net freight operating income was consumed by our 1965 passenger losses of $41.8 million.

And at page eleven of the same report, it was stated:

> Long-haul passenger traffic continued to be a heavy drain on our resources, but we had some encouragement during 1965 of prospects for medium and short-range traffic.
>
> Our passenger operating deficit rose to $41.8 million compared with $34.9 million in 1964.

The shareholders were invited to conclude that the Pennsylvania's net income would have been twice what it was had the carrier not been obliged to operate passenger trains. As chairman of the board of directors, Saunders himself surely knew better.

2. The report, entitled "The Future of Rail Passenger Traffic in the West," prepared for the Southern Pacific by the Stanford Research Institute (undated, but published late in 1966). The authors of this report, whose prognosis of the plight of intercity passenger trains is extremely gloomy, focus on the phony passenger deficit as a most morbid symptom and glibly dismiss critics of the Commission's formula as "informed laymen." The report can be dismissed as specious expertise.

249

that made them useful or attractive to the Post Office Department. Long since, the men who manage the Post Office had been obliged to give serious thought to the pock-marked schedules of the surviving trains, the gross inefficiency of rail terminal operations, the preferred hours of mail delivery, the cost of hauling mail by rail, and the possible advantages of having the mail hauled by some other type of carrier.

Meanwhile the load of mail (most of it junk, to be sure) had enormously increased and the Post Office was rapidly becoming everybody's favorite whipping boy. With increasing frequency, the Post Office decided to cancel its contracts with the railroads for the handling of bulk mail and to award the contracts instead to truckers and, even for ordinary first-class mail, to the airlines.

Predictably, the railroad executives yelped. On the face of it, their anguish was puzzling: from 1958 through 1964 their mail revenues consistently hovered around three hundred and thirty million dollars a year; higher than ever before, more than half as much as the revenues for carrying people; more, it would seem, than the railroads deserved to be paid, after so thoroughly discombobulating the nation's mail service. Why then should railroad executives gripe about an occasionally canceled contract?

An answer can be found in one of the earliest plaints, by the Eastern Railroad Presidents Conference, in February, 1958:

> At recent hearings in the Interstate Commerce Commission's Passenger Deficit Investigation [said a statement by the Conference] it was brought out that frequently the railroads have been forced to discontinue passenger trains because the Post Office Department has taken the mail away.

The unmistakable implication here was that the railroad presidents had been nobly struggling to save the passenger service but that the wicked Post Office had "forced" the defeat of their efforts. This was not true. The Commission knew it was not true and said so (306 I.C.C. 417, at page 471). The railroad presidents also knew it was not true, and so one must ruefully conclude that here is another example of the fact that they tell fibs. Their statement went further:

> On top of this, the Post Office Department has been diverting the more profitable mail to airlines and truckers wherever it feels that it will be to its advantage. . . . [T]he diversion of the more profitable mail traffic away from the railroads will eventually weaken the railroads' ability to provide a national system of mail service and [has] already caused or helped to cause the discontinuance of many passenger trains.

Here was a superb example of the multiple untruth, one that contains in a small compass so much distortion, irrelevance, unwarranted assumption, and flat inaccuracy that it can be properly corrected only by rewriting it entirely and quite changing its meaning and thrust. Yet, in the years that have followed, the railroad executives have nurtured this untruth to a luxurious growth, for it perfectly serves their purpose. Nearly always when a passenger train has been nominated for oblivion, the Post Office has been singled out as the villain responsible, for having withdrawn the lucrative mails from the train in question and thereby made it unprofitable.

As it happens, there is a statute, the Railway Mail Service Pay Act (39 U.S.C. 563), which includes an ominous paragraph putting all railroad campanies on notice that they must "perform mail services . . . when required by the Postmaster General so to do" and warning them that their refusal so to do will result in their being fined one thousand dollars a day. This fearful statute has never been invoked but, just to play it safe, the railroad companies, whenever they have desired to cancel a mail-carrying passenger train, have notified the Post Office of their intention, so that other arrangements for the mail might be made; they have even, on occasion, *first requested* the Post Office to withdraw all mail from the train. The Post Office, ever obliging, has always done so.*

* Indeed, the Post Office has fitted its needs to the convenience of the railroad companies with an almost indecent geniality, remindful of nothing so much as the behavior of the madam of an ill-patronized brothel when the American Legion is in town on convention. The Department

251

This procedure has been invaluable for the railroads. Once the mails have been taken from a train, the railroad company has been able to claim, without fear of contradiction, that the train's operating income has seriously shriveled. Those travelers who opposed cancellation of the train service have naturally assumed that the decision to remove the mails was without the consent and beyond the control of the railroad company (for what sensible company would voluntarily slash its revenues?), and so their opposition has usually collapsed.

But the civil servants at the Post Office came to weary of their role as the bad guys in the steady slaughter of the rail passenger service. They dug back into their files and presently were able to show that, from February 1, 1953, to December 31, 1966, a total of 2,528 mail-carrying passenger trains had been discontinued, of which 1,730 were discontinued after their mail traffic had been removed at the request of the railroads, and 798 were discontinued after their mail traffic had been removed on the initiative of the Post Office.

So all the propaganda from the railroads about the wicked Post Office assays at a little better than thirty-per-cent accurate —which is, to be sure, a phenomenal batting average for truth in the railroad business.

But what about those cases in which the Post Office has itself initiated cancellation of mail by rail? In May, 1966, Daniel P. Loomis, the president of the Association of American Railroads, pounced on what he fancied was a representative cancellation, one he promptly protested to the Postmaster General as "particularly shocking" and "inconsistent with every recognized principle of sound national transportation policy," which involved bulk mail southbound to Florida from a postal facility in Newark, New Jersey. Until April 26, 1966, the mail had been shipped by rail via the Pennsylvania, the Richmond,

once confided to the Interstate Commerce Commission (306 I.C.C. 417, at page 473): "The Post Office Department has accepted what the railroads had to offer. . . . In *no* instance has it used its statutory prerogative to compel the railroads to add trains, change schedules, or make additional station stops."

Fredericksburg & Potomac, and the Seaboard Air Line; thereafter a contract was negotiated with a Philadelphia trucking concern. "Diversion of this mail," Loomis claimed, "will reduce rail passenger revenue by approximately $197,000 per year," and he argued that "any reduction in mail revenue has an immediate and significantly adverse impact on passenger train revenue, so necessary to retention of passenger service over the lines affected." The retort of an assistant postmaster general was acid. Post Office records showed that the railroads had taken from thirty-eight to fifty-six hours to deliver the mail in storage cars, that the Pennsylvania had offered to provide piggyback service in refrigerator vans which were being returned empty to Florida (the vans were used to haul citrus fruit north), but that the Pennsylvania had insisted on the full postal rate (from $438.20 to $516.45 per van). In contrast, the trucker charged only $420 for bigger van loads and consistently delivered the mail to Jacksonville in less than twenty-six hours.

*The Pennsylvania had offered to remove this mail from the passenger service.* Loomis had been the victim of his own propaganda.

Further evidence that, by downgrading the passenger service, the railroad managers were endangering their lucrative mail contracts came with the announcement that the Post Office Department, grown suddenly more severe, had fined nine railroad companies a total of $127,500 for delaying the mails during the first quarter of 1967. (The Burlington was fined $20,000; the New York Central drew the biggest penalty, one of $35,000. Fines were levied when mail trains were late at least half the time.) A few days later a Post Office spokesman gave notice that the mail service on four western roads—the Illinois Central, the Rock Island, the Burlington, and the Milwaukee Road—was to be curtailed or canceled between Chicago, Omaha, and Sioux City. The decision was taken, the spokesman said, because the reduced train schedules made it impossible to move mail when it should be moved, and because the trains still in service were too often too late.

At all events, it seems clear that the mail revenues provide very inadequate support for a healthy passenger service. On January 1, 1967, only eight hundred and seventy-six passenger trains carried the mail, and the number was still shrinking.

During the 1960s the equipment in the passenger service has become older, dirtier, and shabbier, and the industry has done little to refurbish or to replace it. According to the last census of railroad equipment, published by the American Railway Car Institute in 1962, there were at that time about twenty-seven thousand passenger-train cars, of which about eleven thousand were head-end cars (for mail, baggage, and such). Sixty per cent of these cars were then more than thirty years old. In August, 1963, a committee of the National Academy of Sciences, asked by the Secretary of Commerce to study the use of science and technology in the railroad industry, had this to say about the passenger service:

> Research in long-haul passenger equipment in the United States is virtually dead. Of two formerly powerful suppliers of passenger cars, one has within the past three years given up all research and development effort; the other has nothing new or imaginative in its distinctly low-key research program.
>
> It is reasonable to speculate that rail-passenger prospects are on the threshold of a great opportunity as highway programs become overwhelmed by the waves of the new cars of a larger population in the next four decades. Careful research by the rail industry into the economic, social, and demographic forces that may open a door to the railroads might be worth at least a modest effort now. . . .

But the industry had no inclination to make even a modest effort on behalf of the passengers. Within the industry, to be sure, there were still a few companies that welcomed their passengers and afforded them courteous and comfortable service; still a few companies to remind the world that, at their best, the American trains are unrivaled; and of these few one must mention the Atlantic Coast Line and the Seaboard Air Line for their trains to and from Florida (these companies are now merged as the Seaboard Coast Line), the Illinois Central for its trains between Chicago and New Orleans, the Great Northern and the Northern Pacific for their limiteds through the northwest, the Burlington and the Union Pacific for their superior limiteds, and the Santa Fe for its limiteds through the southwest.*

But the industry is dominated by the biggest carriers. As the committee of the National Academy of Sciences also reported:

> A most cumbersome committee-type organism is used for decisions affecting the interrelation of the Class I carriers. . . . There are strong overtones of undue influence wielded by a few carriers. Lack of command, authority, and decision discourages worthwhile expeditious introduction of innovations through the national network.

The many millions of Americans who still prefer to travel considerable distances by rail are convinced that the industry, influenced "by a few carriers," has downgraded the passenger service steadily, persistently, swiftly, and deliberately. They would agree with the analysis of yet another committee that has examined American railroads in detail. In January, 1961, a special study group appointed by the Senate Committee on Interstate and Foreign Commerce concluded, after gloomily inspecting the rail passenger service:

> The very age of the railroad coach is one of its worst handicaps. The coach and the people who operate it seem to have forgotten how to change their habits and to have forgotten that innovation and intelligent improvement have been a hallmark of American business since well before the coach's birth.

So matters stood when, in 1962, Senator Pell published his plan, deplored by most railroad executives but hailed with gratitude by despondent rail passengers all over the country.

---

*I recall how, in the summer of 1964, I told Ernest Marsh, who was then the president of the Santa Fe, that I had never traveled west of Chicago on a train. He gave me a startled look, at once pitying and incredulous. "My friend," he said, "if you have never been on a train west of Chicago, *you* have never *been* on a *train*." I soon found that he was right.

# 15

---

*More on the passenger service. The Pell plan. The industry's trains-off policy. Demonstration project in the northeast corridor. Has the time come to nationalize the passenger trains?*

---

THE PELL PLAN was less important for what it provided than for the discussion it aroused. (The plan envisioned an eight-state public authority, one that was to have owned and operated a high-speed railroad passenger service within Megalopolis—that is, the densely populated region from Boston to Washington; the system was to have been financed by long-term, tax-exempt bonds guaranteed by the government.) No sooner had news of it been published in The New York Times than Senator Pell sensed that he had struck a vein of purest political gold. There was not only the extraordinarily friendly editorial comment in newspapers all over the country. "My office was swamped with letters," Pell wrote, in *Megalopolis Unbound,* the excellent book he has recently had published, "from hundreds of people all over the country who have wanted to offer congratulations, receive more information, or participate in some way in the project that I envisaged."

In the summer of 1962, however, the political wiseacres in Washington doubted that Pell's scheme was high octane. As always, these gentry estimated the puissance of a legislative notion by its sponsorship and the commercial forces rallied to shove it along; and by both these tests the Pell plan was nothing, going nowhere. Who, after all, was Pell? A pleasant young man, to be sure, but an exceedingly junior senator, as yet not even politically pubescent; a member of no committee charged with the grave problems of transportation in the overcrowded northeast. Of the powerful transportation lobbies—highway users, airlines, truckers, automobile manufacturers, railroads, buslines—none was disposed to back Pell's daydream and each could find some reason to oppose it. Pell could be shrugged off and forgotten. His plan was dismissed as a joke, an eight-day wonder, a foolish means of working up publicity by a politician who knew no better.

What the shrewd political thinkers failed to take into account was the widespread popular support for Pell's idea, which was really support for any idea that held a promise of a decent rail passenger service. Moreover, Pell was himself persistent; a kind of cross between WASP and gadfly, he kept pressing the White House for executive action; he nagged, he pestered. And he could marshal battalions of disconcerting facts.

But at first nothing much happened, for the Highway Users Conference (which boasts a lobby second only to the Pentagon's in its influence on Capitol Hill) and the airlines were both suspicious, and the railroad industry was conspicuously indifferent. In the last year of the Kennedy administration, one million dollars were asked and six hundred and twenty-five thousand dollars were actually authorized to study the assumptions underlying the Pell plan, now officially known as the Northeast Corridor Project; in the first year of the Johnson administration, after much prodding by Pell, the Secretary of Commerce announced an ambitious program of research into and development of high-speed rail passenger transportation.

In January, 1965, in his report to the Congress on the state of the union, President Johnson said: "I will ask for funds to study high-speed rail transportation between urban centers. We will begin with test projects between Boston and Washington. On high-speed trains, passengers could travel this distance in less than four hours." *Four hours?* Those unhappy people who still traveled by rail between Boston and Washington were used to the fact that if all went well—which it seldom did—the trip took eight hours and forty minutes. Yet the President reckoned it should take less than four hours? When *that* came to pass, his would not be merely a Great Society, it would be a Naked Miracle.

The administration's bill, which authorized ninety million dollars for new passenger equipment and further research, slid easily through the Congress, assisted now by the Railway Progress Institute (the association of railway equipment manufacturers, each of whom was eager for a contract), by the steel industry, by the railway labor unions, and, mirabile dictu, by the railroads. Stuart Saunders, of the Pennsylvania, urged passage of the bill and said he knew of no railroad official who implacably opposed it. After all, the only railroads directly involved in the Northeast Corridor Project were the Pennsylvania and the bankrupt New Haven.

On September 30, 1965, before a throng of congressmen, railroad presidents, and other dignitaries assembled in the East Room of the White House, President Johnson ceremoniously signed the High-Speed Ground Transportation Act. A big moment; a speech. Ritual pens handed out, hands shaken, smiles exchanged, a buzz of happy talk. The congressmen took their leave, among them Senator Pell, who had briefly glittered in the Presidential spotlight; but the railroad presidents lingered, awaiting their cue.

At the President's chummy invitation, the railroad men then moved to another room of the White House, where he talked with them for a time, in the persuasive manner for which he is celebrated. The performance was private, but some of those who were present later sketched, with some awe, its main features. The President praised them warmly for bringing their companies through a time of lean pickings, expressed concern over the problems posed by their competition, wagged his head over the difficulties of regulation, mentioned the profits flooding in on the wave of current prosperity, and commented that the railroads were unexcelled at carrying large numbers of people from here to there. Then, in a marked manner, came the Presidential request: any further reductions in the passenger service must at all costs be avoided. Did they not agree that it was essential to keep the passenger service at its current level? Perhaps even to restore some of the trains that had already been discontinued?

At this point, some of his guests seemed rather uncomfortable. The President suggested that he would like to see a report on the whole question of the passenger service, its future, how it could be made to work—and who better to prepare such a report than the leaders of the industry?

Before they left, the railroad men had agreed to reconsider the problem of the passenger service and report to the President in three months—by January, 1966.

However inopportune, here was another of those magic occasions when the railroad men had it at their command to obliterate the errors and stupidities of the past; no questions asked, no blames assessed, no guilts imputed. If they had treated their passengers shabbily, the public, through its elected representatives, had agreed to forget all the old animosities and had whipped up a good deal of excitement over the brave new trains promised for the future. If the government in Washington had treated the railroads unfairly, if federal funds had been inequitably sluiced to their competitors, now the seasons had wheeled through an equinox, and at last the railroads were once again sharing in these federal bounties.

It was not much, but it was a beginning. When ninety million dollars were to be spent for a demonstration project in the Washington–Boston corridor, how much more might not soon rain gently down on the other excrescential urban clusters—San Diego–Los Angeles–San Francisco, South Bend–Chicago–Milwaukee, Jacksonville–Tampa–Miami, Pittsburgh–Cleveland–Detroit, Dallas–Fort Worth–Waco–Austin, Albany–Rochester–Buffalo–Cleveland, even Cheyenne–Denver–Pueblo? And if new, fast, profitable trains could connect the cities of these clusters at short range, why should not new, fast, profitable trains also connect the clusters themselves at long range? In short, had the President not invited the railroad executives to assist at a renascence of the passenger service?

Moreover, if they chose so to construe the President's request, the railroad men had just to the north of them a spectacular example of how they might revive the passenger service, modernize it, and make it both popular and profitable: the example of the Canadian National.

The CN is the world's biggest railroad. It operates more than thirty-two thousand miles of track that reach through all ten Canadian provinces and into some of the northern United States as well. Unlike its chief competitor, the Canadian Pacific, the CN is (and has been since 1919) nationalized, but it is nevertheless highly competitive. In 1950 the government appointed Donald Gordon to be the road's president. Gordon is a big, burly Scots-Canadian, a banker by training and a canny gambler from the same mold as George Stephen (later Lord Mountstephen) and Richard B. Angus, the two Scots-Canadian bankers who backed James J. Hill on the wild venture that resulted in the Great Northern. Gordon approached his new job with all the conservative prejudices of railroad men about their passenger service. Like James J. Hill before him, he dismissed the passenger service as a nuisance that would incur only deficits; like the presidents of nearly every railroad in the United States, he accepted the creed that the passenger service was doomed to eternal damnation by the power and the glory of the automobile and the airplane, for ever and ever, Amen. For ten years Gordon cursed the passenger service and reviled it as contemptuously as did his counterparts south of the border; for ten years he devoutly prayed, as they did, that on some soon and blessed morning he would wake to find that he had nothing left to fret his mind except freight. "By 1961," Gordon recalled later, "we had dropped twenty-five per cent of our passenger service and we hoped to get rid of the whole works."

In 1961, however, the Board of Transport Commissioners, which is the Canadian analogue of the Interstate Commerce Commission, blew the whistle on any further quick discontinuances of Canadian passenger trains. Canadian railroads had suffered from the same gnawing competition as had Amercan: Canadian ownership of automobiles since 1950 had soared four hundred per cent, Canadian air travel was up seven hundred per cent, and the railroads' share of Canadian travel revenues had plummeted to less than four per cent; nevertheless the Canadian railroads were warned by their regulators that all future discontinuances would be sharply challenged. The effect of this caveat on Donald Gordon of the CN was remarkable. If he was stuck with a passenger business, by Heaven he would try to make it pay.

Gordon began with a simple, basic precept: he who wants a profit need only offer a better product at a lower price. Fares were slashed; at first experimentally, then all over the dominion; as much as fifty per cent. Equipment was modernized; trains began to move on faster schedules; train crews got new uniforms, and were sent to four-day seminars to learn how to be both efficient and courteous; the public was invited to buy tickets by mail and on credit; a Car-Go-Rail plan enabled passengers to take their automobiles with them and find them, freshly washed, at their destination. Passengers flocked to the CN trains, to the Ocean Limited (Halifax–Montreal), to the Panorama (Montreal–Vancouver), to le Champlain (Montreal–Quebec), and most of all to the Rapido (Montreal–Toronto).

The Rapido went into service in October, 1965, just as the American railroad presidents were beginning to wonder what they should say to President Johnson about the American passenger trains. The Rapido at once became the fastest intercity train in North America, running the three hundred and thirty-five miles between Montreal and Toronto in five hours, which was one and one quarter hours faster than the train it had replaced. Its first-class passengers paid a fare of fifteen dollars, which included an excellent dinner; a coach seat, without dinner, cost eight dollars. "This train is going to hurt the airlines," said a businessman, on one of its first trips. "It doesn't take that much longer, it's relaxing, and we're sure of getting there whatever the weather." He spoke sooth: the Rapido proved so popular that soon it was necessary to reserve space on it a week in advance. And Air Canada ruefully reported that fewer people were flying between the two cities. (By contrast, the New York Central's Chicagoan takes six hours to run the three hundred and forty miles from Cleveland to Chicago; its first-class passengers pay $25.74, the coach fare is $16.25, and any meals are extra; there is no rush to clamber aboard the train.)

No sooner was the Rapido an assured success than the CN announced it would be replaced by five turbine-powered trains, built of aluminum, designed aerodynamically (by United Aircraft) with a suspension system that would permit a smooth ride at speeds up to one hundred and sixty miles an hour, and able to cut the time between Montreal and Toronto to *four* hours. "The most significant railway passenger-service innovation in the last one hundred years," Gordon boasted; and he is confident his turbo-trains will make the CN's passenger service profitable by 1970.

Was there here a lesson for American railroad executives? Or could they learn anything from the resounding success of the Japanese Tokaido line, which shoots a handsome train called the Bullet three hundred and twenty miles between Tokyo and Osaka in *three* hours? Possibly; but the chief executive officers of the great American railroad companies have on their minds more exigent matters than the performance of passenger trains in foreign countries. They delegated the task of drafting the report for President Johnson to their general counsels, to officials of the Association of American Railroads.

In due course the report ("On the Intercity Rail Passenger Train Situation, and Certain Other Railroad Problems") was approved, neatly typed, and, on January 5, 1966, delivered to the White House. It was a pedestrian document; a rambling recapitulation of all the industry's fancied grievances against regulators, tax assessors, tax legislators, competitors, and architects of the so-called federal transportation policy, if any; yet, as the months passed and their report provoked no official reaction, the railroad men bridled. They believed they had proffered substantial pledges and had also suggested, discreetly, that their posture on fundamental issues was radically altered. Why then were their tenders ignored?

In the face of a frosty silence at the White House, the railroad men themselves made public their revolutionary about-face. It was that they no longer insisted on the absurd estimate of the so-called passenger deficit computed by the Commission's formula (which in 1965 amounted to four hundred and twenty-one million dollars); they now admitted that their actual, out-of-pocket losses amounted to only forty-four million dollars. (Even this estimate is probably exaggerated.) The broad implication was that any administration which wished to preserve the passenger service in its status quo, and which at the same time was paying out zillions of dollars of federal funds to build highways and to subsidize airlines, could easily afford to pick up the tab for such a trivial deficit.

But the White House had declined to jump at the bait. Obviously the report was not the "imaginative solution" to the rail passenger service problem that President Johnson had sought.

Stalemate.

Notice should be taken of the brave pledges made by the industry, to wit:

> The railroad industry . . . pledges itself to cooperate with the Administration by making every reasonable effort to place its intercity passenger service on a paying basis and not seek to discontinue any trains that produce revenues in excess of the cost of operation.
>
> The rail carriers further agree that they will from time to time review passenger service along their respective lines and where by reason of changed conditions it appears there is economic justification for the inauguration of changed or additional intercity passenger service, they will take steps to that end.

In March the Pennsylvania announced cancellation of its Spirit of St. Louis, an action rejected by the Commission. Later in the year the Pennsylvania sought to discontinue a pair of Buffalo–Baltimore trains, claiming lack of patronage; the baggage master on one of the trains testified it was sometimes so crowded that as many as twenty-seven passengers would have to ride in the baggage car.

Also in March the Rock Island announced it would seek to cancel all its long-distance passenger service; its Twin-Star Rocket (Kansas City–Fort Worth) and its Rocky Mountain Rocket (Chicago–Denver–Colorado Springs) were both discontinued.

In May the Delaware & Hudson sought to discontinue its famous Laurentian Express, a chief link in the service between New York and Montreal. The New York State Public Service Commission perceived deliberate efforts to downgrade the service and rejected the railroad's request.

In June the Erie-Lackawanna sought discontinuance of its most celebrated passenger train, the Phoebe Snow. By November it had disappeared.

In July the New York Central announced it would seek to cancel all its long-distance passenger trains, including the Twentieth Century. At the time there was an airline strike, so the Century was crowded. A reporter from The New York Times talked with a few of the passengers. "I never ride this train," said a Toledo businessman; "it's too damn dirty and the service is lousy." Other passengers, however, mourned the threat of imminent cancellation.

In August an officer of the Denver & Rio Grande Western wrote the Post Office, asking to "be relieved of responsibility for handling mail on all of our passenger trains." Later came petitions to discontinue such trains as the Prospector (Denver–Salt Lake City), citing cancellation of mail contracts by the Post Office.

Also in August the Western Pacific requested that it be permitted to discontinue its share of the operation of the California Zephyr, the fine train run between Chicago and San Francisco by the Burlington, the Denver & Rio Grande Western, and the Western Pacific. The case was unusual for several reasons. No downgrading of service was charged; on the contrary, its passengers praised the train. The Zephyr operates virtually at capacity during the summer; the annual number of its passengers has held steady since 1950, the first full year of operation. The Burlington's officials maintained that, on an avoidable-cost basis, the train returned them a profit; the Western Pacific's officers, however, were able to show an annual operating deficit in the neighborhood of half a million dollars. The Commission found that the Zephyr was "a unique national asset" and ordered its operation continued for one year; the Commission also emphasized that during that year the public authorities in the affected region should explore possible programs of assistance, and that the Western Pacific would have to consider fare changes and more efficient use of personnel.

In October the Illinois Central announced it would seek to discontinue several trains.

In November the Frisco filed a petition, asking that its last four passenger trains be discontinued. The Commission turned the petition down.

Other companies, the Boston & Maine, the Southern, the Seaboard Air Line, also discontinued trains during the year, but of all the railroad companies the Southern Pacific was easily the most energetic and resourceful in its efforts to boot passengers off its trains and keep them a secret from potential passengers. A typical instance has to do with a pair of trains between Tucumcari, New Mexico, and Phoenix, Arizona, part of a through service between Kansas City and Los Angeles. (Kill part of the service, you kill it all.) The SP, which used to have a huge billboard that read "s.p.—YOUR FRIENDLY RAILROAD" atop its main office building in San Francisco, discouraged passengers from using these trains by eliminating all mention of them in published schedules, instructing ticket agents to deny the trains existed, closing the ticket office two and one half hours before time of departure, and occasionally forcing the stubborn passengers to ride in a caboose. The Commission ordered the trains continued.

The SP also did everything in its power to downgrade services on the Shasta Daylight, a train from Oakland to Portland through some of the most spectacular mountain scenery in the world. The Commission instructed the company to keep the train in service during the summer months.

The SP's Sunset Limited between San Francisco and New Orleans used to be one of the country's finest trains. In January the company dropped its dining-car service and a month later it pulled off its sleeping cars, alleging a need for economy. (The SP is the most profitable railroad in the country.)

In June the SP was working hard to shoot down the Lark, its famous overnight train between San Francisco and Los Angeles. SP advertisements advised everybody to fly. (One full-page advertisement the SP inserted in a travel magazine called the train traveler "The Vanishing American" and blamed him for high freight rates.) Service on the Lark was all but eliminated. Dinner, so-called, was served on paper placemats and was limited to four items: bacon and eggs ($1.85), ham and cheese sandwich ($1.65), hamburger ($1.50), and sirloin steak sandwich ($3.25). Of this last item, Stan Freberg, the humorist, said: "The only thing tougher than that steak is the heart of a Southern Pacific ticket agent." A photograph of the Lark's dining car was printed in The Los Angeles Times; it showed only one customer, an elderly lady. "Hell," said a brakeman, "they took that picture five minutes after the car had been closed." An editorial writer for The San Francisco Chronicle noted, as in an obituary: "Somewhere along the line, the public necessity and the convenience of passengers have been sidetracked and forgotten." At a hearing before the California Public Utilities Commission, the SP produced executives from eighteen California companies; as one man, they complained that they were paying unnecessarily high freight rates just to keep the nasty old Lark rolling back and forth. The commission was not impressed. It assailed the carrier for its efforts to downgrade the Lark and ordered a resumption of advertising and promotion and a consideration of reduction of fares.

And still the officers of the SP were not finished. They engaged the Stanford Research Institute to prepare a study called "The Future of Rail Passenger Traffic in the West," sixty

266

pages of imperial octavo stuffed with charts, tables of statistics, and prognostications of ineffable gloom; selective in its research, tendentious in its hard-nosed conclusions, but having on the unwary a considerable impact, as do all exercises supposedly rooted in fact. Its authors acknowledge in their introduction a debt to "many officials of the Southern Pacific Company . . . for the assistance given in this study," and, indeed, it seems to the prudent reader that the Stanford Research Institute has carefully fed back to the Southern Pacific precisely those ideas that have governed the policies of the Southern Pacific for a decade or more. The burden of the report is that the long-distance rail passenger service is dead, unburied, and beginning to smell. The argument is that *all* western railroads should get out of the business at once. The report seems to have had no effect whatsoever on those roads that are committed to promoting their passenger service. Officers of, for instance, the Santa Fe insist that they seek as many passengers as they can possibly fit into their excellent trains.

Meanwhile, the Commission has been taking a long, hard look at the Southern Pacific and its passenger-service policies. The state regulatory bodies of California, New Mexico, and Arizona are hot after the SP's steady, consistent, determined tactic of throttling its passenger service, and the public interest and convenience may yet prevail.

Whether or not they do, what price the pledge of the railroad industry, so recently proffered, that it would make "every reasonable effort to place its intercity passenger service on a paying basis and not seek to discontinue any trains that produce revenues in excess of the cost of operation"?

There are, of course, other ways to alienate the would-be passenger. Some of them, petty enough to begin with, are yet such ingenious provocations, so marvelously brought up to the highest possible amperage of infuriation, that it is quite impossible to believe they were not purposefully planned.

Take, for example, the process of calling on the telephone for some scrap of information about a passenger train—the

267

fare, its time of departure and destined arrival, how to make a reservation. (And bear in mind that such information is quickly and cheerfully given, twenty-four hours a day, by every airline.) Some railroad clerks are evidently instructed to take their phone from its cradle, or hook, and then to forget it; in this way any persons who call are repulsed, hour after hour, by a busy signal, until 5 p.m., when a recorded voice instructs them to start trying again at 9 a.m. the next morning. Other railroad clerks, themselves impervious to minor irritations, simply ignore a ringing phone, hour after hour. Governor Richard J. Hughes, of New Jersey, found not long ago that he had to wait forty-five minutes before a clerk at the Pennsylvania Railroad station in Trenton would answer his call. Because he is a public official who is trying to improve the passenger service, the governor's frustration was duly reported in the press; but his experience was not exceptional, nor was the apathy of the clerk who eventually took his call.

Another stratagem is the disruption of train schedules, or calculated snafu. Suppose you wish to travel overnight by train from Washington to Memphis. There is no through service, but the Southern Railway has a Birmingham Special that arrives in Chattanooga at 8:10 a.m., or ten minutes *after* the train to Memphis has left. The Southern Pacific's Sunset Limited has been so rescheduled that, eastbound, it no longer connects at New Orleans with the Gulf Wind, the Louisville & Nashville's overnight train to Jacksonville; westbound, the Sunset leaves stranded in New Orleans for about fifteen hours those passengers coming from the east on the L&N's Crescent or the Southern Railway's Southerner. The story of broken connections in Chicago is an old one to Americans; not so to a large party of European travel agents who recently inspected our transportation system with an eye to stimulating the flow of European tourists in our country; the agents found our patchwork of disconnections incomprehensible.

At the least, we must agree it is discouraging.

On October 3, 1966, one year after the High-Speed Ground

Transportation Act had been signed, Senator Pell was pleased to invite the attention of his colleagues to a report of what had been done to improve the rail passenger service in the northeast corridor. Some brave first steps had been taken.

A program of research and development had been launched, with emphasis on railroad technology but geared to explore some fairly unconventional high-speed systems as well. Experimental cars were to be built, crammed with hundreds of electronic sensors and other delicate instrumentation, and set to testing every imaginable aspect of high-speed rail transportation, from the depth of ballast in the roadbed to the interaction of pantograph and catenary in the overhead grid of electric cables; track profiles, level, warp, and alignment; types of wheels, trucks, traction motors, suspension systems, and brakes; levels of vibration and noise; even the tint of the quarter-inch safety glass in the windows; this time nothing was to be left to chance or to guesswork.

The lessons of all this belated research were to be embodied in three demonstration projects. One is designed to explore the feasibility of hauling passengers *and* their automobiles, in specially designed double-decked railroad cars, from Washington to Jacksonville over the tracks of the Seaboard Coast Line. Once on board the train, passengers will be able to get out of their automobiles, stroll about, leave their children to romp in supervised play areas, relax in a lounge car, watch television, and eat their meals in a cafeteria car. The trip will take about twelve hours. The demonstration is planned to begin sometime in 1968.

The other two demonstration projects were, of course, designed to speed and otherwise improve rail travel in the northeast corridor; and in these Senator Pell could take an almost paternal pride. By November, 1967, both projects were to be in experimental operation.

Because of the deplorable financial condition of the New Haven, the demonstration project between Boston and New York is necessarily limited in scope. Moreover, the tracks of the New Haven curve and wind along the shore line, meandering over one hundred and twenty-nine grade crossings and one hundred and seventy-nine bridges which are from fifty to seventy-five years old. The road itself was in wretched condition. How could anyone imagine that trains could be moved over it fast enough to clip an hour from the time the trip has always taken? The challenge was accepted by the United Aircraft Corporation Systems Center. The company has designed and built two small, very light train sets of three cars each, powered by aircraft turbine engines that weigh only two hundred and fifty pounds apiece, and has suspended the trains so that they swing inward as they bank around curves. Thus they are able to negotiate curves thirty per cent faster than trains of conventional design. (Here is an instance of the engineering ingenuity so conspicuously lacking in the railroad industry for so many decades.) The United Aircraft trainsets can zip along at 150 mph over the New Haven's existing tracks, but they will be held to about 110 mph. The state of Connecticut, through its Transportation Authority, has paid out five hundred thousand dollars to make structural improvements in the roadbed. The federal government, through the new Department of Transportation, has made contracts with the New Haven, specifying standards of on-time performance, cleanliness, and those other considerations necessary to a proper test of public reaction to the experimental service.

It is, however, the demonstration project between New York and Washington, over the tracks of the Pennsylvania, that affords the richest promise for a better rail passenger service not only in the northeast corridor but all over the country. This is because the officers of the Pennsylvania are sharply aware that everybody in the railroad business, indeed everybody in the transportation business, in this country and abroad, is taking a lively interest in just what kind of a passenger service the Pennsylvania will offer, after so many years of slovenry and neglect. And anyone who thinks that in these circumstances the Pennsylvania Railroad Company will not try its damnedest to do its best simply does not know the Pennsylvania Railroad Company.

The outward and visible signs of this inward and corporate grace are an improved catenary system, two hundred thousand tons of ballast for a stronger roadbed, hundreds of miles of continuous welded rail, four reinforced bridges, and raised platforms in the depots at Washington, Baltimore, and Wilmington—a list of items that cost the Pennsylvania more than twenty-five million dollars. Other visible signs are the fifty cars—ten parlor cars and forty coaches, twenty of them equipped with quick-service food counters—carpeted, quiet, and comfortable; self-propelled, able to cruise at 150 mph, coupled in pairs, operating in trains of four, six, eight, or more, and slicing about an hour off the old time for the trip. They cost the Pennsylvania more than eleven million dollars.

The demonstration is to run for two years, during which the railroad has agreed (by contract with the Department of Transportation) to experiment with the price of fares, the schedule of stops at intermediate depots, the kind of meals to be served, methods of selling tickets and making reservations, and the possibilities offered by on-board entertainments of various kinds. Those railroad employees who deal with passengers will have been schooled in such old-fashioned virtues as courtesy. Thirty of the cars have telephones; the system permits passengers to receive calls as well as make them. The trains may run on even swifter schedules during the last phase of the demonstration, perhaps fast enough to speed between Washington and New York in two hours and twenty minutes, every hour on the hour.

The aggressive co-operation of the Pennsylvania with the Office of High-Speed Ground Transportation does not mean that Stuart Saunders, the Pennsylvania's chief executive officer, has suddenly moved to the Amen corner and will now whoop it up for the passenger service; he is still inimical to the long-distance passenger train, and he regards the commuter train with considerable loathing; but he deplores our irrational, wasteful devotion to the automobile. ("We are blacktopping ourselves to death," he has said. "Los Angeles now gives sixty per cent of its land to highways, streets, and parking lots. This

271

is land removed from productive use and from the tax rolls. The cloverleaf has become our national flower.") But he has perceived an economic justification for beefing up the rail passenger service in a densely populated, 226-mile strip of urban sprawl.

And so the project has become a true demonstration. The Pennsylvania has always been the most influential company within the industry; always, even in its glum days of deficit, the most powerful; always proud of its claim to be the Standard Railway of the World; and its merger with the New York Central is certain to give the company even greater consequence and its officers even greater panache: if the Pennsylvania (or the Penn-Central) shows the country what can be done with a well-planned passenger service, the other carriers across the country will inevitably come under pressure to do likewise. *Quod erat demonstrandum; quod demonstrabit Pennsylvania.*

The pressure on other carriers is already mounting. In January, 1967, a group of civic and state organizations held a Midwest High-Speed Rail Transit Conference in Chicago; a paper was read by Robert A. Nelson, the able and imaginative director of the Northeast Corridor Project; another paper, by W. W. Hay, professor of railway civil engineering at the University of Illinois, argued that the relatively flat terrain of the middle west is perfectly fitted for high-speed trains, and urged that after a few curves had been reduced, some welded rails laid down, some bridges strengthened, some crests and sags removed, and some grade crossings eliminated, trains run at a top speed of 125 mph could reduce the time of trips between

—St. Louis and Chicago from five and one half to three hours,

—the Twin Cities and Chicago from six and one half to four and one half hours,

—Detroit and Chicago from five and one half to three hours, and

—Cleveland and Chicago from six to three and one half hours.

"These improved times," Professor Hay noted, "would all be

272

competitive with modern jet air schedules."

William B. Johnson, the president of the Illinois Central, also read a paper in which he predicted train speeds up to 170 mph by 1970; but trains running at top speeds of only 125 mph over improved tracks of his own Illinois Central could reduce the time of trips between

—St. Louis and Memphis from six and three quarters to three and one third hours, and

—Memphis and New Orleans from six and three quarters to four and one quarter hours;

and even greater reductions could be scored between others of the dozens of big, proximate cities that have grown up, largely because of the railroads, all over the country.

It is worth noting that the railroads have long been technologically capable of operating trains at high speeds. Thirty years ago trains of the C&NW, the Burlington, and the Milwaukee Road all regularly hit 100 mph on the run between Chicago and the Twin Cities; fifty years ago speeds of more than 100 mph were routine for passenger trains on straight, level stretches of track; in 1905 a train of the Pennsylvania Railroad attained 127 mph over three miles of track in western Ohio. Trains are slower today only because the companies that operate them have deliberately downgraded the service.

The debate about public transportation goes on, and it will never be resolved to everyone's satisfaction.

In terms of efficiency, of safety and dependability in all weathers, of financial economy, the railroads are first and their competitors nowhere in sight; but in an affluent, spendthrift society such arguments as efficiency and economy carry little weight.

What counts in this debate are incontrovertible facts like the steady deterioration of the fleet of passenger cars and the appalling cost of replacing that fleet. If a determination of public policy is not made very soon, there will be no more rail passenger service simply because the cars to carry passengers will be too decrepit for the demands made upon them. To

273

tempt the large sums of capital (public as well as private) needed to build and buy a fleet of new, comfortable, clean, quiet passenger cars, there must be unmistakable evidence of a public demand for an improved rail passenger service, and the demonstration project in the northeast corridor, it is hoped, will supply such evidence in abundance.

But there are other problems that attend any renascence of the passenger train. One of them has been defined by William H. Tucker, who has been the chairman of the Interstate Commerce Commission during 1967.

> This is the problem [Tucker said recently] of educating—or, more accurately, uneducating—the public to the realities of the rail passenger business. Such an "uneducating" process is essential to offset a deeply ingrained public conception of rail passenger service as a third-rate operation begrudgingly performed. Certainly the industry's performance to date in this area has not been exciting. But I hope its history will not trap the railroad industry in a posture of failing to take all steps necessary to convince the public, through an aggressive program of promotion, that rail travel over essential and potentially viable routes can and will become much more responsive to the needs and demands of the user.

Commissioner Tucker has also described what he means by a "viable, modern" passenger service. It must include, he has said, "both a vastly improved medium-range, high-speed intercity train service within the conglomerate megalopolitan zones, and a basic core of long-distance trains connecting the megalopolitan areas to each other in overnight service."

It may be doubted that the railroad companies will undertake any such service unless the federal government makes it quite clear that they will be allowed to cancel no more intercity trains, that they are in the passenger business to stay. But even if the industry succeeds in uneducating the public, even if new equipment is put into service, tracks and roadbeds are improved, and schedules speeded up, everything in our past experience shows that the passenger service nationally will have to be supervised or at least sharply scrutinized by an

274

appropriate federal agency, just as the conduct of the demonstration projects in the northeast corridor is now being supervised by the Office of High-Speed Ground Transportation.

Surveillance is mandatory, for the business of railroading is in truth two quite different businesses—the hauling of freight and the carriage of people—with quite different managerial functions. The hauling of freight is a wholesale, industrial function. It has been well described as a factory that produces transportation in trainload lots for a relatively few customers, the shippers; this factory also functions for the same few customers as a mobile warehouse. The carriage of people, however, is a retail function, more like a specialty shop that sells custom-made goods to an exacting clientele. To ask one man to manage both enterprises is rather like asking the same actor to perform roles written for, say, John Wayne and Doris Day. Moreover, since the revenues from the passenger service in 1961–1965 were only about thirteen per cent of the revenues from the freight service, it is not hard to guess how the one manager of both services will spend his time and his energy and his capital funds—unless an unwinking eye is on him, watchful lest he give less than his wholehearted and zestful best on behalf of his passenger service.

And if the masters of the railroads resist such supervision, if they complain of further intolerable regulation, they must be reminded of what they have studiously ignored and hoped everybody else has forgotten: that the railways are public highways, laid down for the convenience of the general public, required to respond equably and equitably to the public necessity, and administered—at least theoretically—in the public interest. Eighty years ago, in the full wrath of our sovereign majesty, we decreed that the railroads must be regulated by a public authority, the Interstate Commerce Commission, and ever since the masters of the railroads have attempted to squirm out from under this authority, to subvert it, or to overthrow it. Now that we have built other highways on the ground and invented still others to fill the air, we have grown careless of our dominion and permitted, without rebuff,

275

an insolence from those who administer the railed public highways. In this way, through their contumacy on the one hand and a reckless squandering of our sovereign power on the other, we have reached a crisis in the business and the pleasure of traveling from here to there and back again.

In this crisis, time is a factor that can no longer be controlled. The equipment to operate a national passenger service has been allowed to deteriorate beyond patchwork: it is no longer obsolescent or even obsolete: it is all but extinct. No longer do we have a choice. We must once again exert our sovereign power. We must bid our government rule that the railed highways shall remain open for passengers. Once the masters of the railroads have been given their orders in unmistakable terms, they must find the ways to revive the passenger service. If they cannot, they must be relieved of the responsibility, and the passenger service must be nationalized.

# 16

*Commutation. A brief account of the seven railroads that carry the most commuters. The future of mass rapid-transit.*

As to commutation, one fact has always seemed to be beyond dispute: the commuter train rolls in the red; it cannot make a profit for its owner. "There is no way on earth," Stuart Saunders told the stockholders of the Pennsylvania Railroad Company at their annual meeting in May, 1965, "[by which the operation of commuter railroads] can be made profitable." A year later he said much the same thing to a subcommittee of the Senate's banking and currency committee. "Unfortunately," Saunders told the senators, "the economics of rail commutation are such that it is no longer a profitable enterprise for private business."

The mayors of New York City, Philadelphia, Boston, and several smaller cities agree: they have arranged in various ways to subsidize the commuter railroads that serve their cities. The governors of Pennsylvania, New Jersey, New York, Connecticut, and Massachusetts agree: in selfless, bipartisan fashion they have got their bipartisan legislatures to vote huge sums of public money so that the commuter railroads may somehow limp along. The federal government agrees: the Congress, enthusiastically propitiated by the railroad lobbyists, has authorized even huger sums of public money to improve urban mass transportation, some of which, of course, is the carrying of people to and from the big cities on commuter railroads.

All quite clear? Commutation is a losing proposition; it must

277

be subsidized; everybody agrees that it cannot make money.

What is puzzling about this unanimity is that a few commuter railroads *do* make money, and without subsidy.

There are several ways to explain why commuter railroads cannot make a profit for their private owners, all of them having to do with the cost-price relationship. To try to establish that relationship with any precision, however, is another exercise in futility, for the railroad managers have traditionally kept their cost data as murky as possible, hiding whenever possible behind the distortions of the formula invented by the Interstate Commerce Commission (see pp. 246–249), and for its part the Commission has done little or nothing to develop the cost data needed for its own regulatory purposes. When the Senate's Special Study Group on Transportation Policies (better known as the Doyle Committee) came in 1960 to investigate the complex of questions about urban transportation, suburban transportation, and commutation, they were quite cross because of the Commission's delinquencies. They growled about "outmoded accounting and costing practices suitable [only] for monopoly regulations." They urged: "Steps should be taken at the first opportunity to revise railroad accounting from the workman in the repair shop on up" and that "costs should be distributed by type of service from the first compilation forward." They noted that the only attempts at cost-finding studies of commutation had been pressed by the Public Service Commissions of New York and Pennsylvania, and that these efforts had been prejudiced by "the lack of original records and other empirical accounting data" that are now routinely accepted as necessary by financial officers in other industries. In short, the railroad managers had once again contrived to obscure the facts.

But if the statistics on passenger expenses are useful only as they show relative changes over the years, the data on commutation revenues are reasonably trustworthy. Those that deal with coaches and first-class accommodations are included for purposes of comparison:

Revenue per Passenger-Mile (in Cents)

| | Commu-tation | Coach | Parlor and Sleeping Cars |
|------|------|------|------|
| 1941 | 1.01 | 1.64 | 2.28 |
| 1951 | 1.71 | 2.47 | 3.27 |
| 1961 | 3.07 | 2.86 | 3.96 |
| 1966 | 3.33 | 2.99 | 3.84 |

In the last quarter century, then, the unhappy commuters have had their fares hiked faster even than have the intercity passengers; commutation fares have gone up faster, indeed, than the costs the railroads claim their passengers have burdened them with.

But how could the fares for commuters have been pegged so low to begin with? For many years, going back to the nineteenth century, railroad management regarded commutation as a by-product of the intercity rail passenger service. Fares were deliberately priced low, both to fill empty seats as the intercity trains approached their terminals and also to stimulate suburban development along the railways; it was not uncommon for a railroad company to give free passes, for as long as three years, to those who built houses in the new suburbs. Before long the by-product had become a full-fledged service that required its own trains, tracks, sidings, stations, and personnel to operate it. Still the railroad managers made no great effort to raise commutation fares, for they were clearing a nice profit by supplying the thriving suburbs with freight—especially coal for heating the suburban homes. Moreover, the revenues from passenger travel even in the off-peak hours remained fairly substantial. So the managers of the commuter railroads were content with a policy that would have scandalized more sensible businessmen: they gave the lowest rate to those of their customers who rode during the busiest hours of the day and charged the highest rate to the occasional off-peak customers. It is as though they had never heard of supply and demand.

Times change. Coal for heating gave way to oil or gas or

electricity, and suburban freight dwindled; the off-peak passenger, lured by no incentive fares to the railroad, took to her automobile; but still the railroad management clung to low fares for commuters, and to the old rattletrap equipment in which the commuters rode.

Until the 1940s, when suddenly they awoke and began howling for higher fares, fares that would begin to cover their costs.

Railroad companies, because of their considerable investment in plant and equipment and because of the ossified work rules in the contracts covering their employees, have high fixed costs and low variable costs. This means that their unit costs could be wonderfully reduced if only their officers could somehow figure out how to improve their utilization of plant and equipment. "The crux of the [commutation] problem," Saunders, of the Pennsylvania, told a group of senators in April, 1966, "is utilization of equipment. Far and away the greatest volume of traffic is moved in about four hours—inbound in the morning and outbound in the evening. For the rest of the time, the expensive equipment and the crews are comparatively idle, as fewer and fewer people seem willing to use commuter trains for any purpose other than traveling to and from work."

The better utilization of their equipment is a problem that increasingly vexes all railroad operators, and especially those in the east. In public they complain that their expensive commuter equipment is used only four hours a day, five days a week, and is hence a hideous drain on their treasuries; but in private they wag their heads over a far more distressing fact; to wit, that their loaded freight cars move, on the average, *only twenty-three and one half miles a day,* which means that in every twenty-four hours they are moving during only one hour and twenty minutes. Commuter trains are used only twenty hours a week, and that is serious, but freight trains are used, in Official Territory, only *nine hours and twenty minutes a week,* and that is appalling.

Faced with this frightful performance of their freight service, the best railroad brains have been throbbing furiously to improve matters, with, however, only indifferent success. (The figures for movement of loaded freight cars used above are for 1965, and they represent progress of only one half mile, or one minute, over the comparable figures for 1955. But just give the railroad operators a few more decades; they're trying, at least they're in there trying.) Faced with a performance in their commuter service only half as bad, the best railroad brains sag limp. They are complacently defeatist. Most of them can imagine only two alternatives: (1) get out of the business entirely, or (2) demand public money for subsidies. The first of these alternatives is, of course, so callous a defiance of the public interest as to be unthinkable (although the carriers have already managed to scuttle a large number of commuter trains, especially since the passage of the Transportation Act of 1958); but the second alternative is feasible, especially since everybody agrees that private enterprise cannot operate commuter trains profitably.

Meanwhile, what about those few commuter railroads that *do* make money? There they are, shining illustrations of what is best on the commercial American scene; they simply cannot be ignored or swept aside; and at least one of them is very profitable indeed. But perhaps they are special cases, atypical. Perhaps there are circumstances that dictate which commuter railroads must be unprofitable and which can somehow make a dollar or two. Let us, then, have a look at the biggest commuter railroads, beginning with the biggest of all—

*The Long Island Rail Road: approximately 170,000 daily passengers.* The Long Island was launched, improbably, by a wealthy manufacturer of combs whose name was Adolph Poppenhuser. It was Poppenhuser's shrewd conceit that, if he laid rails all over the north shore of Long Island, he could soon stud his combs with diamonds. He was right, but his sense of timing (1878) was wrong. J. Pierpont Morgan took

---

*As this figure is used here and as it will be used later, it must be understood to include all those holding multiple-ride tickets, whether or not on commutation fares.

281

over the infant road and dandled it on his knee for a time; eventually, in 1900, fifty-six per cent of its stock was bought for about eight million dollars by the Pennsylvania, which wanted the Long Island for its freight terminals in Brooklyn and because it was part of an imperial scheme of the Pennsylvania to make a rail connection with the New Haven and so increase the interchange of traffic with New England.

Unlike other railroads, the Long Island must live on its passenger service—less than one-eighth of its income is from freight—but, like every other commuter railroad, its tracks are paralleled by highways and expressways. In addition, the Long Island must compete on some of its lines with New York City's subway system. Its owners never did much to improve the Long Island's corduroy roadbed, or to keep it supplied with up-to-date equipment: it was the Pennsylvania's neglected stepchild. These factors, in combination, proved too much for the road. It collapsed into bankruptcy in 1949, which was also the first year that air-conditioned coaches were put in service. Trains customarily ran late; sometimes they failed to run at all. In 1950 two wrecks killed one hundred and ten people.

In 1952 the state government offered to buy the road from the Pennsylvania for twenty million dollars; the offer was rejected. In 1954, however, an arrangement was negotiated by which the Long Island became a railroad redevelopment corporation; the Pennsylvania agreed to forgo the $2,092,000 in annual interest due on its bonds, while the state agreed to forgive $2,260,000 in annual taxes. The state also gave the road sixty-five million dollars for a program of modernization: two hundred and forty new air-conditioned coaches were bought, and other old coaches were refurbished. More aid came from New York City and from the two suburban counties through which the road runs. Permission was given for six fare increases within eleven years.

But in 1964 the Long Island was back in the red again—by more than two million dollars—and the officers of the Pennsylvania were muttering about the unpaid interest on their bonds. Once again bankruptcy beckoned.

In February, 1965, Governor Nelson A. Rockefeller said he would ask the legislature for money to buy the Long Island if a "reasonable price" could be negotiated.

In May, 1965, representatives of the state of New York began to bargain with officers of the Pennsylvania. The dickering must have been delightful. Here were a reluctant but necessitous prospective purchaser and an eager prospective seller, chaffering over a property that had demonstrated time and time again its unprofitability. Should not Stuart Saunders, for the Pennsylvania, have pressed money on anyone so insane as to take this burden off his hands? To be sure, the Pennsylvania held notes and bonds of the Long Island alleged to be worth $53,800,000 and stock of the Long Island purportedly worth $47,600,000, but nobody took those numbers seriously.

The state is a public enterprise, however, not a private one, and so its representatives do not always drive quite so sharp a bargain. The terms of the sale, as announced in June, were these: the state to buy the Long Island for $65,000,000; the Pennsylvania to retain ownership of the Long Island's freight branch into Brooklyn, and of the freight yards, and of the air rights over about sixty-five acres in the borough of Queens, all suitable for exploitation by real estate operators; the state to amend its tax laws so as to provide tax abatements for the Pennsylvania Station *and* for the Grand Central Terminal (owned by the New York Central) on the theory that these are both "principal passenger stations"; the state to lease, for ninety-nine years, the use of tunnels under the East River and facilities at the Pennsylvania Station, at a rental fee of $581,000 for 1966 and $800,000 for every year thereafter.*

Both parties to the agreement hailed it as in the public interest, and—who knows?—they may both have been right. The only complaint came from a Manhattan councilman, Paul

*The official historian of the Pennsylvania, H. W. Schotter, wrote that the cost of building tunnels under both the Hudson and the East Rivers, and of building the Pennsylvania Station in Manhattan, was $112,965,415. (See his *The Growth and Development of the Pennsylvania Railroad Company 1846–1926*, p. 318.)

O'Dwyer, who insisted the road should have been acquired under condemnation proceedings "for no more than a token price of one dollar." No one heeded him.

At all events, the state, by way of a Metropolitan Commuter Transportation Authority, now proposes to funnel another two hundred million dollars (to be raised by a sale of more bonds) into the Long Island in still another effort to make the railroad profitable. Another tunnel is to be dug, another station will go up in Manhattan, five hundred new coaches will be bought, self-propelled cars will whiz along at 100 mph, everything will be automated, Long Island trains will move over the tracks of the New York subway system, everything will be peachy.

Governor Rockefeller was asked if state ownership of the Long Island were not "creeping socialism." He did not smile. "I've been trying to avoid this for six years," he said. "The alternative is pretty grim."

*The Chicago & North Western Railway: approximately 80,000 daily passengers.* In 1956 the C&NW ranked seventh among commuter railroads and operated that service at a whacking deficit.

In 1959 the C&NW ranked fourth and showed a marginal profit.

In 1966 the C&NW ranked second only to the Long Island in the number of commutation passengers and cleared a net profit of more than $2,000,000 on revenues of $16,600,000. On the C&NW's commuter service, everything is up—the number of daily passengers, the revenues, the profits, the morale of the employees, and the spirits of the passengers. The railroad gets no subsidies and wants none. Was it Stuart Saunders, of the Pennsylvania, who said the commuter railroad cannot make money? Mr. Saunders, meet Mr. Ben W. Heineman, chairman of the board of directors of the C&NW.

Journalists from all over the country have pestered Heineman with questions about his company's remarkable performance. His answers border on the banal. Why had he not tried to get out of a business which, in 1956, was costing the C&NW more than two million dollars a year? "We did not think we could get out of the business," he says; "politically, it was impossible, and it would have caused too much ill will. Since we were going to stay in the business, we concluded we should run it as well as possible." What is the Heineman formula for making a commuter railroad profitable? "The formula of any successful merchant: sell a good product, advertise it, and satisfy the customer."

Specifically, when Heineman took over the C&NW in 1956 it was nearly bankrupt. He borrowed fifty million dollars to buy double-decked, air-conditioned, well-lighted, comfortable coaches, and he persuaded the Illinois Commerce Commission to permit a fare increase based upon a novel theory: he proposed to sell not rides by the mile but transportation by the month. Before long he was mailing his commuters their monthly ticket before the first of each month and giving them ten days to pay for the service, like any other merchant. After studying his customers carefully, he concluded that what they wanted was a comfortable, dependable, prompt ride, shorn of frills and gimmicks. No canned music in train or station. No advertisements in the coaches. Trains on time; and if one was so much as thirty seconds late, its crew had better have a good explanation on tap.

Good equipment, prompt service. The C&NW needed both, when Heineman took over, for two new expressways were a-building next to C&NW tracks, and by 1961 the competition was hurting badly. After two profitable years, the C&NW once again tasted red ink. "We are," says Heineman, "incomparably superior to any expressway during the rush hours," and he undertook to sponsor two different helicopter traffic-control programs on Chicago radio stations so that he might get his message through to the sullen motorists stuck in expressway traffic jams or slipping in expressway slush. "How's the driving?" coos an announcer. "Got you hot and bothered? Why not try a North Western streamliner—warm all winter, cool all summer." When the weather forecast predicts rain, the announcer is sure to remind the motorists that they will find it easier in a C&NW train; and if it *does* rain, the C&NW passengers will find a stack of umbrellas in the C&NW station, with a sign inviting them to "Help Yourself." (The umbrellas are those that have never been claimed from the railroad's lost-and-found department.) When the Chicago area was snowbound for ten days during late January and early February, 1967, the C&NW's three commuter lines carried forty per cent more passengers than usual, on one day setting a record of one hundred and thirteen thousand contented customers.

That number, one may hazard, will grow.

*The Pennsylvania Railroad: approximately 75,000 daily passengers.* The Pennsylvania's policy is to get out of the commuter business where possible; where not possible, to raise fares or, failing that, to seek public subsidies. Since 1949 the number of commutation passengers using the Pennsylvania has declined about forty-five per cent, and the company's officers have been able to control their grief over this trend. A reporter for The Philadelphia Bulletin asked whether the Pennsylvania wanted more passengers, as the C&NW so obviously does. Well, he was told, the Pennsylvania would welcome more riders during off-peak hours when trains are idle, but not during rush hours when they would only require more equipment and so add to operating costs. Had the Pennsylvania considered spending fifty million or so on new commuter equipment, as had Heineman of the C&NW? No; the Pennsylvania would get a better return on such a sum by investing it in its freight service. As for any obligation to the public, the Pennsylvania spokesman observed: "There is no obligation to the public when the public itself has assumed obligations in all other areas—highways, air, water. In fact, all forms of transportation are being subsidized, but in the case of railroads the subsidies come from the railroad owners."

In the case of the Pennsylvania Railroad, the subsidies are coming not from the railroad owners but from the public, by way of city, county, state, and federal governments. City officials of Philadelphia were imaginative enough to pioneer a solution. When the Pennsylvania in 1956 sought another fare increase and threatened to curtail service again, Richardson Dilworth, then the mayor, and the city council made a counter proposal: they would spend about five hundred thousand dollars a year to experiment in maintaining and even extending rail commuter services. By 1960 the city officials were satisfied that their experiments would work; a nonprofit corporation, the Philadelphia Passenger Service Improvement Corporation, was formed and contracts signed with the Pennsylvania (and also with the Reading, another railroad that carries Philadelphia commuters). The city would buy fast, comfortable, air-conditioned electric coaches (called Silverliners), which would be added to the current schedules; the railroad would lower its fares, improve its stations, and provide more space for parking automobiles around them; the city would, with federal assistance, pay the expenses of the program.

This plan was adopted by the Southeastern Pennsylvania Transportation Authority, which represents the state, the city of Philadelphia, and four surrounding counties, and before long the Pennsylvania had been given an operating subsidy of $1,545,000 to help pay the cost of serving twenty thousand commuters in one hundred and sixty-eight trains a day. The subsidy was later increased to $4,163,000 to cover forty thousand commuters on four hundred and fifty trains.

A demonstration project between Trenton, New Jersey, and Philadelphia, financed jointly by local governments and the Federal Housing and Home Finance Agency, showed that a commutation traffic that had shrunk to 381,000 passengers a year could be raised by 1965 to 1,571,000 passengers and proved that the customers had always been there if only the service were tolerable. Moreover, the Pennsylvania's former deficit of $1,400,000 a year had been reduced to an estimated $400,000. (These deficit figures were computed, of course, according to the Interstate Commerce Commission's fragrant formula; by more sensible accounting procedures it is likely that the deficit has completely disappeared.)

The state of New Jersey was next to subsidize the poor Pennsylvania: Governor Hughes announced in October, 1966, that he had ordered several dozen new commuter coaches (for five million dollars of state funds, matched by another five million of federal funds), which would each be leased to the railroad for one dollar a year.

It would seem that the Pennsylvania has been able to reduce the old tug of war—the one between the compelling desire for private profit on the one hand, and on the other the irksome obligation to serve the public interest—almost to a mathematical formula. As Saunders told a stockholder at a recent annual meeting, the Pennsylvania prefers to make investments in operations and facilities that will yield a twenty-five per cent return, or ten times as much as the possible return from the passenger business.

*The Illinois Central Railroad: approximately 72,000 daily passengers.* Until recently the Illinois Central offered proof that a dependable, reasonably efficient service might be all that was needed to keep a commuter business profitable. The number of their passengers was only half what it was in 1949, and no new coaches had been installed since the postwar years, but commutation still returned a small profit in 1965, the sixth consecutive such profitable year. The IC's officers continued to insist they would have recourse to no subsidies of any kind; they hoped, they said, to stay out of the red by shaving the costs of their commuter business even further. They pinned their hopes on an expensive automated system of selling and acknowledging tickets.

Unhappily, somebody goofed. The electronic system did not cut costs but added to them. In 1966, despite the fact that there were actually more riders than in 1965, the IC's commuter business dipped into the red by some $350,000.

Also in 1966 the IC got a new president, William Johnson, whose experience as an executive was acquired while he climbed up the rungs of the Pennsylvania. If the officers of the IC had once eyed the splashy success of their neighbor, the C&NW, with considerable envy, they no longer do so. Johnson has said that the IC is determined to get new commuter coaches, but he has given no indication that he will authorize IC funds to purchase them. Instead, officers of the Illinois Central, like the officers of the Pennsylvania before them, are learning the names and faces and procedures of bureaucracy, learning to identify the button which, when pushed, will result in a shower of federal funds.

So have been protected the stockholders of the Pennsylvania; so will be protected the stockholders of the Illinois Central. The public interest will have been preserved, and the general taxpayer will have paid.

*The New York Central Railroad System: approximately 70,000 daily passengers.* Time was, the New York Central fetched and carried five times as many commuters; but that was forty years ago. Today, like its merger partner the Pennsylvania, the New York Central wants out of the commuter business "because it loses money," but the company is nevertheless far readier to experiment and far more willing to risk its own money in testing the viability of commuter traffic than the other eastern carriers.

This corporate amiability is something new. In the 1950s Robert R. Young and his aides tangled constantly with the courts and the regulatory commissions of New York and New Jersey; trains were discontinued in defiance of court orders; when Young was instructed by New York authorities to resume operation of some commuter trains on the West Shore division, he had the trains run as far as the New Jersey state line and then stopped, far from any station, just as his predecessor, Commodore Vanderbilt, had done nearly one hundred years before.

The Central's war against its West Shore commuters began in 1954, soon after Young won control of the system, and it was bitterly fought for five years until at last the Central succeeded in destroying a vital part of the service, the ferry from the west shore of the Hudson to Manhattan. The several thousand commuters did what they could—once one hundred of them attended a hearing of the New Jersey Public Utilities Commission masked like pigs, in mockery of Young's celebrated slogan, "A hog can cross the country without changing trains—but you can't"; later, when their ferry was under attack, they crossed the Hudson masked like fish, to dramatize their plight—but all to no avail. The Congress passed the Transportation Act of 1958, which took the question of train discontinuances out of the hands of the state authorities and gave it to the Interstate Commerce Commission. By March, 1959, the West Shore division was dead, and New York City's streets were presently clogged with more thousands of automobiles.

Meanwhile, a relentless campaign of fare increases in Westchester County, accompanied by a steady deterioration of service and equipment, further reduced the number of the Central's commuters and jammed the streets of the metropolis more intolerably than ever.

Who was in charge here? Eventually the state and city of New York realized that they might placate the New York Central by reducing its taxes. In 1959 and 1960 certain laws were passed and, after a time, sure enough, the Central began to show signs of being mollified. Alfred E. Perlman, the Central's president, accepted the first of eighty-seven new, air-conditioned, stainless-steel coaches bought and paid for by the New York Port Authority and leased to the Central under enabling state legislation. "We're trying to give Westchester the best commuter service in the United States," Perlman purred. Since then new trains have been put in service, experimentally, occasionally; the company has also tinkered with schedules and with fares, testing whether its service cannot be better fitted to the public convenience; and in 1966 the company spent nearly two million dollars of its own money to renovate forty cars (removed from the elegance of its long-haul passenger service on such trains as the Twentieth Century) for the commuter trade. To be sure, at least one of the experiments in improved commutation was paid for by state and federal subsidy; and a thorough rehabilitation of all its commuter facilities and equipment, long overdue, undoubtedly awaits further state and federal grants; but it is pleasant to detect a small measure of co-operation, even if it turns out to be no more than a suave job of public relations.

*The New York, New Haven & Hartford Railroad: approximately 66,000 daily passengers.* It seems incredible today, but in 1955, when A. C. Spectorsky wrote his amusing and penetrating social study, *The Exurbanites,* he was able to report that the New Haven was "the best equipped and most punctual commuter line" in the New York area. The next year, 1956, was the last in which the New Haven has been able to report a profit.

In truth, the unhappy New Haven has never known a prolonged period of prosperity since J. Pierpont Morgan and his office boy, Charles S. Mellen, wrecked the property more than fifty years ago. In the intervening years its shareholders have only once—in 1928—been paid a dividend. In the 1930s there was a bankruptcy, a hurricane with losses in the millions, and a reorganization that was completed in 1947, after which the "special-situation" men moved in, licking their lips, and whetting their knives to strip the carcass. First came Frederick C. Dumaine, a New England financier with a reputation for fattening off moribund properties; next came the ineffable Patrick B. McGinnis; and finally there was George P. Alpert, a Boston lawyer. McGinnis lasted as president of the New Haven for only twenty months, but his tenure was by all odds the most vivid. He paid himself first fifty, then seventy-five thousand dollars a year; he went on the payroll of subsidiary companies; he was also paid "expenses" at the rate of forty thousand a year. He maintained a suite of rooms in two different New York hotels simultaneously; the decoration of his executive offices in the Grand Central Terminal cost the company one hundred and twenty thousand dollars. More important, he squandered millions on cheesy passenger trains, speculated in his company's securities, and deferred maintenance in order to show inflated earnings. He resigned in January, 1956, to become president of the Boston & Maine.*

His successor, Alpert, distinguished himself by hiring, to run the road, some men whose experience as operating executives of the Chicago & North Western coincided with that road's brush with bankruptcy. Alpert's function with the New Haven was that of undertaker, and for the job he was paid sixty thousand a year under a contract that expired June 1, 1961. His contract also provided that he was to receive twenty-five thousand a year for the subsequent twelve years as severance pay or as deferred compensation. By March, 1961, the New Haven was worthless and was losing money at the rate of more than a million dollars a month. Alpert hung on grimly. "I am satisfied," he told a congressional committee, "there will not be a bankruptcy." His contract having expired, Alpert had the New Haven file for reorganization under the Bankruptcy Act in July, 1961. Later he sued to collect three hundred thousand dollars due him under his contract. A federal judge rejected his claim.

The New Haven has been gradually dismembered. Its station in Boston has been sold; its Boston commuter line has been sold to the Massachusetts Bay Transportation Authority; its commutation service to New York staggers along, supported by subsidies from every governmental agency in sight and assisted by some stupendous financial legerdemain. What will happen to its passenger service and its commutation service is in the womb of the future, but already the states of New York and Connecticut have proposed to take over the services —if the federal government will put up most of the money.

The New Haven is slated to become part of the gigantic Penn-Central, when those two big railroad companies are finally merged; after that, who is to say how big will be the price tag put on the New Haven's commutation service by

---

*McGinnis and two associates were subsequently convicted of accepting kickbacks on the sale of B&M passenger cars; the three men copped a plea on two other indictments. McGinnis was fined a total of five thousand dollars and sentenced to eighteen months in prison.

Stuart Saunders of the Pennsylvania and Alfred Perlman of the Central?

*The Erie-Lackawanna Railroad: approximately 56,000 daily passengers.* The late William White, who was chairman of the board of the Erie-Lackawanna, used periodically to offer to give his passenger cars to any public agency or individual who would operate them without loss to the railroad. No agency, no individual wanted the rolling stock, and for an excellent reason: the Erie-Lackawanna didn't own a single passenger car that was less than thirty-five years old, and most of them were older.

White used to claim that the company was losing fabulous sums of money every year on its commutation service. Sometimes he would say it was eight million dollars a year; later the figure crept up to twelve million a year. He tried to cancel the entire service in 1966, despite the fact that the state of New Jersey had handed over a subsidy of more than fourteen million dollars from 1961 onward. The Erie-Lackawanna was operating four hundred and fifty-one trains in 1966, and the state's Public Utility Commission astonished White by permitting him to cancel two hundred and fifty-six of them; later he sought judicial permission to cancel the rest.

Finally, in January, 1967, New Jersey's brand-new Commuter Operating Agency signed a revolutionary agreement with the railroad company. David J. Goldberg, the state's new commissioner of transportation, announced that the agency would pay the Erie-Lackawanna $4,244,658, that the railroads would once again operate forty-seven of the trains it had canceled four months before, that the state would purchase and lease to the railroads new passenger cars and other equipment, and that the state would assume "general supervisory direction" of the commutation service. A few months later Goldberg announced that the state would further subsidize the railroad to the tune of at least sixteen million dollars a year for the next five years, emphasizing that his agency would supervise the commutation service closely. Erie-Lackawanna officials had for years resisted such control, calling instead for bigger annual subsidies. But the state of New Jersey has at last insisted on taking authority in return for its cash. The Commuter Operating Agency will be the boss, with power to fix fares, demand service, and set schedules. Moreover, if trains are consistently late, or enough cars are not provided, or service is otherwise unsatisfactory, the agency is authorized to impose financial penalties on the railroad.

Since the public is paying, its representatives are going to get tough.

These seven railroads are responsible for almost eighty per cent of the rail commutation traffic in the country, and on balance their performance over the last ten or fifteen years can scarcely reassure advocates of private commercial enterprise. The only company that has undertaken, without subsidy, to improve its service is also the only one that shows a steadily growing profit and a steadily growing clientele. For the rest, one is owned by the state, another operated by the state, a third marginally profitable but unequal to the task of modernizing its equipment unaided, and the others increasingly anxious to suckle the public teat.

Another seven roads—the Burlington, the Southern Pacific, the Reading, the Rock Island, the Milwaukee Road, the Central of New Jersey, and the Boston & Maine—account for nearly all the rest of the country's rail commuter traffic. Of these, the Burlington and the Milwaukee Road have shown small but consistent profits over the last few years, and the Southern Pacific's revenues have also steadily increased despite a dwindling patronage. The others are not so healthy. Officers of one, the Central of New Jersey, filed a petition for reorganization under the Bankruptcy Act in March, 1967.

All are in transition to a future that none can define with any precision. In the vast urban sprawl that surrounds New York City there must eventually come into being some sort of authority, perhaps patterned on the Tri-State Transportation Commission already established by the legislatures of New York, New Jersey, and Connecticut and already functioning to a limited extent; an authority that will be able to rationalize the chaotic muddle of railroads, subways, bus lines, highways, bridges, tunnels, and airports; that will be able to finance the meliorations and expansions already desperately needed by most of these so-called facilities; that will be able to harness and curb the rampaging private automobile and return the carriage of large numbers of people to the mass-transit modes that once, within the memory of men still living, were proven to be clean, comfortable, reasonably swift, and aesthetically pleasant. Such an authority is mandatory in Chicago, as well, and in Washington and Boston and Philadelphia and Cleveland and Detroit. Los Angeles appears to be doomed: every attempt to plan and promote a sensible mass rapid-transit system in southern California is routinely squashed by an all-powerful cabal of automobile dealers, highway contractors, and automobile clubs; even the commuter rail service between San Diego and Los Angeles (on the Santa Fe) is disappearing without any public outcry.

The contrary example of San Francisco is at the same time a warning to the other urban areas around the country.

In and around San Francisco and Oakland, on a seventy-five-mile, billion-dollar Bay Area Rapid Transit system (nicknamed BART), cars controlled by computers will start to move, if all goes well, sometime in 1971. They will move at 70 or 80 mph on a headway of only ninety seconds, connecting ten or more sizable cities in three counties, zipping through sixteen miles of tunnels and subways, for four miles in a tube under the San Francisco Bay, smoothly, swiftly, quietly, over the first completely new rapid-transit railway to be built in the United States since 1907. Naturally, this mammoth venture has not proceeded without controversy. Architects have wrangled with engineers, civil rights proponents with businessmen, Oaklanders with San Franciscans, bankers with politicians, everybody with anybody. Nevertheless it is a hugely exciting project, one that has caught the imagination of all transportation executives, one that is expected to influence every urban mass-transit project, certainly for the balance of this century. If all

295

goes well, BART will be a jeweled crown on a lovely city—and a grim caveat to every crowded metropolis.

For what has been the time lag between conception and reality? The system was first suggested in the 1940s, and schematic planning began in 1950; it will certainly not be completed before 1971. Twenty-one years, to build an urban railway. The subway system planned for Washington, D.C., will be twenty-three years from legislation to operation. In short, any effort by metropolitan man to impose order on confusion takes a generation.

One may hope that a transportation authority will come for New York and Chicago and the other cities plagued by problems of commutation sooner than later.

But it must be a public authority. Private enterprise, especially as exemplified by the lords of the railroads, has shown only too clearly that it is unequal to the task.

# ENVOY

TRAVEL in our incomparable republic, whether of a leisurely turn or more sternly utilitarian, is less likely to be pleasant than it used to be. Getting from here to there is almost never fun any more. When we expect travel, as travel, to be an agreeable experience, we go abroad. At home we know better.

Until recently I had imagined that in holding these beliefs I was one of a persnickety minority, but an upwelling of angry comment in newspapers, magazines, and ordinary conversation has convinced me that nearly everybody who moves about in this country, whether by airplane, automobile, bus, or train, is thoroughly disenchanted with the process of travel. That process, most people seem now to agree, is either boring and uncomfortable or downright dangerous: it must be got over as quickly as possible. Speed! Turnpikes bulldozed straight and level through homogenized landscapes, to accommodate swifter automobiles; supersonic airplanes at no matter what cost to the serenity of those who live below; and still the Red Queen keeps crying, "Faster! Faster!"

And so the relaxed, reflective journey disappears, lost in the blind haste of getting there. What once was a pleasure and an excitement has been transformed by progress into a gritty chore.

When, after listening to my friends complain about crowded highways or how airline attendants have misplaced their luggage, I have suggested the possibility of train travel, I have noticed that at once a clamor burst forth:

"Did I tell you about my last trip on a—"

"Listen! This is incredible. I was on a—"

"No, but wait till you hear what happened when I—"

It is like listening to people boast about their operations.

Now as it happens I have several impressive scars myself, for I am as stubborn in hoping my next train trip will be a good one as most railroad managers are in frustrating me. This livid scar here, for example; see? Eight stitches. It still aches, whenever the weather blows in wet from the northeast.

My wife and I had been invited to dine with friends who live in a suburb of New York and, since we were reluctant to drive in the thick press of commuter traffic, we elected to take a New York Central train for the short ride into Westchester County. Our train was scheduled to leave the Grand Central Terminal a few minutes after six. A few minutes before the hour I presented myself at the information booth to find from which track our train was to leave. Ahead of me was a young man, and I overheard this dialogue:

YOUNG MAN: Which track for the train to Chicago—the Twentieth Century?

CLERK: Don't shout at me!

YOUNG MAN [much puzzled]: I didn't shout. I just want to know which tra—

CLERK: Whyncha take the bus?

YOUNG MAN [with a glance at the overhead clock]: Please, the train leaves in a minute or two. . . .

CLERK [very deliberately]: Track thirty-four.

It was now my turn, and I asked about my suburban train. The clerk eyed me with the disgust he doubtless reserves for all cretins. "Go down to the lower level," he snarled, as who would say, Go to hell, and turned to his next petitioner.

298

Below, we found our train and boarded it. We left on time. We had nineteen miles to go, and we had covered about fourteen of them when our train slowed to a firm stop far short of the nearest station. Here, our friendly conductor informed us, we would stay until some flaw in the third rail had been corrected. Five commuter trains stood still ahead of us, the conductor remarked chattily, and of course others were piling up behind us. There was nothing to do but to wait, especially inasmuch as a summer thunderstorm had now broken and was inundating everything for miles around.

What, we wondered, would our hostess think?

We sat.

After thirty minutes, I rebelled. Others had left the train and hiked up the right of way over the gravel and broken stone; why should my wife not do likewise, in her high heels? After all, the rain had nearly stopped. . . .

After sixty minutes, she agreed. We picked our way the six hundred yards to the station, were lucky enough to find a ride, and were greeted by our imperturbable hostess precisely three hours late. Our host, who had been stranded on the same train, got home thirty minutes later. I was astonished to find that our host, our hostess, and their other guests were all quite inured to such a disruption of their social round and were themselves surprised that I should consider it unusual.

Next day I found a paragraph in The New York Times: the third rail had lost its power at 5:30 P.M., or *thirty-three minutes before* our train had been waved out to its standstill several miles short of its scheduled stops. Had the stationmaster known we would be so stuck? Of course. Did he, or any of his subordinates, warn us of our certain delays, so that we might find better ways of reaching our destinations? Of course not. Why should the New York Central fret over the comfort of fifteen thousand of its commuters?

In 1964 my wife and I had a fine trip by rail, all around the country, and we enjoyed every minute of it. The Twentieth Century to Chicago, the San Francisco Chief as far as Kansas

City, to Tulsa and back on the Oil Flyer, then on out to Los Angeles on the Super Chief, with a one-day visit at the Grand Canyon on the way; the Coast Daylight north to San Francisco and, a few days later, the Shasta Daylight north to Portland, breaking the ride with a two-day stopover at Crater Lake; back to Chicago on the Empire Builder, and home to New York on the Broadway Limited.

But how much longer will such a trip be possible? The New York Central is anxious to be rid of its Twentieth Century; the Santa Fe has already briefly withdrawn its Oil Flyer and may decide to cancel it permanently; the Southern Pacific has downgraded the service on its Coast Daylight and has for years been trying to cancel its Shasta Daylight.

It is quite clear that railroad management no longer consider themselves obliged to supply transportation for people. A few years ago Ben Heineman, the chairman of the Chicago & North Western, told a Senate committee that it was the policy of his company to eliminate through passenger trains "as promptly as possible." The committee counsel pursued this point:

> COUNSEL: Mr. Heineman, I take it as a common carrier you feel that you have some responsibility toward the traveling public that want to use railroad passenger service; do you not?
> HEINEMAN: . . . I am no longer prepared to say to you, sir, that the railroad industry, as you put it, as a common carrier, has the obligations that it once had to the traveling public, as you put it, because of the fact that neither the U. S. government, nor the state governments, nor the traveling public, have protected the railroads against the most destructive competition in our economic history. . . . And I am afraid that I would have to answer your question, no, that we have no greater responsibility to carry the passenger, the traveling public, in through passenger service than the common carrier trucks do, or than the common carrier barges do.

In short, the railroads are to be common carriers of freight only. And Heineman has successfully obliterated the C&NW's intercity passenger service.

The management of the Southern Pacific also consider that they are in no wise obliged to carry people in their trains. They also believe in direct action and, according to the Public Utilities Commission of California, their *"actions,* resulting in hundreds of thousands of passengers being inconvenienced, were accomplished purely by a stroke of the pen of management without any consultation with any of the agencies that supposedly regulate it." Whenever feasible, the management of the Southern Pacific have removed or consolidated passenger trains without reference to the Interstate Commerce Commission or any state regulatory body. According once again to the California commission, the Southern Pacific takes "a well patronized passenger train, and, by a series of unilateral and unauthorized management decisions, downgrade[s] its quality of service, thereby decreasing its patronage. It is," the California commission added, "only remarkable that patronage still exists, in spite of the carrier's action."

What then can the common passenger do about the common carrier? The common carrier has, in flagrant derogation of charter and common law, forsaken the passenger. Some of the state regulatory commissions have fought hard on behalf of the passenger; but the Congress, in its shifting wisdom, has vested the power to abolish even intrastate trains in the Interstate Commerce Commission; and the Commission, seeking to implement the vague and ambiguous language of the national transportation policy (which now prefaces the Interstate Commerce Act), has usually surrendered to the pressures of the railroad industry and piously assisted at the slaughter of the rail passenger service.

What resource has the passenger against this multi-billion-dollar industry and this acquiescent bureaucracy?

He has, in fact, one slim chance. In the spring of 1967 a handful of intransigent rail passengers met in a room of the Hotel Plaza, in New York City, to form an organization which they christened the National Association of Railroad Passengers. It is the first group ever to have been launched on behalf of the bedeviled passenger.

The infant N.A.R.P. is predicated on the assumption, probably conservative, that ten million Americans, through choice or necessity, regularly use the railroads to travel between cities. The N.A.R.P. is in business to speak on their behalf: to fight for what passenger service still exists and to work for its improvement and expansion. The men who formed the N.A.R.P. seem to be sensible and practical. They are not out to get the railroads. They realize that the railroad companies face inequities at the hands of federal and local tax officials, that government funds for research and development have gone to support air travel and highway travel, that the railroads face competition that has been unfairly boosted by a confused federal policy. But they are determined to do whatever can be done to maintain a viable rail passenger service.*

One tenet of the N.A.R.P.'s program is the establishment of a public corporation to acquire and maintain essential passenger equipment, which would be leased to and operated by the railroad companies. Although the word is scrupulously avoided, this notion serves to introduce the ticklish subject of a subsidy.

In the past, railroad men have unanimously spurned any suggestion of a subsidy, fearing that here was a wedge that would open the way to nationalization of the railroads. Nor has the Congress been any more eager to legislate subsidies, since they would appear to be a premium awarded the railroad companies for their stubborn inefficiency. Indeed, it is hard to escape the conclusion that to subsidize the passenger business is to guarantee the stockholders of a railroad company fatter dividends from the profitable freight business. Does the railroad not have a duty to perform useful services for the public, even if those services may be unprofitable? Justice Frankfurter thought so. He once declared, in an often-quoted opinion: "Unlike a department store or a grocery, a railroad cannot of its own free will discontinue a particular service to the public

*The N.A.R.P.'s executive director, Anthony Haswell, is a lawyer with railroad experience who has earned a considerable reputation for pugnacity on behalf of the railroad passenger service. The association's central office is at 333 North Michigan Avenue, Chicago, Illinois 60601.

302

because an item of its business has become unprofitable."

Subsidies from the state for private enterprise? The thing seemed somehow un-American; it smacked of creeping socialism. Nevertheless, in recent years the idea has caught hold and is now flourishing, especially in the Official Region, especially on behalf of commutation. One of its most eloquent advocates is Stuart Saunders, the chairman of the Pennsylvania Railroad; it is instructive to follow the semantic twists and turns in his statements on the subject. Here is Saunders, talking to a subcommittee of the Senate Committee on Banking and Currency, in April, 1966:

> I am convinced that participation in governmental aid programs will not lead to nationalization of the railroads. On the contrary, these programs are necessary and practical steps for the preservation of free enterprise in the railroad industry.
>
> This kind of assistance is not a subsidy for the railroads; it is a means of relieving the railroads from a subsidy they had been paying for the benefit of the public. [This was a reference to the argument, by railroad men, that the freight business subsidizes the passenger business.] It preserves under private management, with its operating efficiencies, a public service which ranks in necessity with highways, airports, or fire and police protection.

Call it subsidy or call it participation in governmental aid programs, the fact is that commutation in the east is now supported by public funds; so also is the demonstration project for passenger service in the megalopolitan corridor between Boston and Washington. Judged by the standard of the public welfare, this development is unquestionably a sound one; it seems also to have been necessary, since the private entrepreneurs who operate the railroads either could not or would not maintain the services unaided.

These private entrepreneurs have demonstrated time and again their skill at forcing such developments of public policy. A case in point is the seven-per-cent investment-tax credit, originally legislated to tempt more spending of capital funds by businessmen. Thanks to that tax credit, the railroad industry spent huge sums—as much as two billion a year—to refurbish and replace its fleet of antiquated freight cars. In 1966, when he perceived what he thought was an unhealthy trend toward inflation, President Johnson got the Congress to suspend the credit. The railroad entrepreneurs were stunned. They still desperately needed more freight cars, and 1966 had been one of the most profitable years in their history, but without their tax credit they simply sat on their hands. Terse announcements from one railroad company after another made it clear that the flow of new freight cars had been stopped. Orders were canceled. President Johnson got the message: he asked the Congress to restore the credit. The Congress, chivvied gently along, decided to make the restoration retroactive to the date of its suspension. At once, orders worth scores of millions of dollars were placed for new freight cars and new, more powerful locomotives. Clearly, the railroad industry can still summon up, when necessary, its oldtime powers of persuasion. The whole affair, as Chairman Wilbur Mills of the House Ways and Means Committee observed, was not "a very happy chapter in the nation's fiscal history."

In the last few years the railroad companies have spent precious little money on such expensive trinkets as new passenger equipment. It is entirely possible that the railroad men have been deliberately awaiting the provenance of some such solution as the one now tentatively put forward by the new National Association of Railroad Passengers.

Quite evidently the railroad managers are not interested in grappling with the manifold problems of a better rail passenger service. They have weightier matters on their minds: how to maintain their rising profits; how further to merge and consolidate their sprawling properties, especially in the western region; how to beat back the economic demands of their employees; whether they should seek another general increase of freight rates from the Interstate Commerce Commission or raise the rates of only a few commodities, selectively; how to cope with their competitors, the barge lines and the truckers; how to contrive to keep their loaded freight cars moving more

304

than ten or twelve hours in any given week; what will happen to their lucrative freight traffic when, or if, the war in Vietnam ever comes to an end. . . .

As for the passenger service, someone else will have to worry about it. The National Association of Railroad Passengers looks like the best bet, especially if it succeeds in rallying a substantial number of members to its brand-new banner. A likely slogan lies ready to hand:

Passengers of America, unite! You have nothing to lose but your trains!

# AN ANNOTATED BIBLIOGRAPHY

Despite the enormous literature that deals in one way or another with the railroads, there is no comprehensive general study which is thoroughly satisfactory. Some are too technical, some too prejudiced, some addressed only to the substantial army of railroad buffs, and the best are out of date. In their time the most useful were:

Charles Francis Adams, Jr., *Railroads: Their Origins and Problems*, 1878.
Arthur Twining Hadley, *Railroad Transportation, Its History and Its Laws*, 1886.
Robert S. Henry, *This Fascinating Railroad Business*, 1942.
Stewart H. Holbrook, *The Story of American Railroads*, 1947.
William Z. Ripley, *Railroads: Rates and Regulation*, 1914.
———, *Railroads: Finance and Organization*, 1915.
Slason Thompson, *A Short History of American Railways*, 1925.

Adams devoted much of his life to the railroad business—as journalist, state commissioner, mediator of rate wars among the trunk-line railroads, and even, for a brief time in the late 1880s when Russell Sage and Jay Gould found it expedient to step aside, as president of the Union Pacific—and he wrote several books about it. Perhaps the best-known is *Chapters of Erie*, written with the sometime assistance of his brother Henry; later historians have been unable to improve upon this stinging indictment of the Erie War, Vanderbilt against Drew,

307

Gould, and Fisk. Hadley is of course the respected historian who subsequently became president of Yale University. Ripley, like Adams, had close associations with railroad executives; his two volumes offer the best analysis of the industry in the decades before the War of 1914-1918. Henry's book suffers from an uncritical attitude; he was for several years the concertmeister of publicity and propaganda for the Association of American Railroads. Holbrook's history is instructive and in some respects invaluable (e.g., in his handling of the callous disregard by the railroads of the safety of their employees and their passengers), but it is marred by the amiable superficiality of a book written for buffs.

The earliest American railroads have each their historians. To pick out a few at random, there are:

Alvin F. Harlow, *The Road of the Century: The Story of the New York Central,* 1947.

———, *Steelways of New England,* 1946.

Edward Hungerford, *The Story of the Baltimore & Ohio Railroad,* 1928.

———, *Men and Iron, A History of the New York Central,* 1938.

———, *Men of Erie,* 1946.

Wheaton J. Lane, *From Indian Trail to Iron Horse: Travel and Transportation in New Jersey, 1620-1860,* 1939.

Edward H. Mott, *Between the Ocean and the Lakes: The Story of Erie,* 1901.

H. W. Schotter, *The Growth and Development of the Pennsylvania Railroad Company 1846-1926,* 1928.

Frank W. Stevens, *The Beginnings of the New York Central Railroad,* 1926.

W. B. Wilson, *History of the Pennsylvania Railroad Company,* 1895.

Harlow's is the best account of the Central; Mott's, of the Erie. What is most interesting about this brief list is that no properly searching account of the most important railroad company in the country, the Pennsylvania, has yet been published.

Of the early masters of the railroads there is a dearth of material. Irene Neu has had published a brief monograph on Erastus Corning; most of the others are referred to only glancingly or bob up from obscurity abruptly in such works as Thomas C. Cochran's *Railroad Leaders, 1845-1890: The Business Mind in Action*, 1953, an essay to which there is a wonderful appendix of three hundred pages, containing extracts from the letters of sixty railroad presidents. When it comes to Commodore Vanderbilt and his descendants, the historians have been more properly respectful. For example:

Wayne Andrews, *The Vanderbilt Legend*, 1941.
W. A. Croffut, *The Vanderbilts, and the Story of Their Fortune*, 1886.
Edwin P. Hoyt, *The Vanderbilts and Their Fortunes*, 1962.
Wheaton J. Lane, *Commodore Vanderbilt*, 1942.
Arthur D. Howden Smith, *Commodore Vanderbilt*, 1927.

These efforts, and many others, came about because the Commodore made his plenty and hung onto it. Poor Daniel Drew, on the other hand, died a bankrupt and so has been most shabbily treated by history. *The Book of Daniel Drew*, by Bouck White (1910), is the only full-length account of his life, and it is mendacious and malicious from beginning to end.

Special mention must be made of Lee Benson's first-rate study, *Merchants, Farmers & Railroads: Railroad Regulation and New York Politics, 1850-1887*, 1955, which with lucidity and scholarship shows how, especially under Commodore Vanderbilt and his son William, the New York Central corrupted the state, impoverished its farmers, and provoked its merchants to insist upon regulatory legislation.

The building of the Union Pacific and the Central Pacific (the latter road later absorbed by the Southern Pacific) attracted the interest of several historians, among them being:

Stuart Daggett, *Chapters on the History of the Southern Pacific*, 1922.
Robert W. Fogel, *The Union Pacific Railroad: A Case Study in Premature Enterprise*, 1960.

309

John Galloway, *The Transcontinental Railroad,* 1950.

Wesley S. Griswold, *A Work of Giants: Building the First Transcontinental Railroad,* 1962.

Robert W. Howard, *The Great Iron Trail: The Story of the First Transcontinental Railroad,* 1962.

Oscar Lewis, *The Big Four,* 1938.

Edwin L. Sabin, *Building the Pacific Railway,* 1919.

Neill C. Wilson and Frank J. Taylor, *The Southern Pacific,* 1952.

As I have indicated in the text, the transcontinental railroad also attracted the attention of three congressional committees, none of which, unhappily, was able to get to the bottom of the Credit Mobilier scandal. Nor, to my satisfaction, have any of the historians listed above. Fogel's book is in many ways the most entertaining, for he has been able to convince himself that the insiders of the Pacific ring made no extraordinary profit.

The six men who were the railroad kings of 1875 have not uniformly aroused the curiosity of biographers. William H. Vanderbilt has ever stood in the shadow of his father; Tom Scott lacks any biography at all, and this is a great shame; Collis Huntington has been sketched best by Oscar Lewis, whose book is cited above; John Murray Forbes was given a most deferential treatment by his daughter, Sarah Forbes Hughes, who edited *The Letters and Recollections of John Murray Forbes,* 1899, and by Henry G. Pearson, *An American Railroad Builder: John Murray Forbes,* 1911; Russell Sage, as I have said in the text, was so secretive that only one biographer, Paul Sarnoff, has ventured to explore his career (*Russell Sage: The Money King,* 1965). The notorious Jay Gould has fared better: at least four studies have been made of his curious life, of which by all odds the best is Julius Grodinsky's *Jay Gould: His Business Career, 1867-1892,* 1957. It should be added that Grodinsky is the author of two other excellent books about railroad affairs: *The Iowa Pool, a Study in Railroad Competition, 1870-1884,* 1950, and *Transcontinental Railway Strategy, 1869-1893, a Study of Businessmen,* 1962.

For my account of the Granger movement, I have drawn on the general studies listed above, on contemporary congressional investigations of the railroads, on Lee Benson's monograph cited earlier, and, as I have indicated in the text, on C. Vann Woodward's *Reunion and Reaction* (1951). For the strike of the railroad workers in 1877 I have depended upon Robert V. Bruce's *1877: Year of Violence* (1959) and upon some of the sources Mr. Bruce listed, especially Ida M. Tarbell's *History of the Standard Oil Company* (1904). For the revolt of the merchants, which led to the Interstate Commerce Act and the establishment of the Interstate Commerce Commission, I leaned most heavily upon Lee Benson's monograph and the reports of the various committees of the Senate, beginning in 1873 with the Windom committee and ending in 1887 with the Cullom committee.

Writers of widely divergent viewpoints have dealt with this gamy period of industrial growth. The contemporary accounts include such gossipy and untrustworthy memoirs as Henry Clews's *Fifty Years in Wall Street* (1908), J. K. Medbery's *Men and Mysteries of Wall Street* (1870), Rufus Hatch's *Sayings of Uncle Rufus* (1882), and, covering a slightly later period, C. W. Barron's *They Told Barron* (1930) and *More They Told Barron* (1931), which do not, however, tell how Barron accepted $133,000 within seven months to print matter slanted in favor of the New Haven Railroad and against its critic, Louis D. Brandeis. Gustavus Myers's *History of the Great American Fortunes* (Modern Library edition, 1936), while tendentious, is a remarkably diligent and painstaking research into court records and congressional investigations to which every subsequent historian owes a debt. Lewis Haney's *A Congressional History of Railways in the United States* (2 vols., 1908-10) is another such thoroughgoing study. Later have come such books as Matthew Josephson's *The Robber Barons* (1934), Stewart H. Holbrook's *The Age of the Moguls*

311

(1953), and Ray Ginger's *Age of Excess* (1965).

J. P. Morgan has had several biographers, among them:

Frederick Lewis Allen, *The Great Pierpont Morgan*, 1949.
Lewis Corey, *The House of Morgan*, 1930.
Carl Hovey, *Life Story of J. Pierpont Morgan*, 1912.
Herbert L. Satterlee, *J. Pierpont Morgan*, 1939.
John K. Winkler, *Morgan the Magnificent*, 1930.

Hovey's book has the reputation of being at least semi-official; it contains several intimate glimpses which seem to have been told the author at first hand. Corey's economic analysis is persuasive and his research is well documented. The great figures of this time have had each their biographers: George Kennan wrote *E. H. Harriman* (1922) and Otto H. Kahn wrote a brief memoir, *Edward Henry Harriman* (1911); J. G. Pyle wrote *The Life of James J. Hill* (1917) and Ray Ginger, *The Bending Cross: A Biography of Eugene Victor Debs* (1949); Cyrus Adler put together *Jacob H. Schiff: His Life and Letters* (1928) and J. B. Hedges wrote *Henry Villard and the Railways of the Northwest* (1930). The reorganization and consolidation of the railroads has been explored by Stuart Daggett in *Railroad Reorganization* (1908), Edward G. Campbell in *The Reorganization of the American Railroad System, 1893-1900* (1938), and John F. Stover in *The Railroads of the South, 1865-1900: A Study in Finance and Control* (1955). John Moody wrote two invaluable little books that cover this same period, *The Railroad Builders* (1919) and *Masters of Capital* (1919); but I prefer the series of magazine articles Moody wrote in collaboration with George Kibbe Turner for *McClure's Magazine* (1910-1911): it covers much the same ground but includes material that was later cut. Also for *McClure's Magazine* there were written articles by Ray Stannard Baker ("Railroads on Trial," 1905-1906) and Burton K. Hendrick (articles on "The Vanderbilt Fortune" [1908] and on E. H. Harriman [1910]).

The years when the railroad industry was nationalized have been best reported by William G. McAdoo in *The Crowded*

*Years* (1931) and Walker D. Hines in *War History of the American Railroads* (1928); the industry's side of that episode was presented by Julius Kruttschnitt in The Atlantic Monthly (January, 1922); the disposition of all claims by railroad companies was given in the administrator's final report, dated December 31, 1924.

The industry's postwar problems were discussed by William Z. Ripley in The North American Review for April, 1922, and were also described by Donald Richberg in his autobiography, *My Hero* (1954). I depended to a great extent on the investigations by the Wheeler Committee (referred to in the text) for my account of the imperial scrambles of the railroads during the 1920s; the many articles published in Fortune magazine were also most helpful; and a case study of one railroad company, the Milwaukee Road, during this time, Max Lowenthal's *The Investor Pays* (1933), was extremely illuminating.

For my handling of the more recent history of the railroad industry I have drawn on the reports and dockets of the Interstate Commerce Commission (usually referred to in the text), speeches by various railroad and transportation executives and especially those by the late Morris Forgash, articles in various periodicals and especially Fortune, The New York Times, The Wall Street Journal, Railway Age, and sundry other trade and financial magazines, and on the occasional reports and studies made for the Congress. Of these last, by all odds the most valuable has been the so-called Doyle report, referred to in the text. This research was supplemented by interviews with various men in Washington and in the transportation industry. I am especially obliged to officials of both the American Trucking Association and the Association of American Railroads. The A.A.R. has been particularly helpful in supplying me with clippings from periodicals, with statistical material, and with the plentiful output of its own publicity department. I am sure that these kind and cooperative men would be the first to agree that the conclusions I have drawn in this book are my own and that the responsibility for them must be assumed by me alone.

# INDEX

315

317

Grand Trunk Railway, 80n
Granger laws, 69–75
Grangers, 68–71, 129
Grant, Ulysses S., 53, 60, 72
Great Depression, 158n, 166, 168, 169–71, 192, 207
Great Northern Railway, 97, 98, 105, 122, 124, 133, 237, 255, 260; struck, 109; shares control of Burlington, 114, 120
Greeley, Horace, 29
Greyhound: Northland Greyhound, 237–38; Pennsylvania Greyhound, 238; Pacific Greyhound, 238
Guaranty Trust Company, 174–75

Harding, Warren G., 154
Harlan, John M., 106
Harriman, Edward H., 51, 102–3, 104, 147; his reported group of railroads in 1902, 113; battles Hill, 114–125; grows more powerful, 131–32; is investigated, 133; dies, 134
Harrison, Benjamin, 45n, 123
Haswell, Anthony, 302n
Hay, W. W., 272
Hayes, Rutherford B., 72–75, 81, 84
Heineman, Ben W., 284–85, 286, 300
Hepburn, William P., 129–30
Hepburn committee (New York State), 86–87
Hewitt, Abram, 72
High-Speed Ground Transportation Act, 258, 268–69
Highway Users Conference, 257
Hill, James J., 50, 97, 98, 105, 108, 260; his reported group of railroads in 1902, 113; battles Harriman, 114–25; quoted, 223
Hocking Valley Railroad, 100, 114n, 160
Hoffa, James R., 204
Hoffman, Wayne, 227
Hoover, Herbert C., 162
Hoover Commission, 247
Hopkins, Mark, 31, 60, 61
Hopkins, John P., 111

Hosmer, Howard, 233
Hudson River Railroad, 18, 20–22, 28
Hughes, Richard J., 268, 288
Huntington, Collis P., 60–61, 69, 71, 73–74, 88, 97, 98, 115; and the Central Pacific, 31–35; in the Pacific Ring, 40–51 passim; sketched, 54–57; dies, 116

Illinois Central Railroad, 6, 15, 68, 98, 102, 115, 253, 254–55, 265, 273; controlled by Harriman, 132; as a commuter road, 288–89
Illinois Commerce Commission, 285
Indianapolis & St. Louis Railroad, 80
Industrial Commission, final report, 112–14
Interstate Commerce Act, 95, 98n, 106, 111, 301; amended, 233, 248–49
Interstate Commerce Commission, 3, 4, 134, 136, 137, 138, 140, 167, 172, 174, 175, 176–77, 182, 183, 188, 190–91, 196, 199, 202, 203, 205, 206, 212–13, 229, 231, 232–33, 250, 251–52n, 260, 263–67, 274, 275, 278, 287, 290, 301, 304; legislated, 95; shorn of power, 106–7; futility of in 1904, 127–28; gathers strength, 129–31; investigates Harriman, 133; raises rates and fares, 149, 151; bidden to plan railroad consolidation, 152–53, 158–59, but is derelict, 162; reports a futile plan, 165; reports a second plan, 166; permits fifteen raises of the rate, 1945-58, 189; permits mergers, 216–21; ups fares, 242–43; and the passenger service deficit, 246–49
Interstate Commerce Railway Association, 97
Iowa Central Railroad, 98
Iowa Pool, 58–59, 60, 67

Jenkins, James, 107–8
Jersey Central. See Central Railroad Company of New Jersey

318

319

National Academy of Sciences, 207, 254, 255
National Association of Railroad and Utilities Commissioners, 248
National Association of Railroad Passengers (N.A.R.P.), 301–2, 304, 305
National Board of Trade, 24
National City Bank, 115, 119
National Republican, The, 83
National Research Council, 207
Nationalization of railroads, 140–48; abroad, 11; efforts in the U.S., 13, 24, 172
Nelson, Robert A., 272
New Haven. *See* New York, New Haven & Hartford Railroad
New Jersey Public Utilities Commission, 289–90, 293
New York & Erie Railroad. *See* Erie Railroad
New York & Harlem Railroad, 15, 20–21, 27n
New York & New Haven Railroad, 15
New York Board of Railroad Commissioners (1855), 15–16
New York Board of Trade, 85
New York Central Railroad, 14–28 passim, 36, 44, 48, 50, 52, 76–77, 80, 85–87, 97n, 98, 103, 114n, 130, 143, 145, 147, 160, 163, 164, 200, 204n, 209–10, 211n, 213–17, 220n, 221; rows with the Pennsylvania, 90–92; as part of the so-called Vanderbilt group in 1902, 112; Harriman buys into, 132; status in 1920, 156; taken over by Young, 181–82; in the red, 193–94; hope for merger with the Pennsylvania, 194; merger with the Pennsylvania approved, 218
And the passenger service, 227, 230–31, 232, 236, 238, 240, 241, 243, 244n, 245, 253, 262, 264, 272, 283, 300; as a commuter road, 289–91; an experience on, 298–99
New York Chamber of Commerce, 86
New York, Chicago & St. Louis Railroad. *See* Nickel Plate

New York, New Haven & Hartford Railroad, 134–36, 164, 193–94n, 215, 221, 238, 258, 282; and demonstration project, 269–70; as a commuter road, 291–93
New York State Public Service Commission, 264, 278
New York Stock Exchange, 17n, 20–21, 47, 51, 247–48
New York Sun, The, 45, 72
New York Times, The, 19, 49, 106n, 227, 228, 241–42, 256, 264, 299
New York Tribune, The, 69
New York Trunk Line Association, 77
New York, West Shore & Buffalo Railroad. *See* West Shore
New York, Westchester & Boston Railroad, 135
New York World, The, 69n
Nickel Plate, 89–90, 155n; bought by Van Sweringens, 156, 161; merged with N&W, 215–18
Norfolk & Western Railway, 156, 163, 165, 209, 213–14; absorbs the Virginian, 215; absorbs the Nickel Plate and the Wabash, 216–18; plans to merge with C&O-B&O, 220–21
North Western Ring, 23–24, 36, 71
Northeast Corridor Project, 257–58, 272
Northern Pacific Railway, 42–43, 47, 51, 80, 97, 98, 125, 133, 134, 155n, 193–94n, 255; reorganized, 104–6; struck, 107–8; shares control of Burlington, 114, 120; secretly bought in by Harriman, 120–22
Northern Securities Company, 122–23, 131; dissolved by the Supreme Court, 124

Oakes, Thomas, 98
O'Dwyer, Paul, 283–84
Office of Defense Transportation, 176
Ogden, William B., 23, 35–36, 38
Olney, Richard S., 107–11
Oregon & California Railroad, 133n
Oregon Railroad & Navigation Company, 116

320

Oregon Short Line, 116, 117

Pacific Mail Steamship Company, 60
Pacific Railroad Act, 31–35 passim, 41n
Panic of 1873, 47–48, 58, 62, 69, 166
Panic of 1893, 100, 109, 166
Parton, James, 23
Passenger service, 179–82, 226 et seq.; and buses, 237–38; and ignorance of market, 239; and equipment, 239–41, 254; and fares, 241–43; advertising of, 244; and travel agents, 244–45; and the Post Office, 249–54; and the Pell plan, 256–59; discussed in A.A.R. report, 262–63; and petty vexations, 267–68; and the demonstration project, 268–73; hope for, 301–2, 305. See also Passenger service deficit
Passenger service deficit, 182, 232–33; critically examined, 242–49, 250, 263, 278
Patrons of Husbandry, 68
Pell, Claiborne, 228–29, 233, 255, 269; and the Pell plan, 256–58
Pennsylvania Company, 54
Pennsylvania Fiscal Agency, 37
Pennsylvania Public Service Commission, 278
Pennsylvania Railroad, 9, 19, 36, 42n, 44–45, 46n, 50, 52-54, 69–80 passim, 84, 96, 97n, 98, 103, 114n, 128, 138-48 passim, 157–65 passim, 171, 186–87, 200, 203, 209, 211n, 213–17, 220n, 221; rows with the Central, 90–92; as part of the so-called Pennsylvania group in 1902, 113; graft by officials of, 130; sells its stock in C&O and B&O, 130–31; opposes Transportation Act, 153; opposes labor, 153–55; status in 1920, 156; picks quarrel with truckers, 184–85; in the red, 193–94; hope for merger with the New York Central, 194; merger with the Central approved, 218

And the passenger service, 227, 234, 236, 240–46 passim, 249n, 253, 258, 263–64, 268, 273, 277, 280, 289, 303; buys into and sells out of Greyhound, 238; and demonstration project, 270–72; and the L.I.R.R., 282–84; as a commuter road, 286–88
People's Line, 18
Pere Marquette Railroad, 160–62
Perkins, Charles E., 98, 107, 234
Perkins, James and Thomas, 58
Perlman, Alfred E., 213–17, 221, 290, 293
Pevler, Herman, 220, 221–22
Philadelphia & Reading Railroad, 80n, 91–93, 114n, 147–48, 156, 163, 164, 215, 220, 287, 294; reorganized, 103
Philadelphia Bulletin, The, 83, 286
Philadelphia North American, The, 127
Phillips, Wendell, 54
Piggyback, 188; status in 1957, 200; improved by Forgash, 200
Pittsburgh, Fort Wayne & Chicago Railroad, 80
Poor's Manual, 89
Poppenhuser, Adolph, 281
Post Office Department, 248, 250–54, 264
Potter, Mark, 162
Potter Act, in Wisconsin, 70
Prince, Frederick H., 171
Prouty, Charles A., 127–28, 136, 218
Providence & Stonington Railroad, 18
Pruyn, John V. L., 36–37
Public interest, usually abused or ignored, 12, 13, 19, 21–22, 23, 30, 58, 74–75, 114, 120, 140, 162, 212, 213, 218, 221, 246, 269, 275, 288, 289; "The public be damned," 89–90; reflected in I.C.C., 95; defended by the public, 126–29; a new aspect of, 136; defined, 212n
Public Works Administration, 167, 170
Pullman, George, 44, 61, 109–10
Pullman Company, 148, 245

321